The Official Gu...

Linksys® Networks

The Official Guide

Linksys® Networks

Kathy Ivens

Larry J. Seltzer

McGraw-Hill Osborne

New York   Chicago   San Francisco   Lisbon
London   Madrid   Mexico City   Milan   New Delhi
San Juan   Seoul   Singapore   Sydney   Toronto

The *McGraw·Hill* Companies

McGraw-Hill/Osborne
2600 Tenth Street
Berkeley, California 94710
U.S.A.

To arrange bulk purchase discounts for sales promotions, premiums, or fund-raisers, please contact **McGraw-Hill**/Osborne at the above address. For information on translations or book distributors outside the U.S.A., please see the International Contact Information page immediately following the index of this book.

Linksys® Networks: The Official Guide

34567890 FGR FGR 019876543

ISBN 0-07-222683-8

Publisher:	Brandon A. Nordin
Vice President &	
Associate Publisher:	Scott Rogers
Acquisitions Editor:	Franny Kelly
Project Editor:	Mark Karmendy
Technical Editor:	Davis Storm
Copy Editors:	Lisa Theobald, Dennis Weaver
Proofreader:	Susie Elkind
Indexer:	James Minkin
Linksys Contact:	Mark Wagner (Director of Marketing)
Computer Designers:	Tara Davis, Lucie Ericksen
Illustrators:	Melinda Lytle, Michael Mueller, Lyssa Wald
Series Design:	Mickey Galicia
Cover Design:	Pattie Lee

This book was composed with Corel VENTURA™ Publisher.

Dedication

For Sarah, Amy, and Leah, because they're wonderful, and
bring joy and fun into my life
Kathy Ivens
To my loving wife Danna and the rest of my family
Larry Seltzer

About the Author

Kathy Ivens has been a computer consultant since 1984, and several years ago she began writing books. She has authored, co-authored, contributed to, and ghost written more than forty volumes on computer subjects. Kathy is a frequent contributor to national magazines on computer topics, writing reviews and articles, and is a contributing editor for *Windows 2000 Magazine* and *Windows NT Magazine*. She is the author of *QuickBooks 2002: The Official Guide* and *Windows 2000: The Complete Reference,* among many other best-selling McGraw-Hill/Osborne titles.

Larry Seltzer writes frequently for several computer and business publications, including *Fortune Small Business, PC Magazine,* and *ZDNet,* and consults on design and testing issues. He has been Technical Director in charge of product testing at *PC Week* and *PC Magazine*, and also has worked in corporate and commercial software development. He is also the author of McGraw-Hill/Osborne's *ADMIN911: Windows 2000 Terminal Services*

Contents

Acknowledgments

A lot of people contributed their expertise to create this book, and we owe them thanks and gratitude. At McGraw-Hill/Osborne Publishing, we offer a thank you to Acquisitions Editor Francis Kelly for this opportunity. Executive Project Editor Mark Karmendy did his usual superb job of keeping this book on track through all the stages it takes to produce a technical tome, and Copy Editors Lisa Theobald and Dennis Weaver made sure we looked like smooth professional writers. Our thanks to David Strom for his technical editing skills. At Linksys, we found some super helpful people, and we give special thanks to Mike Wagner, Diana Ying, Elmer Leon, and Chris Chapman for their support and assistance.

Introduction

Welcome to the wonderful world of computer networks! This book focuses on the hardware side of networking, rather than the usual "everything you want to know about, or do with, a network." If you need to know more about network operating system stuff than you can find in your computer's Help files, including all the logon, user maintenance, and other networking functions, see Appendix C for a list of useful books. We wrote *this* book to help you understand how to create, maintain, and troubleshoot the hardware setup for your home network or your small business network. We know from our own experience, and from talking to other users who have created small networks, that the setup stage is the most daunting. As a result, we believe there's a valid reason to offer a book that covers the setup procedures.

Both authors have spent years setting up networks of all sizes for our clients. Both of us maintain our own home networks. In fact, both of us have multiple home networks, including networks that run Windows domains (like those at corporate businesses), and peer-to-peer networks (like those found in homes and small businesses).

Both authors are fans of Linksys hardware, having purchased Linksys products for our own networks for years. Because Linksys is the leading vendor of network hardware for home and small business networks, it seemed natural and appropriate to present information about Linksys hardware in a book that focuses on the hardware side of networking.

Benefits of a Network

We believe that anyone who owns more than one computer should create a network. Creating a network is easy and the resulting benefits are enormous. In fact, there are no "downsides" to moving to a network environment.

Share an Internet Connection

Whenever the subject of connecting computers via a network is discussed, as soon as someone says, "you can share an Internet connection if you create a network," people who own multiple computers listen carefully. That's the big selling point! If we were to list the top ten reasons homeowners and small businesses cite for creating a network, a shared Internet connection occupies reasons #1 through #9 (reason #10 is sometimes printer sharing and sometimes file sharing).

No matter how you connect to the Internet, without a network you have a constant battle among the computer users in your home or business for access to that Internet device. If you use a telephone modem, even if each computer has its own modem, you probably have only one telephone line dedicated to modem use. (If you've installed multiple telephone lines to accommodate multiple computers with modems, buying the hardware for a network pays for itself within a few months; after that you're saving money).

Every time a user wants to use the modem line, he or she must check to see if a user at another computer is connected to the Internet. If so, you're probably used to hearing "get off the modem, I need to get to the Internet." Sharing a connection over a network eliminates that problem. If you have only one telephone line, period, the battle between callers and modem users is probably constant—put a second line in for modem use and share it over a network. This will stop all that yelling you hear so often, "Get off the modem, I'm expecting a call" or "get off the modem, I want to make a call."

If you have a DSL/cable modem, it's connected to one computer. Anyone who wants to go online must use that computer (and, of course, everybody wants to go online all the time). No matter how many computers you own, everybody wants to use that computer. Sharing that device on a network means that anyone can work at any computer and reach the Internet.

Share Printers

Networking means you don't have to buy a printer for every computer. Of course, you may not have adopted that model when you bought your second (or third) computer, in which case only one computer has a printer. Users who want to print documents have to work at that computer or have to save their document on a floppy disk, carry the floppy disk to the computer with the printer, open the software that created the document (the software has to be installed on the computer with the printer), open the document in the software, and print the document. What a pain! (By the way, the technical jargon for a multiple computer setup where users have to walk floppy disks to computers in order to print or to attach a document to e-mail is called a *sneakernet*.)

Many homes and small businesses have a printer attached to each computer, but the printers are not the same. If you're working at the computer with a laser printer but want to print a particular document to an inkjet color printer, you have to wait until the computer attached to the color printer is free.

When you create a network, any user working at any computer can print to any printer. Nifty!

Access Files No Matter Where They Are

In most homes and businesses with multiple computers, each user has a favorite (or assigned) computer. The user (let's call her "Mom") works at that computer (let's call it "den") and saves documents on that computer's hard drive. One day Mom finds Joey Junior working on "den" (there are always more users than computers) when she wants to work on a document she's been toiling over, or she wants to start a new document based on a template she's created (and stored on "den"). She needs to tell Joey Junior to stop what he's doing and give her the computer. If Joey Junior is like most kids, he complains that he can't stop—he's doing homework or he's in the middle of an Instant Message conversation that is so important it will determine his social life and happiness for months to come. Sometimes it works the other way around—Mom is at the computer and Joey Junior comes to whine that he started his homework on that computer and can't work on the computer in the kitchen (and besides, Dad is on that computer).

When you create a network, any document or template that you've created on any computer is available when you work at any other computer. Handy!

Fun and Games

If you have a network, you can play network games, where users on separate computers play against each other. These games are available for download on the Internet, and Windows provides one right in the operating system—Network Hearts. Try it, it's fun!

Is This Book for You?

We wrote this book to explain and simplify the process of installing a network. If you have multiple computers and have been thinking about creating a network, your network will be up and running quickly as a result of the information within these pages.

If you have multiple computers and haven't thought about creating a network, think again! Then read this book!

Conventions and Special Effects In This Book

To make it easier to get through the technical explanations we had to cover in this book, we've done several things:

- Made the language as straightforward and easy to understand as possible

- Provided a glossary of networking terminology (Appendix A)

- Used special treatment for special text:

  - **Bold type** indicates characters you type when you're supplying information to the operating system

  - *Italic type* indicates a "geeky" technical term or jargon (and is accompanied by an explanation of the meaning)

In addition, you'll find some special effects. These effects are set apart from the regular text in the book, with special formatting and placement on the page.

- Tips are nuggets of information that add to your knowledge or make it easier to complete a task.

- Notes are informative tidbits of information that might make it easier to understand a task or to complete a task in a manner better suited to your own situation.

- Cautions are warnings about things that could go wrong, along with an explanation for the steps to take to avoid the problem.

- Sidebars are technical explanations that you don't really have to understand to perform a task, but we thought you might be interested in the explanation anyway.

Assumptions We've Made About You

We're assuming you know how to use a computer but don't have a great deal of expertise on computer hardware, operating systems, or computer communication protocols. We're also assuming you have multiple computers and they may not all be running the same version of Windows.

Considering current statistics on home computers and small business computers, we've concentrated on explaining how to perform tasks in Windows XP and Windows 98SE. However, for some tasks, you'll find references to Windows 2000 and Windows Me, especially when performing tasks in those Windows versions differs substantially from the way you perform the tasks in Windows XP/98SE. We admit that our coverage of Windows 2000 and Windows Me isn't consistent throughout the book, but that's because we know a couple of facts. First, it's unusual to find Windows 2000 running on home computers or in small businesses that don't have networks. Second, Windows Me didn't sell well and has so many problems that many Windows Me users upgraded their systems to Windows XP. That last sentence also tells you something about the authors of this book: We don't mind sharing our opinions, and you'll find we "opine" throughout this book. Our opinions aren't arbitrary; they're based on many years of experience.

Errata

Note that errata and additions can be found at *http://www.admin911.com*.

About Linksys

California-based Linksys is the worldwide leader in the development of both wired and wireless networking solutions for homes, small offices, and businesses. Founded in 1988, Linksys began with the vision that networking should be easy to use and affordable, helping people share documents, files, mail, and most of all—ideas.

In 2001, Linksys captured the #1 worldwide market share position in the shipments of routers and wireless solutions. You'll find Linksys' award-winning products in more than 8,400 retail stores in the US and in 1,100 stores in 54 countries worldwide. Linksys extensive selection of over 150 products are also best sellers on e-commerce websites and through more than 1,000 Value Added Resellers.

Linksys connectivity solutions are designed to enable the sharing of high-speed Internet access, voice, video, and data in your home, at your business, and around the world. All Linksys products include award-winning 24 x 7 technical support to help customers successfully install and use their network.

Part I

Getting Started

Chapter 1

Networking Choices

Before you grab a screwdriver, drill a hole for cable, or open your computer to add networking components, you need a plan. When the ultimate plan is a small network in your home or in your place of business, you need to take a step back and make some decisions before you pick up your tools. (Maybe I should call that a preplan to a plan?) You have a lot of choices about the way you design and install your network, and you can't do anything definitive until you understand them.

In Part I, you'll learn what a network is, how it works, and the pros and cons of the various hardware options. You'll also learn how to install hardware networking components and how to add peripherals (printers, modems, DSL devices, and so on) to your network.

A network is nothing more than two or more computers that are connected so they can exchange data. The largest network in the world is the Internet, which comprises all the servers that provide services to Internet users. The smallest networks are found in millions of homes, where home users have connected two or more computers. In between those extremes are millions of corporate and small business networks comprising anywhere from two to hundreds of thousands of connected computers. What you may not realize is that all networks, regardless of their size, share common characteristics:

- Every computer contains a hardware device that controls communication with the other computers on the network.

- Every computer has a connection method (wireless or wired) that sends data to the other computers, using the hardware communication device.

When you create a home network or a network for your business, you'll be using the same approach as the network designers who create enormous corporate enterprises. As far as hardware and connection requirements, your network is no different than any other network in the world. While this may seem overwhelmingly complicated, you'll be amazed at how simple and logical it is if you take it one step at a time.

You *do* have some decisions to make, regarding the type of connections you want to use between your computers and the way in which users will join the network. This chapter provides an overview of your choices, and all the other chapters in this book will help you implement those choices.

Types of Networks

Networks are designed to be either client/server networks or peer-to-peer networks. Each type has its advantages and disadvantages, but small networks are almost always created as peer-to-peer networks. Regardless of the network type you opt for, the hardware and connection devices you have to install in each computer are the same.

Client/Server Networks

Client/server networks are built for security and controls. A server, equipped with special software tools, checks the computers and users who are logging in to the network to make sure that only authorized components can access the computers and other resources on the network. Information, including names and passwords, about each computer and user is stored in a database on the server. As each computer boots, and each user logs on, their logon data is checked against the information in the database (see Figure 1-1).

The server can also limit the rights and privileges of computers and users who log on to the network. Some users may be restricted from working with files in certain folders on network computers, or they may not be able to change settings

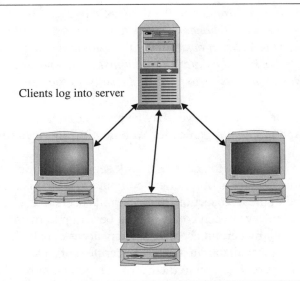

Clients log into server

FIGURE 1-1   In a client/server network, every logon has to be authenticated by a server

on their own computers. These controls are imposed on a computer-by-computer or user-by-user basis, but to make it easier for administrators, computers and users are placed into *groups*. The restrictions applied to a group apply to each member of the group. Assigning rights and privileges on a group basis is easier than dealing with each computer and user one at a time.

Most client/server networks are also designed for server-based work. Servers are set up all over the network (and they must also log on and be authenticated). Most of these servers are assigned a specific task; consider the following, for instance:

- A mail server that holds the company's e-mail software and the users' mailboxes

- The accounting software server, which can be accessed only by members of the accounting department

- Print servers that control the printers attached to them, so users can share printers

- Data servers that hold the documents that users create with software applications such as word processors or spreadsheets

NOTE *In client/server environments, the software that each user runs is frequently configured to save documents to a data server instead of to the user's own computer. This makes it easier to share data among users and also makes it easier to back up the data. (All administrators know that users rarely obey company mandates to perform backups of their own computers.)*

In some large companies, a server may be reserved to host the company's Web site (although many companies let Web hosting services run the company's Web servers).

In addition to being able to access network servers, client computers in a Windows network can access other client computers, which is a peer-to-peer method (discussed in the next section). This permits users to exchange or share data files directly. However, each computer can be set up to maintain permissions that allow access only by certain users, or to deny access to all client computers. (The same controls are available in a peer-to-peer network.)

In fact, users can opt to log on to their own computers, rather than the network, if they wish. They won't be able to access any network resources, but this may still be the way to log on if a server is down or if the user wants to work on software

1

applications that are installed on the local computer without saving the data to a network server.

NOTE
The client/server paradigm described here represents a Windows Network Operating System (NOS), but you may come across a different NOS in corporate environments, such as UNIX, Linux, or NetWare. All of those systems authenticate users to maintain controls and security, but the methods vary. In addition, the client/server relationship is usually absolute, so individual computers on a client/server network cannot access each other in a peer-to-peer fashion, nor can users log on to their local computers— they must join the network. Those last two distinctions enhance the network security.

The biggest advantage of a client/server network is the level of security you can achieve, but for small networks, that advantage is usually outweighed by the cost of buying a server to maintain those controls and the technical knowledge required to set up and maintain the authentication processes. Because small networks have fewer computers and users, the need to develop security controls on a user-by-user or computer-by-computer basis is less daunting.

NOTE
In a Windows client/server network, the servers that authenticate computers and users when they log on are called domain controllers. When you log on to a client/server network, you're logging on to a domain. Peer-to-peer networks log on to a workgroup.

Peer-To-Peer Networks

A peer-to-peer network is exactly what the term implies—everybody is equal. No servers equipped with authentication software utilities interfere with the process of logging on to a computer or to the network. All the computers on the network can communicate directly with all the other computers on the network (see Figure 1-2).

You can apply security measures to resources, such as files and folders, on each computer on the network. In fact, if one user decides that his computer is totally private, he can refuse to share any files or folders on his computer. That doesn't stop him from being able to access resources on another computer, though, if that other computer is sharing resources.

In addition, with peer-to-peer configuration, you don't entirely lose the concept, or efficiency, of a server. For example, you can use any computer on the network as a print server without interfering with a user's ability to work on that computer.

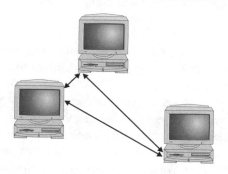

FIGURE 1-2   Each computer on a peer-to-peer network can initiate communication with any other computer on the network

A print server is a computer that has a printer connected to it, and that printer is configured as a shared printer, meaning everyone on the network can use that printer. The user who works at the computer that is connected to the printer doesn't have to share any other resources, such as files or folders, because shared resources are set up on a resource-by-resource basis.

You can also maintain data files for certain software applications on one computer, which essentially treats the computer as a server. For example, many accounting software applications work in this mode (an example is QuickBooks).

In some versions of Windows (Windows 2000 and Windows XP), you can impose security on the logon process, so that nobody can log on except an existing, recognized user who knows the password. In addition, each logged-on user can be restricted in their ability to make changes to the system's configuration.

When you log on to a peer-to-peer network, you join a *workgroup*, which is a group of computers that are connected to each other.

Network Administration

A certain amount of administrative work is involved in creating and maintaining a network. Luckily, if you're creating a peer-to-peer network, most of the administrative tasks don't fall into the category of "real work"; this is all more like "set it and forget it." The fact that administrative tasks must be performed is the result of some important networking concepts and rules, which I'll discuss in this section. This book is really about network hardware, and it won't cover most of the software and operating system issues involved in networking. (See Appendix C for a list of books that cover these issues in detail.) However, it's important to present an overview of what you're going to face as you create, configure, and run your network.

Computer and Workgroup Names

Every computer that joins a network must have a name, and the name must be unique on the network. The computers communicate with each other every time a user accesses any network resource, and the computers don't have a way of determining that you meant this Bob, not the other Bob. One computer named Bob to a network, please. In addition, when you create a network, you must also name the group of networked computers, which is called a *workgroup*.

You can name a computer when you install the operating system, and if you bought a computer from a manufacturer who installed the operating system for you, it may already have a name (something really creative, descriptive, and easy to remember like DEO77495FG077MR). Some people name their first computer Brown, because that's the family name; then when they buy another computer, they name it Brown, and perhaps even when a third computer arrives, it too is named Brown. That's neither unusual, nor harmful, until you decide to create a network with all three computers.

When you install your network using one of the Windows networking wizards (available in Windows Me and Windows XP) or by setting configuration options manually (Windows 98SE and Windows 2000), you can name (or rename) the computer and the workgroup during the network setup process.

It's a good idea to name a computer for the room in which it resides, so there's no chance of duplication and so that everyone understands where the computer is located. For example, Den, Kitchen, Basement, Attic, Garage, Marysroom, and so on, are good choices.

The workgroup name can be anything you want, and each computer on your network must have the same workgroup name (the Windows networking wizards usually suggest something like MSHome or even Workgroup, but you can substitute another name for your workgroup).

Computer and workgroup names cannot be longer than 15 characters, and the following characters are forbidden in the name:

| / | \ | * | , | . | @ | space |

You can change the existing name of a computer (usually a task that's performed because of duplicate computer names) in the following way:

■ In Windows XP, right-click My Computer and choose Properties from the shortcut menu. In the Properties dialog, go to the Computer Name tab (see Figure 1-3). Click Change to enter a new name.

FIGURE 1-3   Click the Change button to change the computer's identification, and optionally enter a description (such as "in the den")

- In Windows 2000, right-click My Computer and choose Properties from the shortcut menu. In the Properties dialog, go to the Network Identification tab and click Properties to change the name.

- In Windows 98SE/Me, open Control Panel, and then open the Network applet. Go to the Identification tab and type in a new name.

User Settings

You can configure any computer to ask a user for a logon name and a password when the operating system starts, and this approach provides several advantages to users and to your efforts to make your computers, and your network, secure.

If more than one person uses the computer, each user's configuration preferences are loaded when that user logs on. For example, desktop icons, the listings on the Programs menu, the personal My Documents folder, and other components are all exactly the way the user wants them. This is called a *user profile*, and each user's profile is stored on the computer.

For computers running Windows XP (and Windows 2000), individual logons also provide security measures that protect the computer, because you can configure the rights and privileges for each user. Users who have accounts configured for limited rights cannot perform certain functions; for instance, they may not be able to install software, and they cannot delete or modify system files (see Figure 1-4). If your network is part of your business, limited accounts make a great deal of sense. Even in a home network, a limited account may prevent damage if one of your household members tends to plunge into computer tasks without enough knowledge

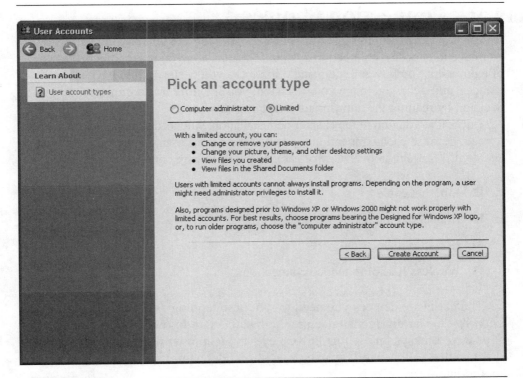

FIGURE 1-4   This user's account is created with limited rights to keep him (and the computer) out of trouble

to stay out of trouble (usually, that means one of the parents—most kids are far more sophisticated about computers than their parents are). All network administrators can identify those users who "know enough to be dangerous"; these are the users they restrict.

For computers running Windows 98/Me, the only advantage to logons and passwords is to load the user profile. There's no security built into these operating systems. Any passing stranger can walk up to a Windows 98 computer, turn it on, and when the Logon dialog appears press ESC or click Cancel, and voila—he's in the computer and can do anything he wants.

It's possible to use logon names and profiles without requiring a password (a user without a password is said to have a *null password*), and this scenario is common in many home networks. However, for a business network, where outsiders may be on the premises, it's a real security risk to permit users to omit passwords.

Network Connection Choices

Before you can do anything about your network—before you buy the hardware— you have to choose a connection system. The decision you make affects the type of equipment you buy and the installation tasks you perform. You have several choices, and once you make your decision, you'll learn how to implement that decision by reading the appropriate chapter in this book.

But before you turn to the chapter on installation, you need to know which chapter to read, because each connection type is covered in its own chapter. To help you decide, I'll present an overview of each of the following connection types:

- Ethernet cable

- Household telephone wires

- Household electrical wires

- Wireless RadioFrequency connections

The hardware devices you need to run these topologies are available from Linksys—the hardware manufacturer both authors of this book prefer (in fact both of us were Linksys fans before anyone ever thought of writing this book). In the chapters that follow, we'll provide Linksys model names and numbers when appropriate.

During the discussion on connection choices, I'll be talking about the speed at which each connection type can transfer data among computers. Network speeds are rated in Megabits Per Second (Mbps). A megabit is a million binary pulses, which doesn't mean anything unless you can think about it in a familiar perspective. The easiest way to do that is to think about a dial-up modem. The fastest dial-up modems available transmit data at the rate of 56,000 bits per second (56 Kilobits or 56 Kbps). If you've ever used a dial-up modem to download a file from the Internet, and you watched the progress bar move rather swiftly as thousands, tens of thousands, hundreds of thousands, and finally millions of bytes were delivered to your computer, think about how fast a megabit must be.

Ethernet Cable

Presenting the pros and cons of choosing Ethernet cable as your network topology is easy: it's almost all "pro" and very little "con." Ethernet is the cable of choice for any network, because it's fast, accurate, and almost always trouble-free; this is

Network Connections Jargon

Even though a complete glossary of networking terms appears in Appendix A, I'll give you a brief rundown on some common terms here, so the section on connection types will be easier to understand (and you won't have to keep flipping the pages to look at Appendix A):

- **Topology** is the configuration of a network, including its layout and the type of connections used to create the network.

- **LAN,** which stands for Local Area Network, is a group of computers that are connected by a topology in order to exchange data.

- **NIC,** which stands for Network Interface Card, is the hardware component that goes into the computer and provides the computer-side connection to the rest of the network hardware. This device gets its name from the fact that until recently, all NICs were installed, as cards, on an internal slot on the computer's systemboard (also called a motherboard). Even though the computer-side connections are now available for other ports (for instance USB ports), we still call the device a NIC.

- **Hub,** which is also called *concentrator*, is a hardware device that is the central point for connecting computers, and all the cable from all the computers on the LAN meet in the hub. When data moves from one computer to another on a network, it moves through the hub, not directly from one computer to another.

the connection type you find in corporate networks. (Instructions for cabling with Ethernet are in Chapter 4.) Absent some good reason, Ethernet is the topology to use for your network. However, I do admit that good reasons exist to opt for another topology, including the following common ones:

- You rent and the landlord doesn't want you to drill holes to bring cable through the walls.

- Your computers are located in places that are difficult to reach with a physical cable.

- The notion of running cable through your home or office strikes you as "too much work."

- The person in your household who has the final word on décor and aesthetic decisions says "I don't want to see cable snaking out of the walls and into the room."

- Your network is made up of portable computers and you never know where any individual computer is going to be used.

Ethernet can transfer data across the network at 100Mbps, as long as the NIC and the hub/switch can support that speed. Some older NICs and hubs can send data at only 10Mbps, but Ethernet NICs and hubs/switches can automatically sense the speed of the Ethernet devices on the network and drop or raise the speed to match the device's capabilities (this feature is called *autosensing*).

Today, Ethernet cable is purchased in the form of *100BaseT cable*, which is also called *twisted pair cable* and *category 5 UTP cable*. The "100" in the name refers to the speed at which it can transmit data (100Mbps); sometimes 100BaseT Ethernet is called *fast Ethernet*. Older Ethernet cable that can transmit data at 10Mbps is called 10BaseT.

The term "base" is short for "baseband signaling," which means that only Ethernet signals are carried on the wires. This differs from telephone wire, which can handle multiple types of signals. (Your telephone service uses only a portion of the wires, and you can use other portions for other technologies, including computer networks, which is discussed in Chapter 6.)

The term "T" means twisted-pair, which is a description of the way the wires are twisted and paired through the cable. (Other wiring types, such as those for fiber-optic wires, which is called 100BaseF, also exist.)

Ethernet cable looks like telephone wire, and the connectors (also called *jacks*, even though the jack is the wall outlet to definition purists) look like the connectors on your telephone cable. However, they're not the same. The wires are twisted differently and the arrangement of wires in the connector is different (a telephone jack is an RJ-11, an Ethernet jack is an RJ-45).

Household Telephone Wires

Household telephone wires are an easy way to connect computers into a LAN, and the technology has come a long way since it was first introduced several years ago. (See Chapter 6 for instructions on creating a telephone line network.) Telephone network cable uses the wires in your telephone cable that voice communication doesn't use, so your telephone lines are still available for normal household telephone use (including a modem and a fax). The available range of frequencies within cable is called *bandwidth*, and you can use the bandwidth your phone services don't use to create a computer network.

There are pros and cons for using your household telephone wires, and they balance rather evenly. On the pro side, the only hardware you need is a NIC and length of plain telephone wire for each computer. Each computer is plugged into a regular telephone wall jack, eliminating the need to buy or install Ethernet cable. You can use your telephone wall jack for both a telephone and a network connection at the same time by installing a *splitter* (really called a *modular duplex jack*) which is a gadget you can buy at your local supermarket. The splitter has a male jack that goes into the wall jack, and it has two female jacks on the outside. Plug a telephone cable into the Phoneline network card into one jack and your telephone cable into the other jack.

On the con side, not every room in your house may have a telephone jack, so you must plan the location of your computers around jack availability. Also, if you have more than one telephone number in your house, all the computers on your network must be connected through the *same* number. Computers can't communicate across different telephone numbers—but then, neither can you. If people are talking on line 1, you can't pick up a telephone connected to line 2 and join their conversation (or eavesdrop).

If your business uses a PBX telephone system, you can't use the jacks for your network, because the wiring is different from regular telephone jacks. PBX jacks are designed to deliver all the services that come with your phone system. In addition, if you have a DSL device for your Internet connection, you'll face some interoperability problems, but the workarounds aren't very complicated (and they're covered in Chapter 6).

NOTE   *Another "con" for using telephone lines is that the maximum distance between any two computers is about 1000 feet—but unless you live in Windsor Castle, that shouldn't be a problem.*

Telephone networks operate at 10 Mbps (although faster devices should be available soon), which is not as fast as today's fast Ethernet (100 Mbps) but matches the speed at which corporate networks operated until the recent introduction of fast Ethernet. In fact, plenty of networked computers still operate at 10 Mbps Ethernet, because the company's Information Technology (IT) professionals decided they didn't have a compelling reason to update the hardware. A connection speed of 10 Mbps is more than sufficient for almost any data transfer tasks. Actually, I don't know whether to call the speed rating of telephone lines a pro or a con.

Household Electrical Wires

You can run a network on the unused bandwidth within your household electrical lines without interfering with any of the work those lines perform to provide power to electrical appliances. In addition, the electrical appliances don't interfere with the transmission of data among the computers on your network. Best of all, since you're not using the part of the bandwidth that supplies power, the network connections don't raise your electric bill.

The NIC in each computer connects that computer to the nearest electrical outlet, and once all the NICs are installed and plugged in, you have a network. The speed of data exchange is about 14Mbps, which is more than fast enough for anything I ever wanted to do on a network. One obvious advantage to this connection type is the fact that at least one electrical outlet exists in every room, so you can put your computers anywhere you wish. Turn to Chapter 7 for instructions on installing your network over your household electrical wires.

Wireless Networking

Wireless networking uses RF (RadioFrequency) signals to communicate among the computers. The advances in wireless networking have been incredibly rapid in recent years, and the technology is becoming more and more popular as each new set of standards increases its power. Chapter 5 provides all the information you need to set up a wireless network.

The NIC has a transceiver (named for the fact that it both sends and receives data) and an antenna, and the data communication rate is about 11 Mbps for 802.11b and 54 to 72 Mbps for 802.11a (discussed more in Chapter 5). The interference problems that plagued early versions of wireless networking have disappeared, and you no longer have to worry that copying a file might open your garage door. In addition, robust security functions are built into the Linksys wireless devices, so you don't have to worry that a neighbor who also uses wireless technology could intrude on your network and gain access to your data.

The downside of wireless communication is that the signal can be interrupted by metal. So if you store your computer under a metal desk, you'll also have communication problems. This is also true if the walls between computers have a lot of metal pipes inside (typical of older homes, before PVC became the standard material for drain pipes). There's also a distance maximum between computers (about 150 feet), but Linksys offers devices that extend the signal.

Mix and Match

Just to make all of these available choices more confusing (or, depending on how you look at it, more reassuring), you can also mix and match these connection types. Both of the authors of this book have been running Ethernet-cabled home networks for years. To write this book, we created separate networks for each of the connection choices, and we also mixed the topology, adding computers that were not running Ethernet to our original Ethernet networks. That action wasn't a "trick" to see what would happen; it was a reflection of reality. Large corporate networks that are grounded in Ethernet are adding other connection technologies to their LANs. The most prevalent example is the addition of wireless technology devices to Ethernet networks so that mobile users who visit the main office can get to corporate data without having to be wired in.

Chapter 2

Purchasing and Connecting Hardware

A ny computer you buy nowadays can be connected on a network, although some are easier to work with than others. In this chapter, you'll learn the basics about computer hardware and how you attach the hardware that communicates with the network to the computer.

Many years ago, adding extra hardware to a computer was tricky and required experience working with computers, but hardware installations have gotten much better. Computer manufacturers, peripheral hardware vendors like Linksys, and Microsoft have all worked to accommodate a Plug and Play feature that allows you simply to plug a hardware device into your computer and it will work. In some cases, you need to open the main system unit of your computer and insert a circuit board, or card, but even this is easy to do.

Desktop Computer Hardware

Most personal computers are of the "desktop" variety. They are meant to be used in a fixed location, probably a desk, and some portion of them will sit on the desk.

Interestingly, the main part of a desktop computer (see Figure 2-1) doesn't usually need to be on the desk. You will likely place the monitor, also called the display, on your desk, along with your keyboard and mouse. But the system unit, which houses the actual computer, is often placed on the floor adjacent to the desk. Other desktop computers are designed so that the monitor sits on top of them.

The keyboard is just a keyboard, the mouse just a mouse, and the display just a display. The system unit contains the actual computer and other essential devices, including disk drives, the plugs for your monitor, keyboard, mouse, and the "slots" into which you may attach networking hardware.

In some rare cases, the display and other parts of the computer are integrated into a single unit for space-saving and fashion purposes. The best-known example of this is the Apple iMac, but such a configuration rarely occurs in the PC world.

Network Adapters

Most computers can't communicate with a network without having more hardware added to them, and that's where companies like Linksys come in. The hardware devices that connect the computer to the network, called *network adapters*, are often referred to as *NICs*, which stands for *Network Interface Cards*. As you will see, though, not all network adapters are cards anymore.

The job of the network adapter is to provide a physical connection—whatever the physical medium—to the network and thereby to the other computers on the

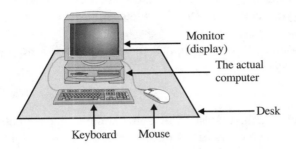

Sometimes the desktop computer's not
on the desktop...

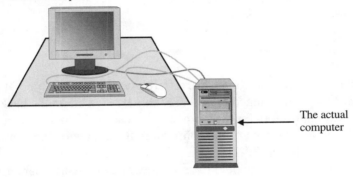

FIGURE 2-1   Desktop computers

network. In the most conventional case, the medium might be network wiring, but
in a home it is likely to be your telephone wiring or a form of wireless connection.
In the case of a wireless connection, the medium is the radio frequency spectrum,
usually in the 2.4GHz range, but we'll discuss this in greater detail in Chapter 5.
Sometimes the word "topology" is used to refer to the physical network medium.

It might be helpful for you to understand that the Internet itself is a network,
so even without a home network, you are using a type of network adapter when
you connect to the Internet. If you have cable modem or DSL service, the device
that connects to your cable or phone lines is a specialized type of network adapter.
Even when you dial up to the Internet on a conventional phone line (what techies
call POTS, for *Plain Old Telephone Service*), the modem acts as a type of network
adapter.

It's also helpful to understand that networking has both a hardware and software
side. Setting up and managing a network has become much easier, because no

matter what type of network medium you use, and no matter what type of network adapter you connect to your computer, Windows lets you treat it in the same way using common network software facilities.

Network adapters connect to your computer in different ways, and you work with them in different ways.

Integrated

The integrated system can be the easiest of all: some computers have networking hardware built right in. In such cases, if the integrated network medium is the same as your network, you can connect to a network without adding any new hardware.

In most cases, integrated network hardware on a computer is for a wired Ethernet network. This type of female connector (shown next) is also called a 10BaseT, 100BaseT, or a 10/100 connector.

Yet another name for the connector, referring to the specific type of plug that fits into it, is RJ-45. The connector will probably be located on the back of the system unit near connectors for the keyboard, mouse, and other devices. Notice that it is an eight-wire version of the common four-wire telephone connector, the plug for which is called an RJ-11.

It's also possible that you could have an integrated network adapter for other network media, such as telephone line networking. In this case, you would probably have two RJ-11 connectors on the back of your system near all the other connectors (shown next)—one for your telephone line and one for a telephone device, such as a phone or a fax.

Line   Phone

In the future, desktop system vendors may start integrating connectors for other types of network media, such as wireless and powerline networking, but we're not aware of any of these types of connectors as of this writing. Many notebook (laptop) computer vendors integrate wireless networking into their systems, and we'll discuss this in Chapter 11.

If you are investigating a new computer that has integrated networking, make sure it is the type of networking you want. Most integrated networking in desktop computers is wired Ethernet and is inappropriate for homes. Adding networking hardware is easy and inexpensive, and doing it yourself gives you the most choice among different types of networks and an opportunity to shop around. (FYI—Linksys has an Ethernet to wireless bridge called the WET11 for just this purpose.)

Cards

Most desktop computers have *expansion slots*. On the back of your system box, you can probably see the outside of these slots, some of them with expansion cards already mounted. Expansion slots are designed to accept "cards"—electronic circuit boards with adapters that can be connected to various devices outside the computer. An example of how expansion slots look is shown in Figure 2-2. These cards add hardware functions to the computer, such as network support, that are not built into the main board, or "motherboard," in the computer. Your computer may have expansion cards installed when you buy it, such as the video card that connects to your monitor.

Before you install a networking card into your desktop computer, you should always make sure to read the instructions that come with the card, but some generic advice follows.

You must open up the system unit to access the expansion slots. First, shut down Windows, and if the system hasn't done it for you, turn off the computer. You may need to disconnect other cables from the system unit, such as the keyboard and monitor, to move the system unit to open it and access the insides. If you disconnect cables, take note of what you are disconnecting so that you can reconnect them correctly. Usually, these connectors are labeled and designed

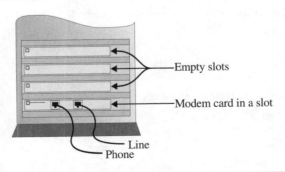

Empty slots

Modem card in a slot

Line
Phone

FIGURE 2-2   Expansion slots from the back of your system unit

so that they can connect only to the proper plug, but some connectors, such as those for the keyboard and mouse, can be identical.

Open the case to expose the insides. This may require tools, such as a Phillips screwdriver, but modern systems from quality PC companies sell "tool-less" cases that may be opened with a thumbscrew or by simply pressing a button.

After the case is open, touch a metal part of the power supply case, which is the box to which the outside power cord attaches. This part is grounded, and therefore touching it will discharge any static electricity you have built up in your body. *Now* you should disconnect the power cord. Continue to have contact with the case as much as possible so that way your body is equalized to the case, thus preventing pesky static build up on your body from going through the case.

Toward the back of the system unit case, probably in a corner, you will see the expansion slots (shown in Figure 2-3).

How to Identify the Inboard Bus (PCI/ISA)   You might see two types of expansion slots on a PC motherboard: ISA (Industry Standard Architecture) and PCI (Peripheral Component Interconnect). An ISA slot (shown next) is based on an old hardware standard devised by IBM back in 1984. These slots' connections can be seen on the back of the computer case. ISA slots are included in PCs these days for

Yuck! What About All that Dust?

If your computer case hasn't been opened for a long time, you may see a lot of dust in there. It's a good idea to clear out this dust, but you need to be careful about how you do it. Some people say to use a can of compressed air and blow the dust off the surfaces inside the PC. I believe it's best to use a handheld vacuum with a small nozzle. (This is the age-old PC "suck vs. blow" debate. Some say that with the "blow" method, you may just move dust into deeper crevices within the electronics of the system unit. With a vacuum, some say that you may suck up something important to the machine—such as a bit of the electronics.)

You need to remember two important things as you're doing this: Don't touch any of the surfaces in the PC with the blower or vacuum, and then make sure the dust gets *out*. Some vacuums can't filter really fine dust, so it may just blow back into the room. If you're nervous about using your vacuum, you can purchase a specially-made computer vacuum unit from many office supply stores. If you're using compressed air, try not to blow the dust toward the power supply or other parts into which it might lodge.

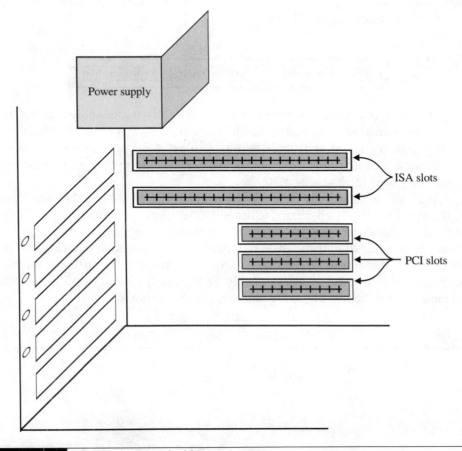

FIGURE 2-3   Expansion slots inside your computer

purposes of compatibility with old expansion cards. No new network hardware that you are likely to buy, and nothing from Linksys, uses ISA slots.

ISA slot

PCI slots (shown next) are shorter than ISA slots and located further inside the case. Some modern systems are equipped with only PCI slots, and almost all modern expansion hardware that uses an internal slot uses PCI. Almost no network hardware you are likely to buy these days will use ISA. (Linksys has an ISA Ethernet card called the LNE2000.)

PCI slot

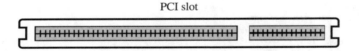

PCI cards (see Figure 2-4) have an edge with tightly-packed gold connectors that are designed to fit into a slot on the motherboard. The slot cover, the metal plate attached to the PCI card, is exposed to the outside of the case after installation so that any outside connectors, such as the network cable, can be plugged into the card via the receptacle on the metal plate.

Finally, you will frequently encounter one other type of slot called an accelerated graphics port (AGP). It's designed to accommodate high-performance graphics cards, so if your system unit has an AGP slot, there's a good chance that a card has already been installed in it and that your monitor is connected to that card. On the motherboard, this slot will probably be brown and set slightly further from the backplate of the case. It will also probably be physically closest to the system unit and memory and the rest of the big chips on the motherboard.

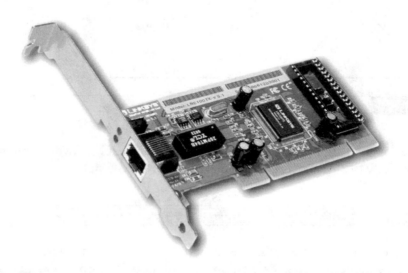

FIGURE 2-4   PCI cards, such as this Linksys network adapter, have a card edge that fits into a slot on the motherboard

Inserting the Card   Here are the basics for inserting the card:

1. Locate an empty slot. You will need to remove a slot cover from an unused PCI slot. Save the screw(s), or whatever connector was used to hold the slot cover in place, as you will use it to hold the installed adapter in place. Usually, any available PCI slot will do, but sometimes certain slots are less accessible than others because of the internal cables attached to them.

2. When you handle the card, try to touch only the slot cover and card, avoiding any of the chips and the card edge—the same goes for the insides of the computer. Don't freak out if you do touch anything; if you've been careful to discharge static electricity, nothing bad is going to happen to the computer. It's just a good habit to try to avoid touching the components.

3. Align the card vertically above the slot. Lower the card so that its edge rests in the PCI slot and so that the slot cover is sliding against the open area on the case, making sure that the card edge is set to insert directly into the slot. Press down on the top of the card to insert it into the slot.

4. Make sure the card is inserted in the slot correctly. The card edge should be inserted completely into the PCI slot; you should be able to see that it can't go down any lower because it is blocked by the lower, nonconnector edge of the card. In addition, check that the slot cover that is pressed against the back of the case and the top, which has a semicircular cut-out to expose the screw hole, is aligned to expose that hole.

5. Reinsert the screw to hold the card in place.

Now that the card is in place, you can put the case back on, reattach all the cables you removed, and restart the system. Windows will recognize the new hardware through the magic of Plug and Play and begin a software installation process to load the device drivers that allow it to work with the new card. This process is detailed in later chapters relative to the various types of hardware you may be working with.

NOTE   *Most new cases from Dell, Gateway, and others do not require screws; they have a piece that will cover all available slot holes in the case.*

Universal Serial Bus

Most people, even computer professionals, don't want to open up systems and mess with cards. That's why the computer industry came up with the Universal

Serial Bus (USB), which is a standard for external devices that connect to the plugs on the computer. You use USB to connect a device to the computer. USB technology has been around since 1996, but it's become popular only within the last few years, as almost all computers sold of late have at least one and probably two USB ports.

USB devices are designed for ease of use. You just plug them in, and they usually just work without further ado. After you plug in the device, Windows detects it and launches the Add New Hardware Wizard (in some versions of Windows this may have a slightly different name, like *Found New Hardware Wizard*) to help you load the device drivers that allow it to communicate with the particular device.

The exact wording in the Add New Hardware Wizard differs depending on which versions of Windows you're using, but the wizard essentially performs the same routine: Windows tells you the name of the device it has found and says that it will now load the driver for that device. A *device driver*, as the wizard says, is a software program that allows Windows to work with the hardware product. You click Next and the wizard will ask you to choose between letting Windows search for the best driver for your device (this is the recommended option) or specifying the type of device you want to load. You almost certainly want to take the default option.

Next, you will be asked from where Windows should search for the driver. The hardware product probably came with a disk—either a floppy disk or a CD-ROM—which contains the device drivers. You tell the wizard whether to use the disk that came with the device or point to a folder on your hard disk that contains the drivers you downloaded from the vendor's Web site. You may also be able to specify Microsoft Windows Update, which is a special site on the Internet where Microsoft stores updates to Windows and many current device drivers. Your best choice is usually the disks that came with the hardware product. Click Next and the wizard completes the installation of the driver. If there are problems, you can visit the hardware vendor's Web site and download the most recent drivers for the device, as they may be more current than the ones on the disk or CD that came with the product.

NOTE   *Later versions of Windows include built-in drivers for many peripheral devices, so there's a chance that as you connect the device, Windows will automatically install it with no need for you to make any choices.*

2

USB devices have an advantage over those that use other types of connections, such as serial ports: USB devices can usually draw power from the system over the USB line itself. This eliminates the need for a separate power supply and one of those bulky transformer boxes that ends up using at least one electrical outlet. Some USB devices, however, require more power than is supplied on the USB line, so they may include their own separate power supplies. USB hard disks and CD-ROM drives are good examples.

A variety of connectors and cables are used on USB equipment. As with almost any cable, USB includes male and female ends, as shown in Figure 2-5. USB goes a step further by defining different types of connectors for the "upstream" (the A connectors) and "downstream" (the B connectors) ends of the cable.

Consider a simple example with a single USB device connected directly to the computer. The computer is upstream, and the device is downstream. The computer and device each contain female connectors, also called *receptacles*, and the cable contains male connectors, also called *plugs*. At the computer, you insert the A plug into the A receptacle, and at the device you insert the B plug into the B receptacle.

Usually, when you buy a USB device, it includes a USB cable with an A plug on one end and the appropriate B connector on the other. You may also occasionally see extension cables, which, like a power extension cable, simply add some length to the connection.

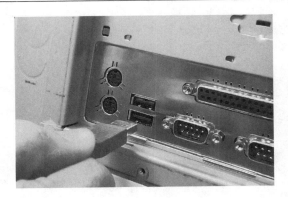

FIGURE 2-5   USB connectors

NOTE
All legitimate and useful USB cables have an A connector on one end and a B connector on the other, or a male A and female A similar to the extender mentioned above. Some vendors sell cables with the same connector on both ends. These can be dangerous; if you were to connect two computers directly via their A plugs, you could create a fire hazard because both ends are supplying power on the line. Special A-to-A cables are available from a variety of vendors, and these include a filter device through which you can connect two computers via USB; doing so directly with a simple cable is dangerous.

Each USB connector on your computer is a separate *bus*. This means that each operates independently and that you can connect, theoretically, up to 127 devices on each connector. Realistically, you can't connect anywhere near that amount, but by attaching what is called a USB *hub* you can add extra devices to the bus.

The hub is a USB device itself, with male connector that plugs into the female receptacle on your system or into another hub. The hub has two or more female receptacles to accept two or more USB devices or more hubs. For instance, the Linksys USBHUB4C Compact USB 4-Port Hub, shown in Figure 2-6, provides four USB ports in a small space. Because the short cable on the USBHUB4C makes it so close to the computer, you may want to buy an extender cable to run between the hub and the system so that the hub is more accessible.

Not all systems come with USB ports, and some systems don't come with enough of them. In any event, you can buy PCI adapters from a number of vendors that

FIGURE 2-6 USB hubs like the Linksys USBHUB4C Compact USB 4-port hub allow you to use multiple devices on a single USB bus on your system

add USB ports to a desktop computer, as well as PC cards to add adapters to notebook computers.

USB 1.1 vs. USB 2.0   There are two major versions of USB.: USB 1.1 (1.0 was never released to the general public) is rated at up to 12 Mbps, but you would probably get only 8 to 10 Mbps. USB 2.0, for which products are beginning to appear in mid-2002, is rated at 480 Mbps. Yes, you saw that right—it's that much faster.

> **NOTE** *You'll see Mbps a lot in networking. It refers to megabits per second, or million bits per second. MBps (note the capital B) refers to megabytes per second.*

Practical terms are somewhat different from these theoretical numbers. With USB, as with most wire transfers (including networks), a certain amount of overhead is involved in organizing the data on the wire (this is called *protocol overhead*). Plus, these ratings are for all devices on the bus, so if you are using a hub and more than one device is sharing the bus, the rated speed (12 Mbps for USB 1.1) is the *combined* limit for all devices on that bus.

Each USB connector on the system is a separate bus, so you may want to give some thought to how you plug in the various devices you have. For instance, some devices, like joysticks and keyboards, use minimal bandwidth and can be combined on a bus easily. But a wireless network can use the whole bandwidth of the USB, so any other devices on the bus with it are likely to impede the performance of the network.

Computers with USB 2.0 ports in them did not appear on the market until 2002, so your computer may not have them. You can, however, buy a PCI adapter or PC card to add USB 2.0 ports to your system.

Portable Computer Hardware

Portable computers, usually known as *laptop* or *notebook* computers, can make a lot of sense for home network use. Notebooks aren't the only computers that are perfectly suited to wireless networks, but they may be the best systems for wireless.

I'm writing this chapter on an IBM ThinkPad computer sitting back in my living room, and the notebook is connected to my wireless network, which is connected to the Internet. In the morning, I read several newspapers online in my kitchen while I eat breakfast. When the ball game is on, I have my notebook handy in the bedroom or living room to browse any of several sports sites to get live statistics.

If a baseball game is not on TV, I can listen to it over Internet radio, through my wireless network, wherever my notebook and I happen to be, including on my deck. This is very cool stuff.

Of course, nothing this good comes for free. Notebook computers, especially quality brand-name notebook computers, are more expensive than desktop computers. But the difference in cost is nowhere near what it used to be. You can purchase a perfectly good notebook computer (it's possible that prices could go up, although that doesn't often happen) from the best companies in the business for $1000–$1200. On the other hand, perfectly good desktop computers start at around $600–$800, including a cheap monitor.

If you don't need or want a wireless network, all the other types of network hardware are available for notebook computers. In recent years, Windows has improved its ability to be disconnected from one networked environment and connected to another. For example, you might be connected to the wired Ethernet LAN at your office. At the end of the day, you can log off, disconnect the wire, and go home. When you turn on the computer back at home, Windows will find the wireless network and you'll be connected to your printer and the Internet through it. Or, you could connect the notebook to the Linksys HomeLink Phoneline or Instant PowerLine network and you'd be working on that. Like me, you might have your own wired Ethernet network (I have a lot of networks at home), and you could use the same Ethernet adapter from work on your home network. Windows will find the right network resources either way.

Some late-model, high-end notebook computers come with "Wi-Fi" hardware built in, and many more come with wired Ethernet hardware. But most users will have to buy a hardware device to get their notebook connected to a network.

PC Cards

A long-established standard for expansion cards in portable computers, PCMCIA is the acronym for Personal Computer Memory Card International Association, the standards body that defines these specifications (or perhaps, as someone suggested at the time of its invention, "People Cannot Memorize Computer Industry Acronyms"). The industry has moved more recently to the name "PC Card" for these credit card–sized adapters, especially for the more recent implementations of them.

PC Card Types

Two types of technical implementations of these cards exist, although the cards themselves appear almost identical. The initial PCMCIA specification defined a

16-bit card type that was very successful. In 1997, a 32-bit specification called CardBus was announced, and all portable computers sold in the last few years have supported this standard. In general, CardBus PC Cards are much faster than the old 16-bit PCMCIA cards and consume less power.

Most 16-bit PCMCIA cards will work in a CardBus slot, although CardBus PC Cards are "keyed" so as not to fit in a 16-bit PCMCIA slot. Some 16-bit cards are still on the market today because of this forward compatibility and the fact that many users still use older notebook computers, but look for the older 16-bit cards to disappear over time. CardBus also requires special support from the operating system or third-party device drivers. All versions of Windows since Windows 98 support CardBus. If your system supports CardBus, you should look for CardBus options.

Although all the cards are the same length and width and have the same dense, two-row 68-pin connector, the three types of available cards offer different levels of thickness:

- Type I cards are 3.3mm thick. They are used for memory devices and you won't likely encounter them when shopping for home networking equipment.

- Type II cards are 5.0mm thick. These are the most popular types of cards and are used frequently for networking equipment as well as for modems and other devices.

- Type III cards are 10.5mm thick, which means they must be inserted in the bottom slot but consume the upper slot's space as well. They were designed for small hard drives, but they are sometimes used for other types of devices as well.

PC Card Connectors

All PC Cards are physically small, and it has been a challenge for vendors to find ways for users to attach relatively large cable connections to them. The initial solution that's still popular is to have a separate attachment with the necessary plugs that connects to the PC Card via a separate small plug to the card. Consider the attachment shown in Figure 2-7. Such attachments are often called "dongles" for their resemblance to devices of that name that were used for security purposes in completely different circumstances. We'll use the more descriptive and accurate name "coupler."

In later years, the industry came up with a more convenient solution than couplers. In these cards, such as the one pictured in Figure 2-8, the cable connections are

FIGURE 2-7   Many PC Cards come with an attachment, sometimes called a coupler, sometimes a dongle, with the receptacles to which cables connect

part of a plastic attachment to the card itself. These are referred to as *integrated* PC Cards. The upside to this arrangement is that you have only one piece of hardware to carry around.

Integrated PC Cards have two potential downsides: First, if you're not careful while the card is installed in the notebook computer, it's possible to break off the attachment. Truth be told, this is also possible with the coupler when it's plugged in, but it's less of an issue because you can detach the coupler without removing the card. So, for example, if you put your notebook in a briefcase, you may want to remove an integrated card entirely from the computer, but you'd only need to remove the coupler from the older type of card. In either case, you need to be careful not to misplace the part after you remove it.

FIGURE 2-8   Other PC Cards come with the receptacles integrated into the card, which can be more convenient, but you must be careful with it

The second potential downside to an integrated card is that the attachments are physically thicker than the cards themselves, so it's not usually possible to install two of them in the same system at once. Some older types of PCMCIA cards, notably those with the "XJACK" type connector, are physically blocked by either the coupler or integrated cards. But this is mostly history; in a home networking situation, you'll likely need to use only one card at a time, and probably just the networking card.

Working with PC Cards

The physical access to PC Cards of all types is identical. The cards slide lengthwise into a slot typically on the side of the computer. You need to press the card all the way in until it won't go any further. At this point, the back end of the card—the point at which either the coupler or the attachment with the connectors attaches to the card—will be even with the outside edge of the computer.

To remove the card, depress the small and inconvenient button just to the side of the PC Card. In most cases, when you press and release the button it will pop further out of the system, but the card will not yet release from the slot. When you press the button a second time, the action will push the card out of the slot and release it from the pressure holding it in place. You can then pull it out the rest of the way with ease.

USB Connections

Most modern notebook computers also come with a USB connection, just like the desktops. The receptacle on the notebook will be an A type (mentioned earlier in the chapter), and the notebook will likely have only one of them installed.

USB-based networking hardware will work fine on a notebook computer, but you will be less free to move about with the computer. At the least, devices will be hanging off the computer. If you keep your notebook computer in one place, a USB solution can be a good one. But if you want to be able to move the computer around and stay on the network, PC Cards are the way to go.

Notebooks often have an expensive option available called a *docking station*. It's a separate part that the notebook connects to via a large, proprietary connector on its back. The docking station, or a cheaper but similar device called a *port replicator*, has connections to printers, networks, and perhaps a full-sized mouse, keyboard, and monitor. The idea is that you can plug the notebook into it and use it like a full-sized computer, or you can detach the notebook and use it by itself.

A USB hub, such as the Linksys USBHUB4C Compact USB 4-Port Hub, can be an effective "poor man's docking station." You can connect a printer, network, keyboard, and mouse to the hub and plug the hub into your notebook when you want to use the notebook in its main location. When you want to move the notebook, all you need to do is detach the USB plug. You will be off the network at this point, though.

Personal Digital Assistants

PDAs, especially those based on Microsoft Windows for Pocket PC, also known as Windows CE, are designed to work on their own and periodically synchronize with a personal computer. But many Pocket PC devices can be expanded through their Compact Flash Type I or II slot, and Linksys makes a Wi-Fi card, the WCF12 (and WCF11) Wireless CompactFlash Card, that can be used to connect a Pocket PC PDA directly to the LAN, and thereby to the Internet.

These devices are expensive, and they would be an extravagant toy to get purely for home use. But you certainly might have one for legitimate reasons at work, and presumably you do go home at night. Why not hook it up to your wireless network at home and surf the Web or send and receive e-mail on it? You can even use a Pocket PC device to control your Windows XP desktop computer over the network. Once again, very cool stuff.

Network Hardware

We've discussed PCs and the different ways to connect peripherals to them, and perhaps you're already familiar with at least some of these concepts. The world of networking equipment has its own set of standard device types that you're likely to run into. In this section, we'll discuss these devices generically. Throughout the rest of the book, we'll discuss specific products of these types that you might use to set up an actual network. But this section will help you to understand what they do.

Network Interface Cards

A Network Interface Card (NIC) is the hardware that performs the actual network communication. As discussed earlier, it might connect to the computer in any number of ways—PCI or USB, for example—or it might come built into the PC.

As discussed in Chapter 1, the type of network with which the NIC communicates could be wired Ethernet, Wi-Fi, your home telephone cables, or even electrical wires. In any case, you need a NIC, and you need a Windows device driver to allow Windows to control the NIC.

Cable

There was a time when many different types of cable were used in networking, but the market has shaken out a bit. In today's world of small networks, you might use two basic types of cable: category 5 (cat 5) and phone line cable.

Category 5

Conventional wired networks usually use cable referred to as cat 5, which specifies a certain level of capacity as well as physical characteristics. The wire itself has four twisted pairs of copper wire with RJ-45 connectors on both ends. RJ-45s (shown next) look like RJ-11 telephone connectors, but they're larger to accommodate the fact that they hold twice as much wire.

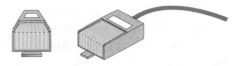

Cat 5 cabling can handle network speeds up to 1000 Mbps (or 1Gbps—gigabit per second), but almost all network equipment sold for small networks operates at 100 Mbps (or at the older standard of 10 Mbps). This speed is fast for any small network, and networking hardware that operates at this speed is affordable, whereas gigabit networking hardware is much more expensive.

When you buy a NIC or other networking equipment, it may come with a length of cable, but you may also need extra cables, perhaps to run at a length greater than the cable supplied with your equipment. You can go to any computer or large business supply store and buy cable, generally labeled as network cable and probably category 5. You can also buy cable from Internet mail-order houses that will have a far greater selection and better prices. My network is probably more complicated than yours, but I find it useful to buy as many different colored cables as possible to make it easier to tell one from the other.

NOTE   *If you buy networking equipment and it comes with wiring intended for use with the equipment, try to use the included wire with the equipment. Strictly speaking, you may not have to use the provided wire, but it is designed for that equipment, so using it decreases your chances of having a problem.*

The ambitious and frugal among you might want to buy raw cable and connectors and make your own, and there are times when this is handy. But for most of you, paying a few extra bucks to get a cable that you can return if it doesn't work is a fair trade-off. If you want instructions on making your own network wiring, see Chapter 4.

Crossover Cables   In almost every case, all cat 5 cables are functionally interchangeable. But in a few situations, you need a special type of cable with a subtly different wiring scheme. It's called a *crossover cable*, and you can use it to wire two computers directly together, NIC to NIC, without any intervening hardware, to create a two-station LAN. (Such a setup is not very flexible or expandable, but it can be helpful in diagnosing some problems.) You might need a crossover cable to connect some DSL and cable modems into a regular port in a hub or to connect two hubs that don't have an uplink port (more on all this later in the "Hubs" section).

It's not easy to tell, just by looking at a cable, whether it's a crossover or a regular cable. In my experience, the cables aren't specifically labeled as such. You may be able to peek into the connector and find the wiring details, but in general I recommend that if you get what you know to be a crossover cable, label it by wrapping a paper adhesive label around some part of the cable and writing "crossover" on the label.

Phone Line Cable

Nowadays, you can run 10 Mbps networking over your regular telephone lines. This networking is designed to work over the same phone lines in your home that already exist for your telephones, so you need only conventional telephone wire. It also uses the standard RJ-11 connectors. And you can still use the same phone lines for voice communications as you always have, even at the same time that the network is in use.

In general, home phone line networking can coexist with Asymmetric Digital Subscriber Line (ADSL) service you might have for Internet access. It can even work on a digital Integrated Services Digital Network (ISDN) phone line. It's possible that this sort of networking could work on phone lines connected through a private branch exchange (PBX), but it would not work well. Connections to different phones are typically physically separated within a PBX, so the phone line networking devices couldn't communicate.

Some home phone systems split the wires in a single cable into two different phone lines, and this can cause a problem for networking. Home Phoneline systems require all four wires.

Hubs

If you have more than one computer you want to connect in a network, your first option is usually to connect them to a hub. A hub is a box (see Figure 2-9) that brings some number of systems in a network together in the simplest way. Hubs are commonly used because they are simple and inexpensive. If your needs are simple, you will probably do well with a hub.

Most hubs have a number of female RJ-45 receptacles and usually an extra connector labeled "Uplink." You use cat 5 cables to connect from the NICs on computers or other devices that you are placing on the network to regular ports on the hub. The uplink port lets you take a regular RJ-45 cable and connect it from a normal port on one hub to the uplink port on another.

When you plan for a hub, it's probably better to plan for room to grow by getting a few more ports than is initially necessary. Although you have the option of chaining hubs together through their uplink ports, this just gets messy and can result in a performance hit.

The more systems and the more traffic you put on the network, the more your performance with a hub will degrade. This is because a hub works kind of like the Chicago Mercantile Exchange: everyone is shouting at everyone else. All data that goes out on the network goes to every other port in the hub, and it's up to the NIC to decide whether it wants the data or not. One approach to this is to use a more expensive type of hub, called a *manageable* or *intelligent hub*, which allows you to

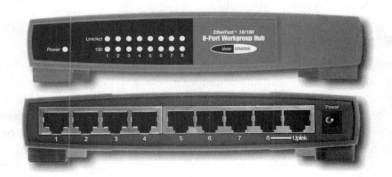

FIGURE 2-9   A hub, such as this Linksys 8-Port Workgroup Hub, has a number of ports for systems to connect to and lights to indicate whether they are connected

turn ports on and off and track the data going through it. Another way to address performance problems on some networks is to use one or more switches.

Switches

A switch performs the same basic function as a hub—connecting networked computers together—but it does it in a faster way. All the systems connected to a hub send all their data to everyone else on the hub. This means all the systems on the network are sharing the total potential throughput of the network, but this causes a problem. If two systems send out data at the same time, a collision occurs: a big part of the Ethernet protocol (CSMA/CD, or Carrier Sense Multiple Access with Collision Detection) is about detecting these collisions and arranging for systems to retransmit data. But the more data being transmitted on a network, the more likely collisions will occur.

Switches work around this problem by creating temporary dedicated connections between systems inside the switch itself. The switch keeps track of the addresses of systems attached to it so that when a packet comes in from one system addressed to another, it can move the data directly to the right port without bothering the rest of the systems. It's as if everyone is hard wired to everyone else. The collision part of the process is eliminated.

You might imagine that the switch performs a more difficult task than does a hub, and you'd be right. A switch has more sophisticated and expensive circuitry, and switches are more expensive than hubs. Few small networks have need for a switch, but if you have unusual needs, such as sending video feeds over a network, you might be able to justify the cost.

Routers

A *router* connects two distinct networks. In the context of small networks these days, this most commonly means connecting your small network to the Internet.

A lot of hard-core techie stuff figures into this. For instance, just because your systems are "on the Internet" doesn't mean they are on the same network as everyone else on the Internet. The Internet is a "network of networks," and the devices that tie all the networks together are routers. When your single computer is dialing into the Internet, you don't need a router because you're just a single client system on your Internet service provider's (ISP) network.

But if you use a network at your home or business, you will use the system's local address that makes your network distinct from the rest of those on the Net. The router knows how and when to let traffic move out to the Internet and how to send it to its destination. It also knows how to route data from the Internet to the correct systems on your network. The typical router (see Figure 2-10, for example) has a connector for the external network, probably the Internet, and one for the internal network.

Routers are often sold combined with other network functions—a switch, for example. If the combined unit has enough ports, you don't have to buy any other hardware to connect your systems to the Internet (apart from a cable modem or other Internet access hardware).

Wireless Access Points

In a wireless network, each system on the network has a wireless NIC. While it's possible to run the network just fine with the individual systems communicating via these cards, it's often a good idea to get a wireless access point—a central antenna that acts as a sort of hub for the wireless network.

You'll probably want to connect your wireless network to the Internet, so wireless access points are frequently sold with integrated routers that you can connect to a cable modem or DSL modem or some other Internet connection. I have mine plugged into a separate hub.

Wireless access points have a few standard management capabilities. To allow client systems to choose from among multiple wireless networks, you can set a name for the network to which an access point belongs. You can also control an encryption capability available to all Wi-Fi networks called WEP, for Wired Equivalent Privacy. We'll discuss all this in greater detail in Chapter 5.

FIGURE 2-10   At its simplest, a router has connections for two networks: the LAN is your internal network and the WAN the external one, probably the Internet

Chapter 3

Internet Connection Hardware

Y ou may want a network at your home or small business for sharing files and printers and such, but most people today want a network to share access to the Internet.

You can connect your network to the Internet in many different ways. While some ways are better than others, not all of them are available to everyone. In fact, your options may be limited, depending on where you live. Such are the laws of economics and physics: high-speed Internet service may be unavailable from your phone company and/or your cable TV company, assuming cable TV is even available in your area. Not everyone can put up a satellite dish, either.

These high-speed services are usually known as *broadband*, a word which alludes to a wider pipe through which data is fed to you. Broadband services are becoming more and more widely available throughout the United States, but it will still be a while before they are available to most U.S. residents.

The baseline for Internet service, telephone dial-up service, will work, even to share access across a small network, but it's the kind of solution that engineers call "suboptimal," meaning that they really wish they had a better option. Once you get a taste of broadband, it's hard to go back to a plain old dial-up modem. Internet access for one user is slow enough through a dial-up connection; imagine how slow it would be with multiple users on your home network surfing the Net.

Depending on your method of connecting to the Internet, you may have more or less freedom in selecting equipment to use. For instance, all large cable modem networks support an accepted standard for cable modems, so you don't have to buy equipment from the cable company. There is no such standard for digital subscriber line (DSL) equipment, so if you are getting DSL service you will likely have to buy equipment for it from the Internet Service Provider (ISP).

In any case, your connection to the Internet is a matter separate from how the computers on your network share that Internet connection, which is accomplished via both hardware and software. Broadband Internet access devices, such as the Linksys BEFCMU10 EtherFast Cable Modem, come with connections that make it easy to work with routers, which connect the network to the Internet. Telephone dial-up modems, on the other hand, don't connect easily to a home network, although you can make the connection by adding software that comes with all recent versions of Windows. Such hardware routers and the software methods are discussed in greater detail in Chapter 8.

Another issue which you should be aware of in evaluating Internet access is *asymmetric transfer rates*. In most cases, the rate of data transfer from you to the

3

Internet (often called the *upstream* rate) will be slower than the rate of data coming from the Internet to you (the *downstream* rate). When the rates differ, the service is called *asymmetric*. When they are the same, it is called *symmetric*. This is not a serious concern, since in almost all cases users receive far more data than they send. But when shopping for Internet service, you should check to make sure that the upstream rate is reasonable.

Normally, a higher upstream rate is required to operate Internet servers, such as Web and mail servers, and few small network operators run such servers. In fact, operating such servers is often a violation of the terms of service for your ISP, so make sure to check your service agreement. Many teenagers join clandestine peer-to-peer (P2P) networks to share music and other files, which can easily consume all of your upstream bandwidth, potentially slowing down everyone else using the Internet. One solution to this is to ban such uses on your network—good luck!

Each computer connected to the Internet needs a unique Internet address, called an IP (Internet Protocol) address. With most Internet service plans, every machine that connects to the Internet gets a temporary address when it connects. These addresses, also known as Dynamic Host Configuration Protocol (DHCP) addresses (see Chapter 8), are yours for only a period of time while you're connected— which means, for example, that you can't register a name (like *www.linksys.com*) and have it point to your systems, because such name registrations always require what is called a *static IP address*—a permanent IP address.

Some classes of more expensive advanced Internet service, especially from DSL providers, will offer static IP addresses. It's possible that you have a legitimate need for this, but few home users do. The applications for which you would need such a feature, such as setting up a mail server, are beyond the scope of this book.

Telephone Modems

If nothing else is available, you can always get telephone-based Internet service. It's available in almost every country across the globe, and at any particular location in the United States you probably have several options. The hardware device you use for this is properly known as a *modem*, which is basically a telephone for the computer.

What's a Modem?

A computer modem has to use the same analog frequencies and other facilities that you use when you make a voice call. (Incidentally, sometimes you'll see conventional telephone service derisively referred to by techies as POTS, for *Plain Old Telephone Service.*)

The word *analog*, a shortened version of *analogous*, is often used in contrast to the word *digital*. Think of the difference between a digital clock, which displays a precise numeric time, and an analog clock, which has minute and hour hands. Since the computer is talking *digital* information over an *analog* phone line, it has to translate the digital data it is communicating into analog sounds that it sends over the phone line. It also knows how to pick up the line, dial the phone, hang up, and so on. At the other end of the line, at your ISP's office (called a *Point of Presence* or POP), are groups of other modems receiving these calls and communicating with your computer and its modem.

When two modems talk, their main job is to turn digital data from the computer, binary 1 and 0 values, into analog data that can move over the telephone lines. This process is called *modulation*. At the other end, the modem receiving the analog signal converts it back into digital data, and this process is called *demodulation*. The shortened combination of these two terms is where the word *modem* comes from.

You can buy modems in two forms, internal and external. An internal modem is inserted as a card in your computer (probably as a PCI card; see Chapter 2 for more detail on such hardware). Many computers, especially portable computers, come with *integrated*, or preinstalled, modems. In either case, an internal modem has two female telephone plugs exposed on the outside—one to connect to the telephone jack on the wall and probably labeled "LINE," and another to be connected to a conventional telephone for voice use when the modem is not being used for data. This other plug is probably labeled "PHONE," or shows a small drawing of a telephone.

External modems connect to the computer via a cable. In most cases, this is called a *serial* cable; on the computer side, it will connect to a 9-pin male plug. On the modem side, the connection will probably be a female 25-pin plug. When you buy the modem, buy a serial cable specifically meant for a modem, because many other types of serial cables are available. Some modern external modems connect to the computer using USB, as discussed in Chapter 2. Such modems use standard USB cables and probably come with one.

External modems tend to be more expensive than internal modems, but they have several advantages: You don't have to open the computer to install it. You can turn it on and off separate from turning the computer on and off, which can be helpful for clearing up certain connection problems. Best of all, external modems have a series of lights that indicate the status of communications. You can see if the modem is on, if it has a connection to the other end, and if data is being transmitted or received.

Modem Speeds

For many years through the '80s and '90s, the industry steadily increased the standard speed of modems, but now they appear to have reached a permanent plateau. The highest data rate you can expect to get downstream is about 53,000 bits per second, or 53 Kbps. The highest upstream rate that is possible with an analog modem is 33.6 Kbps.

You may see many terms referring to modems that fit the current standards, including 56K, V.90, and V.92. The term 56K is a misleading indicator that has somehow stuck with these modems, since it's not possible to get more than 53 Kbps. V.90 is a standard defined by the International Telecommunication Union (ITU). At the time modems of this speed class were released, more than one proprietary definition for them existed, and V.90 resolved the differences between them. You may also see V.92, a compatible standard that reduces the handshake time, which is that period of time during which the modems establish a connection (when you hear the modems screeching at each other).

It's important that you understand that just because a modem is technically capable of speeds up to 53 Kbps doesn't mean that you will get those speeds. The quality of the telephone lines can limit the speed of connection. And even with the highest quality lines, the use of certain telephone equipment, either in your building or by your telephone company, may prevent you from getting greater than 33.6 Kbps downstream speed. (Speeds up to 53 Kbps rely on techniques that are prevented by such equipment.)

NOTE
Your modem may achieve greater throughput than the rate at which the modems are actually transmitting data because some modems compress data before transmitting it on the line.

ISDN

Telephones, as you know, are designed to use analog signals. But a special type of digital phone line is available from the phone company called ISDN, for *Integrated Services Digital Network.*

ISDN provides three channels for communication—one A channel at 16 Kbps and two B channels at 64 Kbps each. ISDN terminal adapters (they aren't "modems" because they don't modulate or demodulate) bond all these together to provide a highest theoretical throughput of 144 Kbps.

> **NOTE** *Some ISDN services don't include all three channels, depending on what your telephone company offers. Also, note that your ISDN-based Internet service is a separate service at a separate cost from your ISDN line itself, and you will not be able to use the ISDN line for conventional voice telephony.*

If you've been shopping around for broadband Internet service using other device types such as a cable modem or DSL (discussed next), you know that 144 Kbps is not a very high speed. In general, ISDN missed the boat as a technology and is not the best option for you unless it is the only option for you. You will have to check with all the potential providers of service to see if this is the case.

The original idea of ISDN, when it was developed in the 1980s, was for it to serve both data and enhanced voice needs, but the telephone companies and hardware manufacturers failed to agree on effective national standards until fairly recently.

Cable Modems

A cable modem enables broadband Internet access through the same cable lines that deliver cable television. In general, considering all the cost and ease of use factors, it's usually the best option for consumers, although the specifics differ from one cable provider to another. For businesses, options can be very different, and once again you have to check the service agreement to see what is legal.

Like telephone modems, cable modems modulate and demodulate data, which actually travels on the wire in a portion of analog television bandwidth. Unlike telephone modems, this data travels at a very fast rate allowing you, potentially, to download several megabits of data per second. Upstream data has a much narrower bandwidth and has to contend with more interference from other devices, which is one reason why cable modem connections are invariably asymmetric: Your downstream bandwidth will be many times faster than your upstream bandwidth.

None of this interferes with your cable TV services on the same wire, and of course, since it doesn't use your phone lines, it doesn't interfere with your ability to make phone calls.

Older One-Way Systems

Few of these exist. Some older cable modem systems use the cable modem only for downstream data and a telephone line for upstream data. Such networks were built only with downstream repeaters to save money because conventional television doesn't require upstream transmission. These systems are relatively rare and rely on proprietary cable modem hardware, so if you are in an area served by such a system you probably have no choice anyway, and your cable company will probably provide your cable modem.

Equipment

The actual cable modem is a device that connects on one end to the cable, just as your television or VCR does, and on the other end it connects either directly to a PC or to some other network device.

The Linksys BEFCMU10 EtherFast Cable Modem with USB and Ethernet Connection, pictured in Figure 3-1, is a perfect example. It is designed to support

FIGURE 3-1   The Linksys BEFCMU10 EtherFast Cable Modem with USB and Ethernet Connection

either a stand-alone PC or to connect a local area network (LAN) to the Internet through the cable system. You have numerous options for how to do this, which are explored here.

The BEFCMU10 conforms to a well-respected standard for cable modems called DOCSIS (Data-Over-Cable Service Interface Specifications), which is administered by an organization called CableLabs (*http://www.cablemodem.com/*). All large cable modem networks will support DOCSIS-compliant modems, such as the BEFCMU10, meaning you don't have to buy or lease equipment from the cable company. All DOCSIS-compliant cable modems should work on any DOCSIS-compliant network. CableLabs tests and certifies the modems before they can be labeled as DOCSIS-certified.

Most cable modems, including the BEFCMU10, are capable of speeds far greater than is allowed on your cable modem network. Cable modem equipment supports standards, including SNMP, which you may recognize as a corporate network management standard as well, to control the speeds at which cable modems operate. They do this mostly to prevent a small number of individuals from consuming a large percentage of their network bandwidth, although even with the restrictions that happens.

Setting Up the BEFCMU10

Connect the power adapter (the thin wire with the transformer block attached) included in the package to the plug labeled "Power" on the cable modem. Then connect the included power cable from the transformer block to a power outlet.

NOTE   *No matter how you connect your cable modem to your PC or network, you're going to need the TCP/IP protocol installed on the PC. If it is not installed, or if you don't know whether it is, read Chapter 8 for installation instructions.*

The BEFCMU10 has four lights on its front panel that represent the following:

■ **Power**   When this light is on, the cable modem is receiving power correctly. It should always be on as long as the cable modem is plugged in.

■ **Activity**   This light indicates activity between the cable modem and the PC or router to which it is attached. It won't be on constantly; it indicates data moving between the cable modem and the computer(s).

■ **Cable**   This light indicates activity between the cable modem and the cable modem network. It, too, will not be on constantly, but only when data is being transmitted.

■ **Status**   This light flashes on and off as the cable modem is turned on and attempts to connect to the cable modem network. When the cable modem has successfully connected to the cable network, this light will stay on constantly. If it keeps blinking after ten minutes, there may be a problem with the cable modem, but more likely with the cable connection. Check the physical cable connection. Try resetting the cable modem by pressing the reset button. If the status light stays blinking, contact your cable company. There may be a problem with the signal.

The BEFCMU10 also has a pinhole on the back labeled "Rst." This is the reset button. If the cable modem becomes jammed somehow (cable network or electrical problems can cause this, but it's rare and impossible to predict), you can use the end of a paper clip or something similarly pointed to depress the internal button in the hole. This will reset the cable modem to factory defaults and cause it to restart as if you powered it up.

If you are connecting the cable modem to an Ethernet adapter in a PC, or if you are connecting the cable modem directly to the network through a router (see "Connecting the Cable Modem to the Network" later in the chapter for more on these options), you do not need to install any drivers or other special software on your PCs. You may need to configure the TCP/IP settings for each PC; we discuss this in detail in Chapter 8.

If you are connecting the cable modem to a PC using USB, you need to install the BEFCMU10 USB device driver. Windows helps you do this. Insert the CD-ROM that came with the cable modem into the computer's CD-ROM drive. If Windows' AutoPlay feature loads the Setup Utility, click the Exit button near the top-right of the window. (If you wish, you can use the Setup Utility to read an electronic version of the cable modem manual, the printed version of which also came in the box with the cable modem.)

> **NOTE**   *You may also need your original Windows CD-ROM. Make sure it's available before you begin installation.*

USB Setup in Windows 98   Here's how to set up a USB in Windows 98.

1. With the cable modem turned on and connected to the cable modem network (both the Power and Status lights should be on and not blinking), connect the USB cable from the computer to the cable modem. Windows will detect the new hardware and load the Add New Hardware Wizard, specifying "USB Composite Device." Click Next.

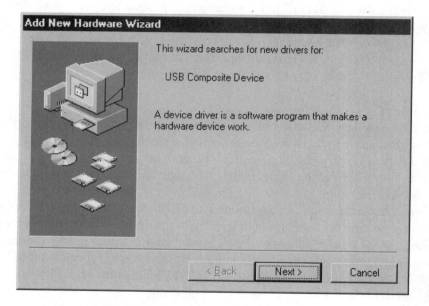

2. The next screen in the wizard asks whether it should search for the best driver or let you specify what driver to load. Almost everyone should leave the default, recommended selection to search. If you're following your own path on the setup and know what you are doing, you can choose the other option (good luck; you're on your own).

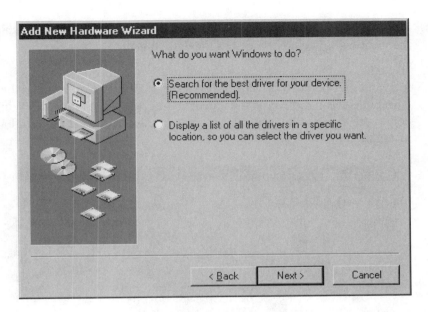

3. Next, you tell Windows where to get the driver. If your cable modem came with drivers on a CD-ROM, select only the CD-ROM Drive option and Click Next. If your drivers are on a floppy disk, insert it, select Floppy Disk Drives, and then click Next.

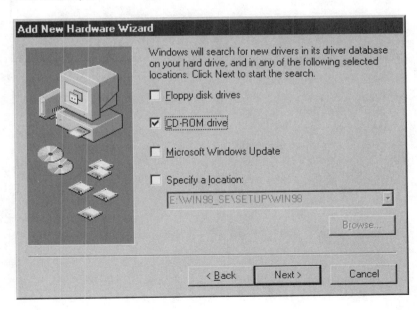

4. When Windows finds the driver on the disk you specified, it will display the location on the next screen as the default choice. Click Next.

5. In the next screen, you are asked specifically to confirm that you want to install the specified driver for the specified device. Confirm that the correct device and driver is indicated, and click Next again. After Windows copies the driver and installs it, you may be asked to insert the Windows installation disk.

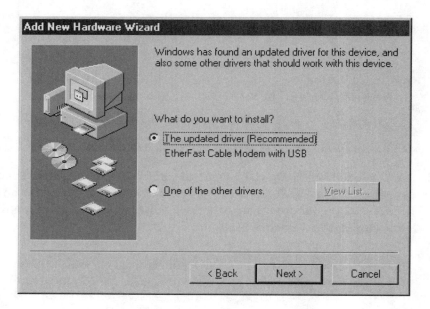

6. Finally, the wizard tells you what driver you have installed. It may then ask you to reboot the computer. Click Finish.

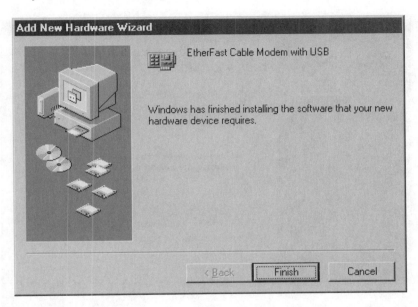

USB Setup in Windows XP Home   Here's how to set up a USB with Windows XP:

1. With the cable modem turned on and connected to the cable modem network (both the Power and Status lights should be on and not blinking), connect the USB cable from the computer to the cable modem. Windows will detect the new hardware. First, a small bubble will pop up in the bottom-right of the screen stating "Found: USB Cable Modem." Then, the Found New Hardware Wizard will start, stating that it will help you to load software for the USB cable modem. So far, so good.

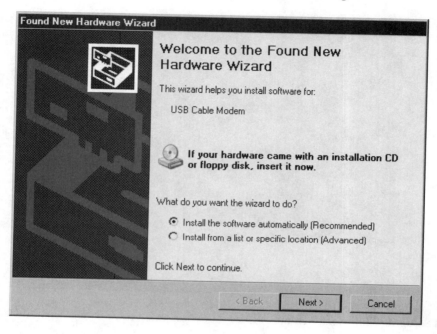

2. As the wizard says, if the driver disk for the cable modem is not yet inserted in the appropriate drive, insert it now. Leave the default selection to Install The Software Automatically (Recommended) and click Next.

3. Depending on the version of drivers that you are running, you may next see a scary dialog box telling you that the drivers for the cable modem have not passed Microsoft's compatibility tests for Windows XP. While it would be nice for the drivers to have passed the tests, it's OK at this point to install them anyway by clicking the Continue Anyway button.

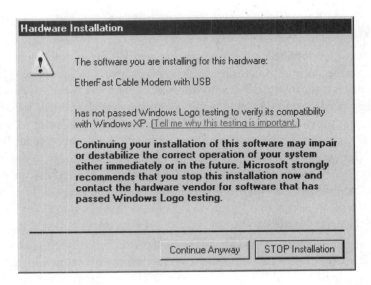

4. Windows copies the appropriate files from the driver disk to the computer and completes the wizard. Click Finish to exit it. Windows will also temporarily pop up another balloon message in the bottom right to let you know that the device has been installed and is ready to use.

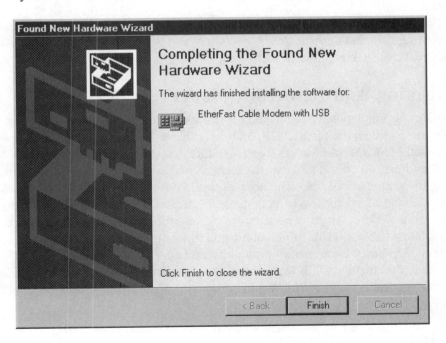

Cable Modem Service Options

Many cable modem services offer one level of service, which makes things simple. But others are beginning to offer multiple service levels to discount service to users who put a light load on the network and to get more from those who use it heavily. They usually do this not by setting a "bit quota" that limits the amount of data you can transmit for a price, but by charging more for faster service. The heavier your use, the less acceptable slower service would be. My philosophy, given such choices, is to try to get along with the slower service, with the knowledge that I can probably move up a service class if I need to. Incidentally, in almost all cases, cable modem service will prohibit you from running servers on your computers.

Business Cable Modem Plans

Read your service agreement: Many cable modem service agreements state that they are intended only for personal use. I know that my cable modem service prohibits the use of Virtual Private Networks on their consumer service. (They probably have no way of enforcing this rule, but if you want to follow the rules it's an issue.)

For this reason, some providers, like mine, have more expensive service plans intended for business users. The business service offered by my provider costs more than twice what the consumer service costs—pretty much just to let you run a VPN. For far more money, perhaps hundreds of dollars per month, my cable modem service, and perhaps yours, will allow you to use servers and many other fancy features such as static IP addresses.

Activating Your New Cable Modem

All network adapters have unique addresses associated with them that are of a different kind than the Internet (IP) addresses discussed earlier. These addresses are called MAC (Media Access Control) addresses. All cable modems have a MAC address, too, because they are essentially network adapters on the Internet.

In the same package as your cable modem, you will find some conspicuous label with the MAC address of your cable modem as well as its serial number. Your cable modem company needs these two numbers to activate your service through that cable modem. If you don't find these numbers separate from the cable modem, they are probably printed on stickers on the cable modem itself. If you don't find them at all, bring the cable modem back to where you obtained it, because it's useless without these numbers.

If you have your cable modem before you call to set up your cable modem service from your cable provider, you can probably provide the cable company with the MAC and serial numbers at the time you set up service. If not, you will probably have to call the customer service or technical support number for your cable company to provide them with this information. There may be a delay of a few hours or perhaps a bit longer before your cable modem is functional on the network.

Connecting the Cable Modem to the Network

To serve a network of users, you can set up your cable modem in two basic ways. The first, and most convenient, way is to connect it to a router, such as the Linksys BEFSR11 EtherFast Cable/DSL Router. This router can then attach to a hub or switch into which you can connect the systems in your network. The router will connect them all to the Internet through the cable modem, as shown in Figure 3-2.

Alternatively, you can use your PC as a router, as illustrated in Figure 3-3. You connect the cable modem directly to the PC, either using the USB connection or to an Ethernet adapter in the PC. Then you need a separate Ethernet adapter in the PC connected to the hub or switch into which all the other systems on the network are connected. At this point, the PC is on both networks: the Internet through the cable modem and the LAN through the hub.

You need routing software, such as the Internet Connection Sharing feature that comes with Windows or third-party software to make the connection between

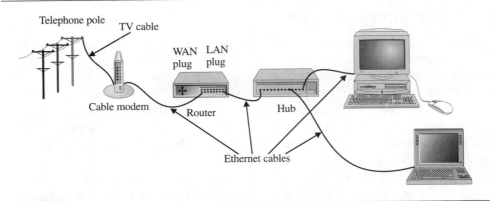

FIGURE 3-2   In a classic cable modem-based small network, the cable modem connects through a router device to a hub (the hub and router may be combined into a single box) to the PCs

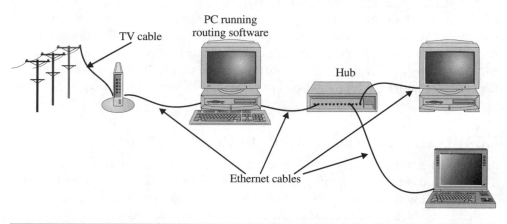

FIGURE 3-3   It's also possible to connect a cable modem directly to a PC and, optionally, run routing software on the PC to connect the rest of the network

the two networks. It's easier to do things the first way, for a number of reasons. First, the PC doing the routing has to be turned on at all times, or the other PCs won't be able to access the Internet. If the routing PC crashes, the Internet connection to the rest of the network goes down. The routing also imposes a small performance burden on that PC.

We will explore more details on how to configure setups such as these in Chapter 8.

Digital Subscriber Line

DSL uses regular telephone lines for high-speed Internet access. Even though you use the same wires, you can continue to use your phones for normal voice and fax equipment because DSL uses different frequencies on the wires.

Different types of DSL service are available, and within each type are often a dizzying variety of service plans available from several ISPs. Fortunately (or unfortunately, depending on your point of view), far fewer companies are in this business today than there used to be, so obtaining such a system isn't as complicated as it used to be.

The quality of DSL service you can get, and whether you can get it at all, depends on the physical distance between you and your telephone central office (CO). This CO is where all the area telephone lines from homes and businesses connect and are switched into the rest of the phone system. Your local phone company and possibly some competitors maintain equipment in these buildings to separate the

DSL Internet signals from the voice transmissions and connect them to the rest of the Internet.

DSL can't operate over lines longer than a certain distance, so if you attempt to order service, the company will figure out what the distance is for you to see what quality of service, if any, you can get. Different phone companies have different distance limits they allow for service, so you'll have to check with your local company, but it's not uncommon for customers to be too far from a CO for service. It's also possible, depending on how the phone wiring was done in your area, that it is incompatible with DSL.

Synchronous vs. Asynchronous vs. IDSL

Three basic types of DSL service are available, but one is more important than the others for most small network customers. Symmetric DSL (SDSL) and Asymmetric DSL (ADSL) are the two main types, with ADSL being far more common, affordable, and reasonable.

With SDSL, transmission speeds are the same for both upstream and downstream traffic. With ADSL they are different, which in reality means that downstream traffic moves faster than upstream traffic, as with most Internet services.

A third type of DSL, called IDSL, works over ISDN phone lines. (See the "Telephone Modems" section earlier in this chapter for an explanation of ISDN.) IDSL is relatively difficult to find and it's expensive, and it makes sense only for users who can't get other types of DSL because they are too far from a telephone CO.

IDSL is limited to 144 Kbps each way, which only looks like a lot compared to regular telephone modems, and cost (not including the cost of the ISDN line) rivals that of far faster ADSL lines. It can be supported a much greater distance from the CO though—up to about 50,000 feet.

How to Shop for DSL

If your local phone company sells DSL, you probably have been getting junk mail about it from them every week for years. The company may be a good choice for DSL service, but it may not be the only one.

As a result of the Telecommunications Act of 1996, telephone companies have to allow third parties, called Competitive Local Exchange Carriers (CLECs, pronounced "see-Leks"), to rent space in the CO to run their own value-added services, including DSL. In the late '90s, many of these companies were formed and many of them went out of business. But a few are still around, the biggest being Covad. You can buy DSL service directly from Covad (*http://www. covad.com/*) or through a large number of ISPs who use Covad for their DSL infrastructure. For example, my ISP is Speakeasy.net (*http://www.speakeasy.net/*), and it handles my e-mail and all the rest of the Internet part of my service, but the actual DSL service is handled by Covad and my local telephone company, Verizon.

Choosing which ISP to use can be difficult. It wouldn't be unreasonable for you to decide that your telephone company is unlikely to go out of business and just go with them. A good Web site with a lot of DSL information, including comparisons of providers, is at *http://www.dslreports.com/*.

NOTE *Remember also to check the service agreement before you sign up for DSL service. It's possible that the ISP does not allow the use of local networks to connect multiple PCs through some of their connection plans.*

DSL Equipment

Unlike with cable modems, no effective standard for DSL equipment is supported by all ISPs and phone companies. As a result, you will have to buy or lease equipment from the ISP or phone company when you get your service. These companies often have special deals for signing up new customers, involving discounted or free equipment, but you don't have the choice to go to third parties to buy equipment.

Like cable modems, the DSL "modem" is technically a network adapter on the Internet. One or more Internet (IP) addresses will be bound to it and it will attach either to a PC or a router, such as the Linksys BEFSR11 EtherFast Cable/DSL Router.

Satellite

If you live out in the middle of nowhere, there's a decent chance you have access neither to cable modem nor DSL service. But if you have access to the sky, you may be able to get broadband Internet service via a satellite dish. We can't provide a full guide to satellite Internet access here, but we will provide a brief overview of satellite issues for Internet access and some issues related to networks.

The main part of a satellite Internet connection is the satellite dish itself, so you will need to be able to mount a dish outdoors, either on your house or in your yard. Many companies provide satellite services, but two major providers work through smaller companies. Hughes Network Systems provides the DirecPC and DIRECWAY satellite services, often through partners such as Earthlink, Pegasus, and AOL. Technical support for the product is provided by the partner. Gilat provides the Starband service.

Many satellite systems operate downstream only, so you need to have a simultaneous telephone connection to transfer data upstream. As you can imagine, this is rather slow. But even satellite systems that support upstream transmission to the satellite have slow upstream transmission. Actual downstream speeds can range from a few hundred Kbps to perhaps 2500 Kbps, but the high speeds come only with a lot of hand tweaking of settings. This is just part of satellite connectivity being generally more complicated than other broadband offerings.

Connecting the Satellite to Your Network

Another complication with satellite Internet connectivity is that current products are incompatible with hardware routers. All satellite systems need to be run in conjunction with software on a PC—specifically, the satellite transceiver, often misnamed "satellite modems," need to be controlled by PC-based software.

Therefore, to connect the network to a satellite Internet connection, you need to run routing software, like Windows' included Internet Connection Sharing or a third-party product. In Chapter 8, we explain how to set up Internet Connection Sharing in detail.

Part II

Installing Your Network

Chapter 4

Installing an Ethernet Cable Network

Now that you've made your decision about the type of network connection you want to use, it's time to install the hardware and hook the computers together. Then, you have to tell Windows that the network exists, so the communication channels can be opened and you can start using your network.

Part II has a chapter for each type of network connection, filled with detailed installation instructions. Then, in Chapter 8, you'll learn how to configure the operating system to run your network, and let every computer share one Internet connection device.

If you decided to use Ethernet cable to connect your computers, you have some work to do, but it's easy, nontechnical work. You have to create the physical plant that runs your network. The central component of the plant is the hub, which accepts the Ethernet cable that arrives from each computer on the network. You have to run lengths of cable between the hub and each computer, and you also need to install a Network Interface Card (NIC) in each computer on the network to accept the computer-side connection of the cable.

The Hub: Central Control

The hub controls the communication among the computers on the network. When one computer sends a data packet to another computer, it's not sent directly (because the computers aren't directly connected to each other); instead, the data packet is sent to the hub, which passes it along to the recipient computer.

Hub Speed

Hubs come in two speed flavors: They operate at a specific speed, measured in Megabits per second (Mbps), or they are Autosensing (each port communicates with each NIC at the speed that NIC can handle). If you're building a new network, all of your NICs operate at 100 Mbps, because that's today's standard, especially for small networks. However, since most Linksys hubs are autosensing, you don't have to hunt for a hub that operates at 100 Mbps; the autosensing hub will know the speed and adjust.

I know a lot of people who created home networks by bringing home computers from work when their companies upgraded hardware. This is a great way to add computers to your home—the price is certainly right. Many of those computers have 10 Mbps NICs installed, and with autosensing hubs, you can certainly use those computers "as is." For the normal file exchanges that take place in a home network, or a small business network, it's unlikely you'll notice the difference in speed. If you sense a difference in the 10 Mbps computer, replace the NIC (see the section "Installing NICs" later in this chapter).

 *Never connect a computer that's powered on to an autosensing hub that's also powered on; turn off the power on one of the devices before inserting the cable connector.*

How Data Moves Through the Hub

A standard hub passes incoming data to all the computers that occupy ports in the hub, but only the computer that's meant to be the recipient pays any attention. Even though that means the hub wastes some communication bandwidth (it splits the bandwidth by sending the data to all the ports), you shouldn't notice any degradation in performance.

However, on some networks (usually business networks), many of the data packets are very large, especially if users are working across the network on large graphics files and the network is busy with lots of data traffic. In that case, you should consider one of the Linksys *switches*, instead of a hub. A switch is a more advanced version of a hub, and it sends data only to the computer marked as the recipient. (See the sidebar "Hubs vs. Switches" if you're interested in a slightly more technical explanation.) This keeps the performance level of your network at a productive rate, even in the face of constant large data packets.

Hubs vs. Switches

In case you're curious, here's an explanation (admittedly oversimplified) of the differences in the methods used by hubs and switches to deliver data. When data is exchanged between networked computers, the data packet (also called a *datagram*) contains information beyond the data—it contains the address of the receiving computer. The receiving computer's address is its MAC (Media Access Control) address, which is unique on the network.

All the steps you take to install the operating system files for your network (running the networking wizards, installing protocols such as TCP/IP or NetBEUI, and so on) are necessary to make sure these functions work properly. The protocol is responsible for determining the MAC address, and to accomplish this it checks a look-up table of computer names that provides all the right technical information. (Remember, in Chapter 1 you learned that computer names must be unique on the network, and if you're using TCP/IP, each computer must have its own unique IP address and MAC address. (MAC addresses cannot be changed; they are encoded into the NIC.)

When the data packet is sent to a hub, the hub ignores the address that's contained in the packet and ships the data through all the ports, sending it to every computer that's connected to the hub. The computers read the MAC address and only the computer that's the designated recipient accepts the packet; the others ignore it.

A switch is a more intelligent device than a hub, because it can store information in its memory. Switches keep their own ARP (Address Resolution Protocol) table, which match the MAC addresses to the port connections. When data arrives, the switch looks up the MAC address in its own ARP table and isolates the circuit (the port and cable) that belongs to the receiving computer, sending the data only on that circuit.

It's important to realize that what I've described here is not only a simple (perhaps simplistic) overview, but it also applies only to simple switches that are commonly found on small LANs. More sophisticated switches are available that perform more sophisticated technical tasks. (And for seriously sophisticated technology, the next step up is a *router.*)

Finding a Location for the Hub

You need to decide where to locate the hub, and you should choose a location that reduces the amount of cable you need to install to connect all the computers to the hub. This setup is called a *star topology* and it requires a length of cable between each computer on the network and the hub (see Figure 4-1).

Star Topology

Years ago, the term *star topology* was applied to distinguish this type of layout (using twisted-pair Ethernet cable to connect computers to a hub) from the layout of Ethernet coaxial cable (a daisy-chain arrangement moving from the first computer on the network to the last). In those days, we used BNC connectors to connect the Ethernet coax, and if any connection along the daisy chain was interrupted, the whole network went down. Users had a wide variety of methods for breaking the connections—tossing a heavy object (like a dictionary) on the back of the desk where it would fall behind the desk and break the connection;

or reaching for something under the desk, and accidentally yanking the coax cable; or, if the connection were within easy reach, idly twirling the connection during telephone calls until it became unscrewed (today they play FreeCell during telephone calls).

With star topology, if you disconnect one computer, the other computers keep working. Twisted-pair Ethernet, hubs, and star topology certainly made my life as a consultant much easier.

The permutations and combinations for network layouts are way too high for me to cover them with explicit advice about the location of the hub. You might have two computers on the second floor and one on the first floor, so it makes sense to locate the hub on the second floor (you'll only have one long cable run). If all your computers are on one floor (typical of a small business network), the logical place for the hub is at the mid-point. However, you can't always measure distances and put the hub in the location that mathematically works best in terms of distances. You have other considerations, which are discussed next.

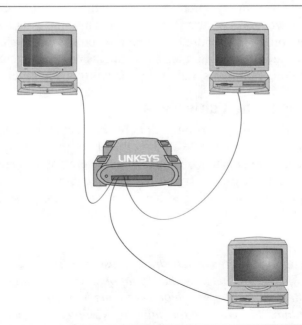

FIGURE 4-1   You need multiple cable runs to connect each computer to the hub

Access Considerations

Access to the hub is not an important issue. The only time you need to work at the hub is when you're plugging an RJ-45 connector into a port (and after you set up your network, you have to perform that task only if you add more computers to the network). There's nothing to do on a day-to-day basis—the hub just sits there, working dependably, without any baby-sitting from you. This means you can put the hub in some nook or niche and save desk space.

Linksys hubs have lights that glow to indicate connections, and they flash to indicate data transfers. When I first installed my Ethernet network, I glanced at them frequently to make sure everything was working. After a few days, I took the reliability for granted and moved the hub off the desktop and tucked it away on a shelf.

Power and Environment

Hubs require electrical power, so the location must have an electrical outlet. This eliminates most closets, which is a shame, because a closet is a great location for a hub. In addition, as with any electrical device, you need to protect the hub from overheating and excess humidity. Keep the hub away from direct sunlight, radiators, and heaters. Don't cover it or wrap it in plastic (some people do that to avoid dust), because there must be some air circulating around the hub to prevent overheating.

And, of course, you must protect it from power surges, so plug a surge protector into the outlet and plug the hub into the surge protector. Also, avoid proximity to other electrical devices that might interfere with data communication—don't put the hub next to fluorescent lights, radios, or transmitting equipment.

Near a Gateway to the Cable Runs

The cables from all the computers on your network meet at the hub, so the hub must be near a place that can handle all the cable. If you're running cable through the walls, put the hub in an inconspicuous corner where you can create a hole large enough to handle multiple cables. If you're running cable along baseboards, locate the hub at the logical place for ending each cable run. Obviously, it's best to locate the hub at the edge of a room, not in the middle of a room where the cables would snake across the floor.

NOTE   *You can add hubs to your network because your network outgrows the number of ports, or because the layout of your cable run works better if you connect one group of computers to one hub, and another group to a different hub, then connect the hubs. See Chapter 10 to learn how to link multiple hubs.*

Installing Cable

The way cable is strung through a building is called the *run,* and you need to create a plan for the run. The plan should match the type of access you have among the rooms that hold computers. For your Ethernet network, you must install multiple runs, one from each computer to the hub.

Types of Cable

4

Two broad categories of Ethernet cable exist: straight-through and crossover. The physical difference between them is the way the wires meet the connectors; the difference to users is the set of circumstances under which each type of cable is used.

Category 5 cable contains eight color-coded wires that run from one end of the cable to the other. You can see the colors easily if you have a piece of cable that doesn't have a connector (you may have to strip the outer insulation of the cable to see the colors of the wires clearly). If you look at a length of cable that has a connector, point the connector away from yourself, with the little plastic tab (it's a spring clip) on the bottom, and wire #1 is on your right. Table 4-1 explains the wiring of cat 5 cable.

NOTE
Two types of cable are available: unshielded twisted pair (UTP) and shielded twisted pair (STP). STP has a metal shield encasing the wires to reduce the possibility of interference from other electrical devices, radar, radio waves, and so on. UTP has no such shield and is less expensive, and it's almost always the cable of choice.

Wire Number	Color	Use
1	white/orange stripe	transmit data
2	orange	transmit data
3	white/green stripe	receive data
4	blue	not used
5	white/blue stripe	not used
6	green	receive data
7	white/brown stripe	not used
8	brown	not used

TABLE 4-1   The Wiring Scheme for Category 5 Cable

Crossover Cable

Crossover cable gets its name from the fact that the wires change position between connectors. (You need to consider only the wires that are actually used for Ethernet communication: 1, 2, 3, and 6.) Wires that start at one position end up at a different position, as follows:

- 1 crosses to 3
- 2 cross to 6

Of course, if you look at the crossover from the other end (the other connector), it's the reverse:

- 3 crosses to 1
- 6 crosses to 2

Crossover cable isn't used for standard network cabling; you don't use it to connect the computers to the hub. It's used for special connections—for example, you may need crossover wire to attach a DSL (Digital Subscriber Line) device to a hub or to link two hubs. The documentation for the hardware device tells you whether a crossover cable is required. It's entirely possible (and even probable) that you'll never need a crossover cable because most hubs have an uplink port which will cross the connection automatically.

Straight-Through Cable

Straight-through cable gets its name from the fact that the wires go through the cable without changing their positions, so that wire 1 at one connector is wire 1 at the other connector. (You need to consider only the wires that are actually used for Ethernet communication: 1, 2, 3, and 6.)

Straight-through cable is the standard, used for Ethernet cable that attaches components of a network together. Taking into consideration the technical nomenclature and the technical jargon, this cable is known by several names, any of which you may hear when you're buying cable or asking for help from knowledgeable friends:

- **Twisted pair**, which is a description of the way the wires are twisted through the length of cable. Insulated copper wires are twisted around each other to reduce crosstalk, or electromagnetic induction, between the pairs of wires.

■ **Category 5** (frequently called *cat 5*), which is an indication of the category (level) of the cable. Other categories of twisted pair cable exist, such as cat 2 for telephone lines and alarm systems. Cat 5e is available for high-speed (gigabit) Ethernet systems, and cat 6 is in the works.

■ **10BaseT**, which is a technical description of twisted-pair Ethernet cable to distinguish it from 10Base2 (coaxial Ethernet cable).

■ **Patch cable**, which is the term for a length of cable to which RJ-45 connectors have been added, so it's ready to use. You can build your own cable by using special tools to add an RJ-45 connector to raw twisted pair cable, but most people find that unnecessary because patch cables are inexpensive.

Measuring the Runs

Cable doesn't run from the hub to a computer in a straight line. It runs along baseboards, up or down walls, and across ceilings, so you can't measure the distance "as the crow flies." The only way to measure properly is to follow the path the cable takes. Don't forget to measure the space between the place the cable enters the room and the RJ-45 connector on the hub or the NIC.

You have one thing to worry about—the maximum length of a cable run is 328 feet (100 meters). It's unlikely that any run would be longer than that in a typical home or small business environment, but you should know that the maximum exists. If you're creating a network in a large house or office building, and the computers are spread among several floors as well as spread among the front and back parts of the building, you may end up with one run that is longer than the maximum distance allowed. The best solution is to use two hubs for the network, and then link the hubs. (Actually, the best solution is to move the computers that can't be connected within the maximum run length, but most people don't like that idea.) See Chapter 10 to learn about using multiple hubs on an Ethernet network.

The space you use to bring the cable from the computer to the hub is called a *chase*. If you're lucky, you'll have a straight-line chase between the hub and each individual computer. The chase may be inside a wall, in a hollow space above the ceiling, through the basement or attic, along the baseboards of a room, or a combination of these paths.

After you measure, you must buy patch cable (cable with the RJ-45 connectors already attached) of the right length. Most patch cable is sold in the following lengths (in feet): 10, 15, 20, 25, 50, and 100. If you need cable longer than that you can order patch cable in custom lengths from most computer stores (both online and brick-and-mortar), or you can make your own (see the sidebar "Making Your Own Patch Cables").

You can connect two pieces of cable with a coupler, which is a small plastic device that has two receptacles that accept RJ-45 connectors. The coupler works much like the couplers you can buy in any supermarket for telephone lines. (Do not use a telephone coupler for your computer cable.) However, couplers don't have a terrific history of reliability. Frequently, when I've encountered problems with network communications, the cause was the coupler. Also, never put a coupler inside a wall or in any other location that's difficult to get to, because if you have to check or replace it, you need access. The best plan is to use a coupler as a temporary measure while you wait for delivery of a custom-made patch cable that's the right length.

Linksys sells a nifty product called Network in a Box, which comes with a hub, two NICs, and two 15-foot patch cables. This is usually sufficient for a small home network in which the computers are in the same room, adjacent rooms, or stacked rooms (one room is directly above the other room).

Making Your Own Patch Cables

If you need an extra long cable, or if you're cabling a lot of computers and want to save money (or if you just like doing it yourself), you can make your own patch cables. You're not making cable, of course—you're adding connectors to lengths of cable. It's actually quite easy—I can't figure out how to use my VCR, but I've been making my own cable connectors for years. You'll need the following supplies and tools:

- Bulk cat 5 cable, which sells for about 10 cents a foot

- RJ-45 connectors, which cost less than 50 cents each

- A wire stripper, which costs a few dollars

- A crimper, which costs about 20 to 25 dollars

The prices really depend on the size of the order, as the more cable and connectors you buy, the lower the unit cost. I have a combo stripper/crimper that was about $35, and it also handles RJ-11 connectors for regular phone cable (I wired my own PBX phone system) in addition to cat 5 cable.

To make a patch cable, follow these steps:

1. Cut the cable to the length you need (plus two–three feet "just in case").

2. Use the stripper to remove about a half-inch of insulation and expose the wires.

3. Push the wires into the holes on the connector (see Table 4-1 for the colors). They slide in easily.

4. Set the crimper for RJ-45 connectors.

5. Position the crimper where the connector and the wires meet, and press firmly.

6. Repeat these steps to add a connector at the other end of the cable.

Assembling Your Tools

Depending on the layout of the building and the placement of computers, you'll need one or more of the following tools to install your network cables:

- A fish, which is a long, thin length of metal encased in a holder (it looks like a steel tape measure on steroids). The metal is thin and flexible but very strong. The front end of the fish is a hook, which can grab cable and fish it toward you through walls. If the distance isn't very long, you can sometimes get away without buying or borrowing a fish (do you have a friend who is an electrician?) or by using a coat hanger you've untwisted (the hook at the end grabs the cable).

- A drill, with a bit large enough to make a hole at least 7/8ths of an inch in diameter. The connector on patch cable is about a half-inch wide, but the little plastic tab may increase the size of the hole you need. You do not want to risk breaking the tab, so drill the holes large enough to avoid that risk. Some people tape down the tab, but that increases the width of the connector, so you still need a generous hole. Also, I've seen the tab break off when the tape was removed.

- Cable staples, which you can use to secure cable along baseboards, quarter-round, or doorjambs.

■   A hammer for installing cable staples.

■   Strong string with a small, heavy weight attached, for vertical chases (it's so much easier to drop the string, attach the cable, and pull up, than to fish the cable up through the wall).

■   A flashlight, for peering into the spaces between walls, or between the ceiling and floor, when you can't figure out where the cable went.

■   Cable covers, which are rubber or plastic devices that are put over cable that has to cross part of the floor after it emerges from its chase (needed when computers aren't located against the wall). Cable covers keep cable from moving, and they keep people from tripping over the cable (they're sloped at the edges to reduce the chance of tripping over them). You can even use them under a rug, which is something you shouldn't do with cable, because the rubbing of the underside of the rug against the cable can weaken or break the cable's insulation.

CAUTION   *Be careful about the way you handle cable as you run it through the chase and around the room. Don't bend cable at a sharp angle. When cable turns a corner, don't pull it taut—give it some slack.*

Cabling Within the Same Room

If all the computers on your network are in the same room (common for small business and home-based businesses), you don't need to drill holes in walls or floors. Put the hub next to one computer, and use a short cable to connect them. Then run longer cable from the hub to the other computers (see Figure 4-2).

Run the cable along the baseboard or quarter-round, instead of running it across the room. If a doorway interferes with a straight chase along the wall, that's the place to put the hub; otherwise, use a cable cover to cross the opening, or run the cable up and around the doorway. If your computers aren't against the walls, use cable covers when you bring the cable from the wall to the computer.

Cabling Between Adjacent Rooms

If your computers are located in adjacent rooms on the same floor, you have to drill only one hole between the rooms (the least noticeable site is to drill through the baseboard, just above the quarter-round). Put the hub in one of the rooms, near

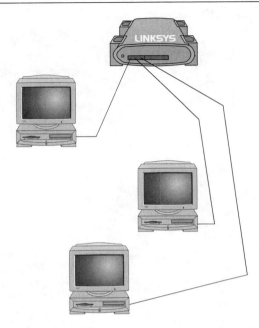

FIGURE 4-2   Network installation is a piece of cake when all the computers are in one room

a computer, and run one short length of cable between them. Run another length of cable to the computer in the other room, through the hole you drilled (see Figure 4-3).

It's easier, of course, if the computers are all located against the common wall. If they're not, run the cable along baseboards or quarter-round, not across the floor.

Cabling Between Nonadjacent Rooms on the Same Floor

If your computers are on the same floor but aren't in adjacent rooms, the most efficient cabling route is a chase along your home's beams. Most houses have beams between floors that run straight through the house, either from front to back or from side to side. You usually can expect a clear chase from one end to the other.

■ If your computers are on the second floor, the best chase is across the attic floor or through a crawl space above the second floor.

■ If your computers are on the first floor, the best chase is across the basement ceiling or through a crawl space below the first floor.

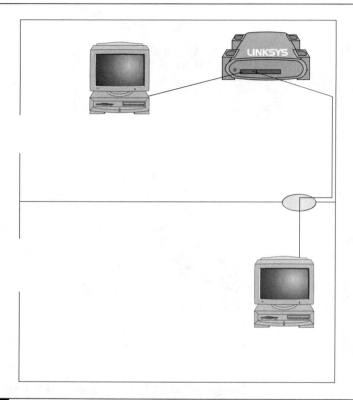

FIGURE 4-3   Cabling between adjacent rooms means drilling one hole

The trick is to get the cable into the chase, and the logical way is to drill a hole in the ceiling or floor (depending on whether the chase is above or below the level you're working on). However, I hate drilling holes in the ceiling because it looks terrible, and even if I paint the cable to match the wall, it's visible. And I have hardwood floors so I shudder at the thought of drilling into them. Instead, I use closets or walls to get to the chase.

Use a Closet to Get to the Chase

Wiring through closets is a great way to hide cabling. If you're lucky, there's a closet in every room that holds a computer. Drill a hole in the ceiling or floor of each room that holds a computer (the choice of ceiling or floor depends on whether the chase is above or below the rooms). Then fish the cable through the chase to the closet of each room that has a computer (if a room doesn't have a closet, just bring the cable directly into the room).

Of course, a portion of the cable has to run between the closet and the computer (or hub, or both). If you have enough clearance under the closet door, run the cable under the door and then attach it to the quarter-round or baseboard with cable staples. If there's no clearance under the closet door, drill a hole in the bottom of the door jamb to bring the cable into the room.

Go Directly to the Chase

For any room that lacks a closet, bring the cable from the chase into the room at a corner, and then paint the cable to match the wall. Run the cable along the baseboard or quarter-round to reach the computer.

Cabling Between Floors

If your computers are located on different floors, your cable length measurement must include the height of the room in addition to the horizontal length required to reach the computer. If one computer is in the basement and another is on the second floor, you need sufficient cable length to make the trip to the hub (which should probably be located midway, to avoid the need to purchase long cable lengths).

If the rooms are stacked one over the other, run the cable through the inside of the walls, near a corner. If radiators or heating pipes are accessible, use the opening around the pipes. If closets are stacked, use them.

If the rooms are on opposite ends of the house, you have to use both walls (closets are better) and ceilings. For the vertical chase, use any openings around pipes that are available, otherwise use the inside of the wall. For the horizontal runs, find a chase above or below the room.

Work from the top down to let gravity assist your efforts. Put a weight on the end of strong string or twine and drop it down to the lower floor. Then, tape the cable to the weight and haul it up.

NOTE *You can also cable through HVAC (Heating, Ventilation, Air Condition) ducts, but many cities and towns have strict rules about this option. Some building codes totally forbid using HVAC for cable of any type; other building codes set strict standards. Never enter the duct system by drilling a hole; instead use an existing entry and exit (look for a grate over the point at which the duct meets the wall).*

Adding a Professional Touch

After all the cabling is finished and the computers are connected to the hub, here's what happens: People in your household look at the installation and are not the least bit impressed with your efforts, or with the new technology available to them. They look at all that cable coming out of walls, closets, and ceilings, and make comments in which the words "ugly" or "sloppy" occur. Somebody remarks that the network at her corporate office doesn't have holes exuding cable. Professional cable installers use faceplates on the wall, and there's no reason you can't put the same finishing touch on your system.

If you run cable through walls, you can terminate the cable on the wall, using an Ethernet socket that is attached to the wall with a faceplate. You can buy sockets and faceplates at any computer store.

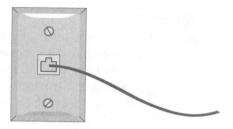

To create an Ethernet socket, pull the cable through the hole in the wall and use a stripper to remove about an inch of insulation from the cable (cut off the connector first). Then insert the wires into the socket and push against the socket to seal the connection (these are similar to electrical connections that just snap into place). Attach the socket to the faceplate, and attach the faceplate to the wall (pushing the wires back into the wall).

Plan Ahead—Bring Up Other Cables

The first time I cabled my home office, I did something really smart: I made my house cable-ready for anything. (I say "the first time" because I've recabled many times, moving from coax to twisted pair, moving offices around the house, creating offices for staff and network entry points for houseguests who brought laptops, and so on.)

In addition to the network cable I hauled up through three stories—and down the hallways of each of the three stories—I brought along telephone cable (8-pair), speaker cable, and electrical cable. I just tied all the cable into a bundle, and hauled away. To accomplish this, I had to drill holes that were a full inch in diameter, but I was able to enter each floor through a closet and then snake each type of cable into the various rooms separately (which meant smaller holes as I entered each room).

After I set up my network outlets, the other cable just sat there, taped to the quarter-round, waiting for me to use it. Whenever I wanted to add a phone jack, the wire was there. When I wanted to pipe the output of my stereo into any room in the house, I just had to bring up speakers—the wire was there. When I called my electrician for new outlets, the wire was there and he could hook up the basement end (the circuit box) and the outlet, without having to fish cable through the walls (at his high hourly rate). I do not do my own electrical wiring—that stuff is dangerous if you're not properly trained.

Installing NICs

Every computer on the network needs an Ethernet network adapter to accept the RJ-45 connection at the end of the cable. Linksys offers a wide variety of Ethernet adapters, so you can mix and match computers on the same network. For example, you can get internal NICs for your desktop computers and a PC-Card for your laptop. If a desktop computer has a USB port available, you may prefer to use it so you don't have to open the computer to install an internal NIC.

The following sections describe the steps you must take to install Internal NICs and USB network adapters. See Chapter 11 for detailed information on installing network adapters on laptop computers.

After you complete the tasks described here (physically installing the NICs and installing the operating system drivers), you must configure the NIC so it can find the other computers on the network. You'll find all the information you need in Chapter 8.

Internal NICs

To install an internal NIC, you must open the computer and insert the NIC into a slot (called a *bus*) on the systemboard (sometimes called a *motherboard*). Some people find the prospect of messing around in the computer's innards rather daunting, but it's really easy, and the only tool you need is a Phillips-head screwdriver. However, pay attention to the following safety tips:

- Don't use a magnetic screwdriver. Magnets and disk drives do not get along well because magnetic forces can delete data.

- Discharge any static electricity in your body before you touch any of the components inside the computer. Touch something metal inside the computer to ground yourself.

- Remove metal jewelry, especially gold (which conducts static electricity), and most especially, rings.

Determining the Bus Type

Depending on the age of the computers in your network, you may need to purchase NICs for different bus types. (Most networks, especially home networks, comprise some older computers and some new computers.) Two types of buses accept NICs:

■ A PCI (Peripheral Component Interconnect) bus is usually white, and it has a crossbar about three-quarters of the way down its length. All newer computers use PCI buses, and some older computers may have a couple of PCI buses.

■ An ISA (Industry Standard Architecture) bus is usually black (an Extended ISA bus is brown), and it has a small crossbar about two-thirds of the way down its length. ISA buses are longer than PCI buses. Older computers contain ISA buses in addition to a couple of PCI buses.

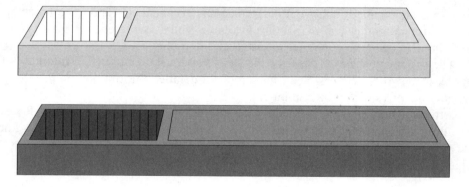

NOTE   *Your computer may also have a bus that's shorter than the PCI bus and is located further away from the back of the computer than the other buses. This is an Accelerated Graphics Port (AGP) bus, and it's used for high-speed video controllers.*

For computers you've purchased within the last few years, you can automatically assume you'll need a PCI NIC. In fact, even though older computers may have PCI buses in addition to ISA buses, you have no way of knowing whether a PCI bus is empty. If only an ISA bus is available, you'll have to use a NIC designed for ISA. You'll also have to make sure you've installed an autosensing 10/100 Mbps hub, not a pure 100 Mbps hub.

NOTE *If one of your computers needs an ISA NIC, I can personally recommend the Linksys LNE2000 for this purpose; it's a reliable workhorse. (LNE2000T is hard to find; LNE2000 is basically the same but easier to find.)*

Inserting the NIC

Use the following steps to install your NICs:

1. Unplug the computer. It's easiest to pull the plug from the back of the computer, rather than from the wall outlet.

2. Disconnect the cables (mouse, keyboard, printer, camera, and so on) that are attached to the ports at the back of the computer.

TIP *As you disconnect each cable, write the name of its peripheral on a small piece of paper and tape the paper to the cable. Then, on the back of the computer, use a felt tip pen to mark the ports, for instance "M" for mouse and "K" for keyboard, "Modem" for the serial port, "Printer" for the parallel port, and so on. You'll have many occasions to thank yourself for marking everything in this manner.*

3. If your computer chassis is on the floor (common with today's tower computer cases), move it to a table to make it easier to work inside the computer.

TIP *When you move the computer to a table, vacuum the area where your computer sits, which almost certainly has a layer of dust (computers attract dust). In addition, use a can of compressed air or a computer vacuum to clean the ports from which you just disconnected cables.*

4. Use the Phillips-head screwdriver to remove the screws that hold the exterior case onto the chassis. Usually, you'll find four or six screws at the back of the case. If your computer doesn't have screws, and instead has a snap-up or pop-up device for opening and closing the case, you can skip this step, of course.

NOTE *Once again, use compressed air or a computer vacuum to clean the inside of the computer, which I guarantee is filled with dust. Don't use a regular household vacuum cleaner or dust-buster to do this.*

5. Remove the metal backplate at the end of the bus slot (at the back of the computer) by removing the small machine screw with a small Phillips-head screwdriver. Newer computers may require you to push out the piece of metal that is attached. Be careful not to bend the slots around it.

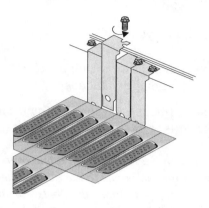

TIP   *When you remove the screw, which is very, very small, place it on a piece of sticky tape. This keeps it from rolling off the table and landing in the rug, where it will probably be lost forever, or from falling on the wood or tile floor and bouncing, landing far away so you have to hunt for it for a long time, and may not ever find it. Then, a week later, when you hear a funny clinking noise as you vacuum your house, you can say, "Oh, that's where that screw went." I'll bet you can guess how I learned these things.*

6. Open the static-free bag that holds the NIC and remove the card. Touch the metal chassis of the computer to discharge any static electricity in your body, try to always have contact with it to prevent any component getting damaged by static electricity.

7. Position the metal edge of the NIC in the open slot at the back of the computer (putting the RJ-45 jack in the rear opening where the metal plate used to be).

8. Position the teeth that are at the bottom of the NIC into the bus, and then push down on the NIC. The NIC is inserted properly when the back of the NIC fits neatly into the slot at the back of the computer, and the flange sits tightly on the metal rim, with the screw hole visible.

9. Replace the screw you removed when you took out the metal plate.

10. Put the cover back on the computer and replace the screws.

4

Install the Drivers

After you reconnect all the cables to the back of the computer, plug the computer in and start it. The Windows Plug and Play feature will discover the NIC when Windows starts. Depending on the version of Windows you're running, you may have to install the drivers for your NIC.

Installing Windows XP Drivers   Windows XP should automatically install the drivers for your new NIC. You may notice that the startup takes a bit longer, because it takes some time for the operating system to discover the new hardware and install the drivers. First, a message appears above the notification area of the taskbar, telling you that Windows has found new hardware, and then another message appears to tell you the hardware has been installed.

If this doesn't occur automatically, you need to install the drivers manually. Windows XP always finds the hardware, but if it can't find the appropriate drivers, it launches the Found New Hardware Wizard so you can perform a manual installation. Put the driver disk that came with your NIC into the appropriate drive (floppy or CD, depending on the type of disk that is in the package). Then follow these steps:

1. Select the option Install From A List Or Specific Location (Advanced) and click Next.

2. In the next wizard window, select the option Search For The Best Driver In These Locations and clear the check box labeled Search Removable Media. In the field labeled Include This Location In The Search, type one of the following:

    - **a:\winxp** if your Linksys drivers are on a floppy disk

    - **d:\winxp** if your Linksys drivers are on a CD (substitute the drive letter for your CD-ROM drive if it's not d:)

3. If the wizard displays a window telling you that the driver is not tested for Windows, click Continue Anyway (don't worry; the driver is exactly what you need for Windows XP).

4. Click Finish in the next wizard window.

Installing Windows 98 Drivers   Windows 98 discovers your new hardware when it restarts, and it launches the Add New Hardware Wizard. Insert the Linksys driver disk into the appropriate drive. Then follow these steps:

1. Select the option Search For The Best Driver For Your Device (Recommended) and click Next.

2. Select the option Specify A Location, and enter one of the following locations. Then click Next.

   ■ **a:\win98** (or win9x) if your Linksys drivers are on a floppy disk

   ■ **d:\win98** (or win9x) if your Linksys drivers are on a CD (substitute the drive letter of your CD drive if it's not d:)

3. Click Next again after Windows 98 finds the driver to begin installing the files onto your hard disk.

4. If Windows 98 needs files from the operating system CD, you'll see a message asking you to insert the CD. The file location should be d:\win98 (substitute the drive letter for your CD for "d:". If you do not have the Windows 98 disk, then try c:\widows\options\cabs, or try specifying the driver location (a:\win98 or d:\win98) if the file that Windows can't find has a .sys or .inf extension).

5. When all the files are installed, click Finish.

You should see a message asking if you want to restart your computer—take the Linksys driver disk out of the drive and click Yes. If you don't see that message, take the Linksys driver disk out of the drive and click Start | Shutdown | Restart. When Windows restarts, your Linksys NIC is installed and available.

Installing Windows 2000 Drivers   Windows 2000 discovers your new NIC when it restarts, and it launches the Found New Hardware Wizard. Follow these steps to install the drivers:

1. In the Install Hardware Device Drivers window, the wizard announces it found an Ethernet Controller. Select the option Search For A Suitable Driver For My Device (Recommended) and click Next.

2. In the Locate Driver Files window, select Specify a Location and click Next.

3. Insert the Linksys driver disk and enter one of the following locations in the text box:

   ■ **a:\win2000** if your drivers are on a floppy disk

   ■ **d:\win2000** if your drivers are on a CD (substitute the correct drive letter for your CD drive if it isn't d:)

4. Follow the rest of the wizard's prompts and click Finish on the last wizard window.

4

Installing Windows Me Drivers   Windows Me discovers your new NIC when it restarts, and it launches the Found New Hardware Wizard. Follow these steps to install the drivers:

1. In the Install Hardware Device Drivers window, the wizard announces it found an Ethernet Controller. Select the option Specify The Location Of The Driver (Advanced) and click Next.

2. In the next wizard window, select Search For The Best Driver For Your Device (Recommended). Also select Specify A Location and enter one of the following locations in the text box:

    ■ **a:\winME** if your drivers are on a floppy disk (may also be win9x or win98 if winMe doesn't work)

    ■ **d:\winME** if your drivers are on a CD (substitute the correct drive letter for your CD drive if it isn't d:—may also be win9x or win98 if winMe doesn't work)

3. Click Next and wait for the wizard to tell you that it has found the drivers; then click Next again.

4. If Windows Me needs files from the operating system CD, you'll see a message asking you to insert the CD. When you do, the system will find the files it needs. If you do not have the Windows ME disk, then try c:\widows\options\cabs, or try specifying the driver location (i.e., a:\win9x or d:\win9x) if the file that Windows can't find has a .sys or .inf extension).

5. When all the files are installed, click Finish.

You should see a message asking if you want to restart your computer—take the Linksys driver disk out of the drive and click Yes. If you don't see that message, take the Linksys driver disk out of the drive and click Start | Shutdown | Restart. When Windows restarts, your Linksys NIC is installed and available.

Installing a USB Network Adapter

The nifty thing about a USB network adapter is you don't have to open your computer to install it. In fact, you don't even turn off your computer to install it. All you have to do is connect the parts together properly, and Windows will automatically discover that you've installed your adapter.

Your Linksys USB network adapter has two connectors, one on each end:

- An RJ-45 connector, which accepts the Ethernet cable you use to connect the adapter to the hub. The RJ-45 connector resembles a telephone jack.

- A USB connector, which accepts the cable that connects the adapter to the USB port.

A USB cable for connecting the adapter to the USB port is included in the Linksys USB adapter package. Connect one end of the cable into the adapter and the other end into the USB port (you can't accidentally put the wrong end into the wrong device).

The Linksys USB adapter package also includes a disk with drivers for the device. As soon as you connect the adapter to the USB port, the Windows Plug and Play feature discovers the new device. At this point, you must install the drivers, using the same steps described in the previous section for installing drivers for internal NICs.

Now that installation is complete, turn to Chapter 8 to learn how to configure the adapter so you can begin communicating with the other computers on the network.

LIKE TO PLAY WITH TECHNOLOGY?

Chapter 5

Installing a Wireless Network

Everyone wants a wireless network. Especially if you have notebook computers, they're just plain cool—and they're affordable. They also have the advantage of not requiring any wiring at all, so you can put computers almost anywhere.

There are some things you need to be concerned about, including security and what type of hardware you need, but we'll explain all the issues and tell you how to set up the network.

The vast majority of wireless networking products are based on a wireless standard known technically as 802.11b and more colloquially as Wi-Fi. The network traffic for these products uses radio frequency in the 2.4-GHz band, the same used by some high-end cordless telephones. The speed of networking for Wi-Fi depends on the signal quality, but in normal conditions it runs at 11 Mbps. This standard is defined by an industry consortium, the Wireless Ethernet Compatibility Alliance (WECA—http://www.weca.net/), and interoperability between products from different vendors is good.

Positioning Computers

There are two issues to consider when deciding where to position computers on a wireless network. One is distance between wireless systems, and the other is potential sources of interference with the wireless radio signals.

Distance can be tricky, although there are usually ways to extend distance using wireless access points, which we will discuss in detail in the "Using Wireless Access Points" section.

Wi-Fi networking can work through most walls and other building structures, but the range is much better in open spaces. Linksys rates the range of their wireless adapters outdoors at up to 1500 feet (457 meters) and indoors at up to 300 feet (91 meters), but the ratings are under ideal circumstances, without interference. The indoor range is the most sensitive and really depends on structural elements in the house.

What to Avoid

Significant amounts of metals in the walls can be a problem for wireless networking. For example, I've seen problems with plaster walls built on a metal lath; however, you can have problems with much less pervasive metal structures. My own house has a small wireless dead zone that I believe is caused by metal ducting from the air conditioning in the walls. (One day I plan to fix it with another access point.)

Wireless networks broadcast on the same 2.4-GHz frequency as many cordless phones. These 2.4-GHz devices aren't supposed to interfere with each other, but I've seen it happen occasionally. It's a good idea to keep wireless network cards some distance from cordless phones, and especially base stations. If you're experiencing interference, you might try changing channels on the network (see the section on "Configuring the Wireless Network" for how to change channels.)

Finally, microwave ovens actually broadcast in the 2.4-GHz band as well, so you want to keep any wireless devices, including 2.4-GHz cordless phones, away from microwave ovens.

Wireless NICs

Every computer on the wireless network needs a wireless network adapter. Linksys offers a wide variety of wireless adapters, so you can mix and match computers on the same network. For example, if you want to use an internal PCI NIC for your desktop computers, you can get the WMP11 Instant Wireless Network Adapter. If a desktop computer has a USB port available, you may prefer to use it so you don't have to open the computer to install an internal NIC. For portable computers, you can get a wireless PC Card. The following sections describe the steps you must take to install Internal NICs and USB network adapters. See Chapter 11 for detailed information on installing network adapters on laptop computers.

After you complete the tasks described here (physically installing the NICs and installing the operating system drivers), you must configure the NIC so it can find the other computers on the network. You may have to do some configuration specific to the wireless network and some related to Windows networking. The wireless configuration information is below in the sections on the Linksys Wireless Configuration utility and Windows XP's built-in wireless networking support. You'll find all the information you need about Windows networking in Chapter 8.

Internal NICs

As a side note, before you start to install the internal NIC, please install the drivers first, which are provided on the CD-ROM that came with the product. The only exception to this is if you're using Windows XP. All other OSs require that you install the drivers first. (To do this, pop in the CD ROM and it should auto-run, then click on the Install option and follow the options.)

To install an internal NIC, you must open the computer and put the NIC into a slot (called a *bus*) on the system board (sometimes called a *motherboard*). Some people find the prospect of messing around in the computer's innards rather daunting, but it's not—it's easy, and the only tool you need is a Phillips head screwdriver. However, pay attention to the following safety tips:

- Don't use a magnetic screwdriver. Magnets and disk drives do not get along well because magnetic forces can delete data.

- Discharge any static electricity in your body before you touch any of the components inside the computer. Touch something metal inside the computer to ground yourself.

- Remove metal jewelry, especially gold (which conducts static electricity) and rings.

Determining the Bus Type

There are two significant types of buses (and expansion cards such as NICS to go in them) in computers:

- A Peripheral Component Interconnect (PCI) bus is usually white and has a crossbar about three-quarters of the way down its length. All newer computers use PCI buses, and some older computers may have a couple of PCI buses.

- An Industry Standard Architecture (ISA) bus is usually black (an extended ISA bus is brown) and has a small crossbar about two-thirds of the way down its length. ISA buses are longer than PCI buses. Older computers contain ISA buses in addition to a couple of PCI buses. Very old computers may only have ISA buses.

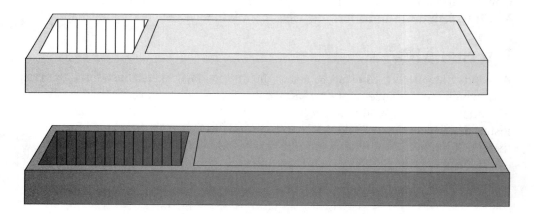

NOTE

Your computer may also have a bus that's shorter than the PCI bus, and is located further away from the back of the computer than the other buses. This is an Accelerated Graphics Port (AGP) bus, and it's used for high-speed video controllers.

For computers you've purchased within the last few years, you can automatically assume that you can use a PCI NIC. In fact, even though older computers may have PCI buses in addition to ISA buses, you have no way of knowing whether a PCI slot is empty without opening the computer.

If only an ISA slot is available, you may have to free up a PCI NIC somehow, because nobody makes ISA wireless network adapters. Your only alternatives are to use a USB adapter (described below) or to use a network adapter of another type, such as an ISA card for wired Ethernet (see Chapter 4), and connect the wired network to the wireless network. At this point, though, you are adding complexity and expense to support an old computer that is probably best replaced.

Inserting the NIC

Use the following steps to install your NICs:

1. Unplug the computer. It's easiest to pull the plug from the back of the computer, rather than from the wall outlet.

2. Disconnect the cables (mouse, keyboard, printer, camera, and so on) that are attached to the ports at the back of the computer.

TIP

As you disconnect each cable, write the name of its peripheral on a small piece of paper and tape the paper to the cable. Then, on the back of the computer, use a felt tip pen to mark the ports—for instance, "M" for mouse and "K" for keyboard, "Modem" for the serial port, "Printer" for the parallel port, and so on. You'll have many occasions to thank yourself for marking everything in this manner.

3. If your computer chassis is on the floor (common with today's tower computer cases), move it to a table to make it easier to work inside the computer.

TIP

When you move the computer to a table, vacuum the area where your computer sits, which almost certainly has a layer of dust (computers attract dust). In addition, use a can of compressed air or a computer vacuum to clean the ports from which you just disconnected the cables.

4. Use the Phillips head screwdriver to remove the screws that hold the exterior case onto the chassis. Usually, there are four or six screws at the back of the case. If your computer doesn't have screws, and instead has a snap-up or pop-up device for opening and closing the case, you can skip this step, of course.

NOTE   *Once again, use compressed air or a computer vacuum to clean the inside of the computer, which I guarantee is filled with dust.*

5. Remove the metal backplate at the end of the bus slot (at the back of the computer), by removing the small machine screw with a small Phillips head screwdriver. Newer computers may require you to push out the piece of metal that is attached. Be careful not to bend the slots around it.

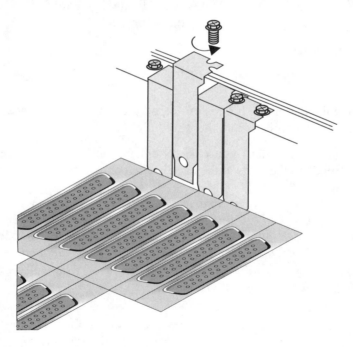

TIP   *When you remove the screw—which is very, very small—place it on a piece of sticky tape. This keeps it from rolling off the table and landing in the rug where it will probably be lost forever, or from falling on the wood or tile floor and bouncing, landing far away so you have to hunt for it for a long time (and may not ever find it). Then, a week later, when you hear a funny clinking noise as you vacuum your house, you can say "Oh, that's where that screw went." I'll bet you can guess how I learned these things.*

6. Open the static-free bag that holds the NIC and remove it. Touch the metal chassis of the computer to discharge any static electricity in your body; try to always have contact with it to prevent any component getting damaged by static electricity.

7. Position the metal edge of the NIC in the open slot at the back of the computer (putting the screw connector for the wireless antenna in the rear opening where the metal plate used to be).

8. Position the teeth that are at the bottom of the NIC into the bus, and then push down on the NIC. The NIC is inserted properly when the back of the NIC fits neatly into the slot at the back of the computer and the flange sits tightly on the metal rim, with the screw hole visible.

9. Replace the screw you removed when you took out the metal plate.

10. Put the cover back on the computer and replace the screws.

11. Take the black antenna from the package the NIC came in and screw it onto the exposed connector on the card.

Install the Drivers

After you reconnect all the cables to the back of the computer, plug the computer in and start it. The Windows Plug and Play feature will discover the wireless NIC when Windows starts. Depending on the version of Windows you're running, you may have to install the drivers for your wireless NIC.

Installing Windows XP Drivers   Windows XP should automatically install the drivers for your new NIC. You may notice that the startup takes a bit longer, because it takes some time for the operating system to discover the new hardware and install the drivers. First, a message appears above the notification area of the taskbar telling you that Windows has found new hardware, and then another message appears to tell you the hardware has been installed.

If this doesn't occur automatically, you need to install the drivers manually. Windows XP always finds the hardware, but if it can't find the appropriate drivers, it launches the Found New Hardware Wizard so you can perform a manual installation. Put in the driver CD that came with your NIC, then follow these steps:

1. Select the option Install from a List or Specific Location (Advanced) and click Next.

2. In the next wizard window, select the option Search for the Best Driver in These Locations and clear the check box labeled Search Removable

Media. In the field labeled Include This Location in the Search, type the following:

■ **d:** if your Linksys drivers are on a CD (substitute the drive letter for your CD-ROM drive if it's not d:)

3. If the wizard displays a window telling you that the driver is not tested for Windows, click Continue Anyway (don't worry, the driver is exactly what you need for Windows XP).

4. Click Finish in the next wizard window.

5. Windows XP may display a message above the notification area of the taskbar that a new network device is available and that you should click the notice to run the Network Setup Wizard. See Chapter 8 for more on the Network Setup Wizard.

Installing Windows 98 Drivers   Follow these instructions if you did not install the drivers first.

Windows 98 discovers your new hardware when it restarts, and launches the Add New Hardware Wizard. Insert the Linksys driver disk into the appropriate drive, then follow these steps:

1. Select the option Search for the Best Driver for Your Device (Recommended) and click Next.

2. Select the option Specify a Location. Enter **d:** (substitute the drive letter of your CD drive if it's not d:), then click Next.

3. Click Next again after Windows 98 finds the driver, to begin installing the files onto your hard disk.

4. If Windows 98 needs files from the operating system CD, you'll see a message asking you to insert the CD. The file location should be d:\win98 (substitute the drive letter for your CD for d:). If you do not have the Windows 98 disk, then try c:\windows\options\cabs or try specifying the driver location (a:\win98 or d:\win98 if the file windows can't find has a .sys or .inf).

5. When all the files are installed, click Finish.

You should see a message asking if you want to restart your computer—click No. (If you do not get prompted, don't worry about it—just follow the instructions.)

After clicking No, go to the utility folder on the Linksys CD-ROM and run the setup.exe from there. You can do this by going to Start | Run | d:\utility\setup.exe. Once you've finished with the setup, take the Linksys driver disk out of the drive and click Start | Shutdown | Restart. When Windows restarts, your Linksys NIC is installed and available.

USB NICs

Installing the WUSB11 Instant Wireless USB Network Adapter is about as easy as can be. The box has the actual NIC and a USB cable. Connect the cable on one end to an available USB connector on the computer or USB hub and to the NIC on the other end. Extend the antenna and you're basically done with setup, although you may want to give some thought to the location for the NIC. Notice that it comes with an adhesive attachment if you want to put it on the side of a cabinet or some such place. You may get a generally better signal by placing the NIC at a greater height and further away from the computer and monitor.

We are writing here about version 2.6 of the WUSB11, which should be the only version available in stores as you read this. Earlier versions worked similarly, but versions 2.5 and 2.6 are certified to work out of the box with Windows XP's built-in wireless support. The current version also has support for 128-bit WEP encryption (see "Configuring Security" below).

NOTE *If you are running Windows 95 or Windows NT, you don't have built-in support for USB. Third-party support for USB on such operating systems is available, but Linksys does not recommend or support them.*

Install the Drivers

When you finish the connection between the USB NIC and system, or if you turn on the system after connecting the NIC while it was off, the Windows Plug and Play feature will discover the wireless NIC. Depending on the version of Windows you're running, you may have to install the drivers for your wireless NIC.

Installing Windows XP Drivers   Windows XP automatically detects the new USB wireless NIC. First, a message appears above the notification area of the taskbar telling you that Windows has found new hardware. At this point, Windows XP launches the Found New Hardware Wizard so you can perform a driver installation. Put the driver disk that came with your NIC into the CD drive. Then, follow these steps:

   1. Select the option Install from a List or Specific Location (Advanced) and click Next.

2. In the next wizard window, select the option Search for the Best Driver in These Locations, and clear the check box labeled Search Removable Media. In the field labeled Include This Location in the Search, type **d:\Drivers** (substitute the drive letter for your CD-ROM drive if it's not d:).

3. If the wizard displays a window telling you that the driver is not tested for Windows, click Continue Anyway (don't worry, the driver is exactly what you need for Windows XP).

4. Click Finish in the next wizard window.

5. Windows XP may display a message above the notification area of the taskbar that a new network device is available and that you should click the notice to run the Network Setup Wizard. See Chapter 8 for more on the Network Setup Wizard.

Installing Windows 98 Drivers   When you're using Windows 98, it is recommended that you install the drivers first, then insert the card. For more information on this, please see the section "Installing the Wireless Configuration Utility."

If you did not install the driver's first, insert the WUSB11, and when Windows 98 discovers your new wireless USB NIC, it launches the Add New Hardware Wizard. Insert the Linksys driver disk into the appropriate drive. Then, follow these steps:

1. In the opening window, the wizard announced that it has discovered a USB Device. Click Next.

2. Select the option Search for the Best Driver for Your Device (Recommended) and click Next.

3. Select the option Specify a Location. Enter **d:\drivers** (substitute the drive letter of your CD drive if it's not d:), then click Next.

4. Click Next again after Windows 98 finds the driver, to begin installing the files onto your hard disk.

5. If Windows 98 needs files from the operating system CD, you'll see a message asking you to insert the CD. The file location should be d:\win98 (substitute the drive letter for your CD for d:).

6. If Windows 98 asks for the location of files that have names that begin with "lne" or "netlne", enter **d:** (or whatever drive letter is appropriate) in the text box.

7. When all the files are installed, click Finish.

You should see a message asking if you want to restart your computer—click No. Go to the utility folder on the Linksys CD-ROM and run the setup.exe from there. You can do this by going to Start | Run | d:\utility\setup.exe. Once you've finished with the setup, take the Linksys driver disk out of the drive and click Start | Shutdown | Restart. When Windows restarts, your Linksys USB wireless NIC is installed and available.

Configuring the Wireless Network

Windows XP lets you configure wireless network adapters using the operating system, but older versions of Windows require that you use a utility program supplied by Linksys with the adapter. The utility program is different for the USB and PCI wireless adapters. Even though you can install the Linksys Wireless Configuration utility on Windows XP, Linksys recommends that you use Windows XP's built-in support.

Installing the Wireless Configuration Utility

To install the utility, place the CD-ROM that came with the adapter in your CD drive. If Windows's Autoplay feature loads the Setup program, click on the Install tab to launch the Utility install program. If not, click Start, select Run, and type **d:\utility\setup.exe** (change the drive letter to the appropriate one for your CD-ROM). Follow these steps:

1. Click Next at the Welcome screen.

2. The next page is the copyright and warranty notices—click Yes to agree to the terms of the warranty policy.

3. If you wish to change the Destination Folder indicated on the next screen, click the Browse button and do so. Click Next when you are satisfied.

4. At this next screen (see Figure 5-1), you need to choose between Infrastructure Mode and Ad-Hoc Mode. If you are using a wireless access point or router with an integrated wireless access point, choose Infrastructure Mode. If you simply have wireless cards communicating directly with each other, choose Ad-Hoc Mode. While this is an important decision for your network, don't get panicky, because you can easily change this setting later.

5. (You will see the area only if you are in AdHoc mode.) In the next window, you select a channel from 1 to 11. In a sense it doesn't matter

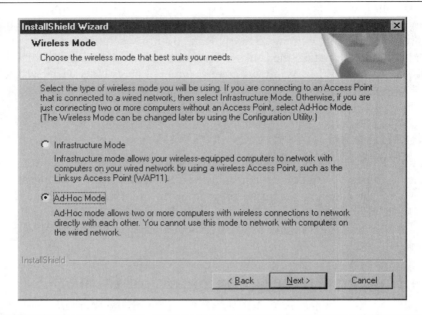

FIGURE 5-1   Infrastructure Mode means using a wireless access point, and Ad-Hoc Mode means wireless cards are communicating directly with each other

which you choose, as long as all your systems and access points are on the same channel. I think it's a good idea to choose something other than the default channel 6 because if there are other nearby networks, they are most likely on the default channel. Admittedly, this may be planning for an unlikely event; however, since you're using an AdHoc network, each computer must be on the same channel. Please make sure to use the same one as the rest of the computers, then click Next.

6. This next screen is important. Here, you enter a Service Set Identifier (SSID), which is basically the name for your wireless network. The default name is "linksys"—leave it as is for now but be sure to read the "Configuring Security" section later in the chapter. Click Next.

7. Now the Install program repeats your settings back to you before copying the files from the install disk. Confirm they are what you wanted and click Next to proceed.

8. If the program asks you to reboot the computer, choose No, then actually shut down the computer.

9. Once the computer has shut down, insert the Wireless adapter and restart; Windows should find the drivers for the product without any problem.

Using the USB WLAN Monitor Utility

The Linksys WUSB11 Instant Wireless USB Network Adapter comes with a configuration utility different from that which comes with the PCI adapter and PC Cards. After you install the program, an icon of a blue computer with an antenna will appear in the system tray. (Actually, the icon is blue when the adapter is connected to a network and red when it is disconnected.) Double-click this icon to launch the WLAN Monitor program (pictured in Figure 5-2).

This opening screen, which you can also reach by clicking Link Status on the right side of the window, shows you the state of the connection: the SSID of the network, whether it is Ad-Hoc or Infrastructure, the speed, the channel, and the WEP status. The Signal Strength and Link Quality indicators will only display in Infrastructure mode. The set of numbers and letters after the SSID is called the BSSID, or Basic Service Set ID, which is a unique number identifying all the systems in the wireless network using the SSID.

Click Connections on the right to bring up a list of wireless networks that are in range. You can connect to any one of them by selecting one and pressing the Connect button. Pressing the Refresh button will cause the program to rescan for

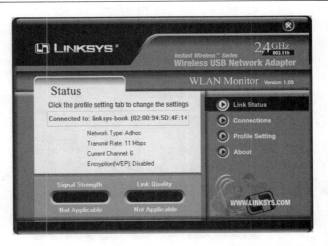

FIGURE 5-2   The WLAN Monitor program displays and lets you change wireless configuration settings on the WUSB11 adapter

available networks and repopulate the list. Selecting Attempt Auto Connect to ANY network in range will cause the program to connect to the closest network.

Clicking Profile Setting brings up a list of profiles. Clicking New or selecting a profile and clicking Edit brings up a screen like that pictured in Figure 5-3.

You can have multiple profiles for multiple wireless networks.

Clicking the Advanced button brings up the WEP configuration screen. See the "Configuring Security" section for full treatment of security issues.

Finally, the About screen shows you the versions of the WLAN Monitor program, the device driver, and firmware.

Using the Wireless PCI Card/PC Card Configuration Utility

The WMP11 and the WPC11 Instant Wireless Network Adapter comes with a different configuration utility than the USB adapter. After you install the utility, a new tray icon appears, although with the WMP11 the icon is green in its connected state and red in its disconnected state. Even though it looks different, the Wireless PCI Card Configuration utility has basically the same features as the USB WLAN Monitor, but in a completely different user interface.

The program opens to the Link Info tab (see Figure 5-4). Here you can see information about the wireless connection, including the channel used (although

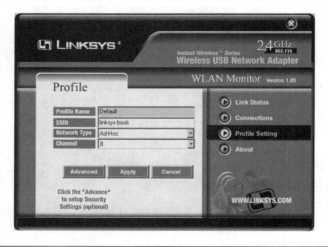

FIGURE 5-3   The Add and Edit Profile screens are where you can set basic wireless network parameters like SSID, channel, and network type

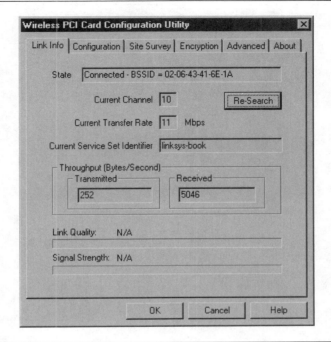

FIGURE 5-4   The Link Info tab tells you the basics of the network connection for the WMP11 card

you can change that elsewhere), the SSID, and the throughput. The Link Quality and Signal Strength indicators only work when the card is in Infrastructure mode.

The Configuration tab (see Figure 5-5) is an important one. Here, you can change the card from Ad-Hoc to Infrastructure mode, set the channel and SSID, and set the transfer rate of the card (although you should almost certainly leave the setting at Auto Rate so that the card can find the highest rate it can handle).

The Power Saving Mode setting is valid only when the card is in Infrastructure mode. If it is available and you set it to Enabled, the card will enter a power-saving sleep mode when there is no data to transmit, and periodically wake up to check for data.

Because the settings on this tab may differ in different environments, you can save them and name them as a "profile." By clicking in the Profile Name field and typing, you can name a profile and then save it by clicking the Create button. By opening the list of names and selecting one, you can then remove it with the Remove button or activate those settings with the Activate button.

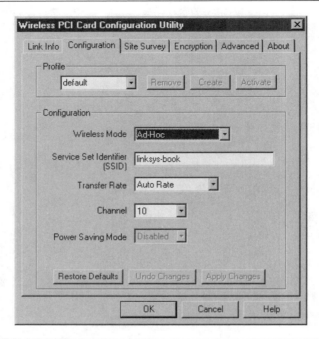

FIGURE 5-5   The Configuration tab lets you change important card parameters like the mode and SSID

The easier way to connect to other networks is on the Site Survey tab (see Figure 5-6). It contains a list of available wireless networks and some information about them. By clicking the Search button, you can rescan the network list. By selecting one and clicking Connect, you can change the wireless connection to that network.

The Encryption tab allows you to implement WEP encryption on the wireless connection. This is important, and we deal with it in the "Configuring Security" section of this chapter.

The Advanced tab has some low-level tweaking functions for the wireless transmission protocols. You should never change these settings unless instructed to by Linksys technical support.

The About tab shows you the versions of the program, the device driver, and the firmware.

Windows XP's Built-In Wireless Support

When you are connected to a wireless network in Windows XP, you will see an icon in the system tray (the icons in the bottom right of the screen) that acts as an

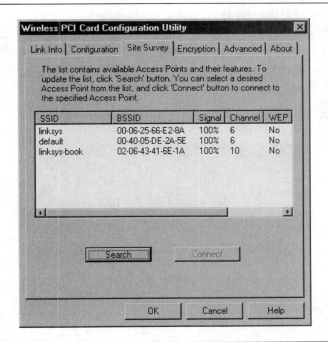

FIGURE 5-6   The Site Survey tab is where you select from active networks and connect to one

interface to your wireless connection. It is a picture of two computers next to each other, apparently networking. Right-click on this icon and a menu appears.

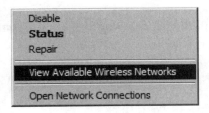

The menu lets you disable the wireless connection, which you shouldn't often need to do. The Repair option resets many settings for the network connection. For example, it renews any DHCP connection, flushes several caches, and reregisters the computer on the network. Repair can be a convenient way to clear up some problems. I will describe the Status, View Available Wireless Networks, and Open Network Connections options next.

The Network Status Dialog Box

Selecting the Status option brings up a dialog box that tells you the status of the connection (connected or disconnected), the duration (how long you have been connected to the network, the speed (which should be 11.0 Mbps if all is well), and a graphical indicator of signal strength. The graphical indicator is something like the signal indicator on a cell phone. If all five bars are green, the signal is at full strength. Fewer green bars mean a weaker signal.

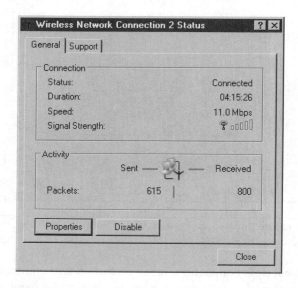

The Activity section shows how many packets or bytes of data have been sent or received through the adapter.

On the Support tab of the Status dialog you can see some configuration information for the network connection, such as the IP address. Click the Details button and you can see more details. There is also a Repair button that performs the same functions as the Repair menu option described above.

View Available Wireless Networks

Selecting the View Available Wireless Networks option opens the Connect to Wireless Network dialog, shown next. The main feature of this dialog is a list of available networks, which are wireless networks in range of this system. The results can be surprising: If you see networks you didn't expect, they probably belong to neighbors. In any event, if you are not connected to a network, you can select the one to which you wish to connect and press the Connect button.

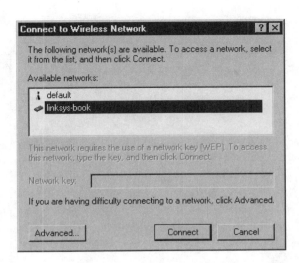

5

Clicking the Advanced button opens up the Windows Properties dialog for the wireless network connection. Most of this dialog does not differ from the functions for nonwireless networks, so you don't need to concern yourself with them. The Wireless Networks and General tabs have some useful features, though.

Preferred and Available Networks   The Wireless Networks tab of the Wireless Network Connection Properties dialog, pictured in Figure 5-7, lets you prioritize your access to wireless networks. The upper list of available networks is basically the same as the Connect to Wireless Network dialog—you can select a network to connect to. Clicking the Refresh button repopulates the list in case some of the networks have gone out of range or new networks have come in.

The lower list prioritizes your access to the available networks. You can manually add or remove entries from the list. The Add and Properties buttons bring up dialog boxes for implementing Wired Equivalent Privacy (WEP) and are described in detail in the "Configuring Security" section.

Open Network Connections

Selecting this option opens the Windows Network Connections window. One of the entries (perhaps the only entry) will be for your wireless connection. Double-clicking on this icon opens up the Status dialog box described previously. If you right-click, you can perform several other options previously described. Selecting Properties opens up the Windows Properties dialog box for the connection, described in the previous section.

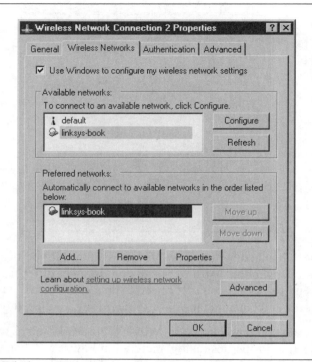

FIGURE 5-7   Windows XP builds in support for managing multiple wireless network connections

Using Wireless Access Points

If your network grows beyond a small number of systems, or if you need to integrate it with a wired network, you need a wireless access point. Implementing an access point moves the wireless network into what is called Infrastructure mode, in which all wireless systems communicate with the access point instead of with each other.

Wireless access points are a good way to expand the range of your wireless network because they act as a central antenna. In Ad-Hoc mode, the maximum range of the network is the longest distance between any two systems. In Infrastructure mode, you can place the wireless access point at the physical center of the home or office and your range moves out from that point.

Expanding the Signal

But you can't just set up a wireless access point as an antenna. It must be connected to a wired network. The access point and any wireless systems connected to it constitute, in Wi-Fi terms, a BSS and all the systems connected to the access point can access wired network resources (including the Internet) through the access point. You can add multiple access points and configure them so that wireless users can roam from one to another—just as with a cell phone, you are passed from one cell tower to another automatically. Multiple BSS setups configured for such roaming are called an Extended Service Set (ESS).

Linksys Wireless Access Points

Linksys makes several wireless access points with a variety of features in them. The basic one, the WAP11 Instant Wireless Network Access Point - Version 2.2, simply connects a wireless network to a wired network. The BEFW11S4 EtherFast Wireless AP + Cable/DSL Router w/4-Port Switch - Version 2 combines a cable/DSL router and four-port switch into the unit. The WAP54A Instant Wireless Access Point is an 802.11a unit that we discuss in detail in the 802.11b (Wi-Fi) and 802.11a section.

Chapter 10 contains an extensive discussion of routers, the main point of which is to connect one network to another—usually your internal network to the Internet. The router features in the Linksys router/access point combination units are similar to those discussed in Chapter 10. We will concentrate in this section on the features of these products that focus on the wireless network.

Setting Up the Access Point

In this section, any screens we display will be from the BEFW11S4 EtherFast Wireless AP + Cable/DSL Router w/4-Port Switch - Version 2, but they should be very similar, if not identical, in other Linksys access points.

The WAP11 access point has just a few connectors and indicators. You connect the power adapter to the power connector (there is no on/off switch) and a regular cat-5 cable from the LAN port on the WAP11 to your network's hub or switch.

The BEFW11S4 has a few more plugs. You connect the power as usual, and use a cat-5 cable to connect from the WAN plug to your cable modem or DSL device (or any other broadband device with an Ethernet connection). The 1–4 plugs can accept any wired Ethernet device or computer and they will be on the same network as wireless systems because of the integrated wireless access point.

You can connect a cable from the uplink port to a data port on a separate hub or switch to extend the wired network, but you cannot use both the number 4 data port and the uplink port at the same time. When the uplink port is in use, the number 4 data port is shut down.

Configuring Clients for the Access Point

To configure the router, you need a client with a network connection to it. You can configure it either from a wired or wireless client. If you use a wired client, plug it into one of the four data ports and set the client to obtain an IP address automatically from the network (that is, to use DHCP). If you are using a wireless client, the access point will, by default, be set up to use an SSID of "linksys" on channel 6. Connect the client to that network.

To actually obtain the IP address from the router you either have to reboot the computer or release and renew your address. To do the latter, open a command prompt by doing the following:

1. Click Start and select Run.

2. Type **cmd** and press ENTER.

3. Type **ipconfig /release**.

4. Type **ipconfig /renew**.

The first ipconfig command should report, after running the release, that you have an IP address of 0.0.0.0—in other words, you have no IP address. The second command should retrieve and report a new address. In all likelihood, you should see an IP address of 192.168.1.101, a subnet mask of 255.255.255.0, and a default gateway of 192.168.1.1. Any IP address beginning with 192.168.1 is good.

The Router Configuration Program

Now that you are on the same network as the access point/router, open a Web browser and enter **http://192.168.1.1/** in the Address bar and press ENTER. First, you are asked to log in. There is no default user name, so leave the field blank and enter a password of **admin**. Press ENTER or click OK. You should see the screen shown in Figure 5-8.

Right there on the Setup tab, in the Wireless section, you will find most of the wireless access point settings with which you need to be concerned. The first, setting enables or disables the access point; please bear in mind that it is enabled by default with no security at all. The next option, Allow "Broadcast" SSID to Associate?, controls whether the SSID of this wireless network is left out for everyone to see. Setting this to No isn't a guarantee of security, but it will make you a much more difficult target because other wireless users won't be able to tell that you have a wireless network. However, you will have to remember the SSID name to manually connect to it from clients.

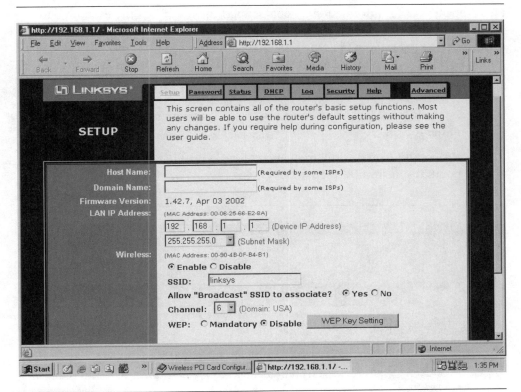

FIGURE 5-8   The wireless and other parameters of the router or access point are programmed through a Web browser

Next is the channel setting, which keeps you from conflicting with other APs or 2.4 GHz devices.

The final settings are the WEP settings. By default, WEP is disabled. By switching this setting to Mandatory and setting the WEP values in the WEP Key Setting page, you can implement encryption on all data on the wireless network. We discuss WEP implementation in the "Configuring Security" section.

If you make any changes in these settings, click the Apply button to save them in the router.

Advanced Wireless Configuration Settings

There are a number of advanced settings for the wireless access point that most users will never use, but which you should know exist. In general, you should not change these settings unless directed to do so by Linksys Technical Support (see Appendix C for information on contacting Linksys). The only exception to this is the Station MAC Filter, which will be discussed in the "Configuring Security" section. At the top right of the browser administration page, click the Advanced link. At the far right of the next page, click Wireless. The screen shown in Figure 5-9 appears.

■ At the top, the page shows the version of firmware in the access point side of the router.

■ Beacon Interval sets the frequency of packets of data sent out by the access point to synchronize the wireless network.

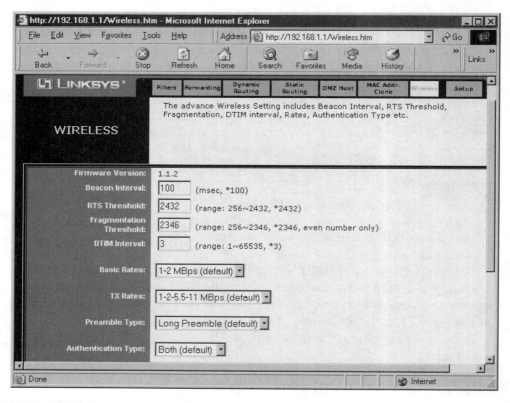

FIGURE 5-9 The settings in the Advanced Wireless screen generally don't need to be changed, but they can help with some unusual problems

■ The 802.11 standard defines the RTS threshold as the packet size at which transmission is governed by the RTS/CTS transaction. Smaller packets need not employ these transactions, thus larger packets involve an added overhead. Each station can have a different RTS threshold. If you ever change this value, don't change it by much.

■ The fragmentation threshold defines the amount of router resources dedicated to recovering packet errors. Changing this setting can increase error rates.

■ The DTIM interval defines the interval for the DTIM, which is a timing packet sent on the network that helps clients to receive broadcast messages.

■ The Basic Rates field lets you lower the speed of the network to be compatible with older 802.11 equipment that couldn't exceed 2 Mbps. The default setting allows for such equipment, but doesn't limit the network to it. You probably don't need to change this.

■ The TX Rates field sets the rate at which the access point will attempt to communicate with the client. You can change this to slow down the network, but why?

■ Preamble type defines the length of the CRC block for packets between the access point and the network card. The CRC is error-checking information. Changing the setting from Long Preamble (default) to Short Preamble will lower network overhead, and thus may be advisable in very high wireless traffic areas, but will also increase the possibility of errors in transmission going undetected.

■ The choices for Authentication Type are Open System, Shared Key, and Both, and the default is Open System. With this setting, the sender and the recipient do not share a secret key; rather, each party generates its own key-pair and asks the receiver to accept the randomly generated key. Once accepted, this key is used for a short time only. Then a new key is generated and agreed upon. Shared Key is when both the sender and the recipient share a secret key.

■ The Antenna Selection field lets you specify which antenna is used to transmit data. By default, both are on (Diversity Spread On). You could change this to only left or right, but I can't imagine why.

■ The Station Mac Filter feature allows you to filter out all wireless traffic except those whom you specify in the Active MAC Table. This is an excellent security feature because it's more difficult to hack than WEP. Clicking the Active MAC Table button opens a window with a list of computers active on the wireless network and the MAC addresses of their network cards. (A MAC, or Media Access Control, address is a unique address in every network adapter.) Copy the address you wish to filter from the Wireless Active MAC Table. To enable the feature, you must select Enable and then click the Edit MAC Filter Setting button. On this page, select "1~10" for 1 through 10, and so on, and paste the appropriate MAC address in the appropriate field. Only Check the Filter check box if you wish to disable that card from accessing the network for a short time (saves time so you don't have to re-enter it later when you wish to have access). Once you've finished the settings here, click Apply to close the window.

> **NOTE**   *This specific filtering only blocks access to the wireless network.*

After any changes in any of these fields, you must also click the Apply button at the bottom of the page.

Configuring Security

If you follow the computer trade press, you've seen many a story about deficiencies in wireless network security. Sadly, it turns out that WEP is not as impenetrable as its designers originally thought. A talented and determined hacker with access to your physical proximity, and with the use of some software tools that are available if you know where to look, can gain access to your wireless network.

How concerned are you about this? It's something to think about. I run a wireless network in my home. I eventually implemented all of the security features described in this section. I haven't always had them running, and they're not an absolute defense against attack. But I'm not going to deny myself the benefits of a wireless network just because it's possible for someone to hack into it. In the same way, I'm willing to live in my house even though it's possible for someone to break in and steal my belongings, even if I have good locks and a burglar alarm (and I do, so don't you go getting any ideas!).

So the good news is that even though security in 802.11 has been less than pristine, it's still possible to protect yourself. Think of wireless security features like The Club for your car: a good car thief can still steal your car, but he's more likely to look for an easier target. So, follow this section and you'll be doing what you can to make your wireless network safe from prying eyes.

Good Practices

Without ever getting into WEP, there are a number of good practices that you can follow that shut off the easier avenues of hacker attacks.

- Adapters, access points, and other hardware all come with default passwords and other settings. You should quickly change these values. Leaving manufacturer default passwords and settings is basically opening up the door to strangers. The most important values to change are the SSID (from the default "linksys") and the access point or router password (from the default admin). As with any important password, don't set it with something easily guessed about you, like your birthday or pet's name.

- If the access point supports it, and some Linksys models do, disable broadcast SSID. If you do this, the client and access point must be specifically set for an SSID rather than picking one up off the Wi-Fi airwaves. You know the SSID you set so it's no problem for you, but disable broadcast SSID and hackers may not even see that there's a network.

- Place your access point as close as possible to the physical center of the home or office. This is good practice anyway in order to give you the best coverage inside your location, but it has the side benefit of minimizing coverage outside of your location.

- In case you're curious enough and have a wireless-equipped notebook, take it outside and walk around. If your signal radiates several houses away, remember that they have access to it, as could someone in a car if they were actually looking. If you live in an apartment building, you have even less wireless privacy. If your access point or adapter has, as some Linksys models do, the ability to decrease transmission power through a software setting, you might want to play with the setting to see how little power you can use and still have the coverage you need.

- Many access points support Media Access Control (MAC) filtering. This feature lets you block out access to the wireless access point except to those adapters specified by their MAC addresses. All wireless adapters, indeed all network adapters of any kind, have a unique address in them called the MAC address, so telling your access point only to support your adapters is the best way you have to keep outsiders out.

5

- Use the longest key length of WEP that your equipment supports. All current Linksys equipment supports at least 128-bit keys (actually a 104-bit user key plus a 24-bit initialization vector, as explained later in this section).

- Change your WEP keys periodically. This can be a pain, since the changed passwords need to be set in every adapter and access point, but even if someone is determined to hack into your network through high-strength WEP, when you change the passphrase and lock them out again.

- When using WEP and a wireless Windows XP computer, be sure to keep the key in document form, such as Notepad or Word, and copy it onto a floppy. This way you can easily copy and paste the key into Windows XP's Zero Configuration utility.

- Check your log files. If your router or access point can create log files, glance at them every now and then to see if there are any systems accessing the network that shouldn't be there.

WEP

WEP is a system for encrypting the data on the wire. The goal behind it is to prevent unauthorized users within range of the network from "sniffing" the data on the network and seeing its contents. If you take some of the other precautions just mentioned, you can make it harder for someone even to see the encrypted data.

WEP's weaknesses aren't its only problem—WEP is not easy to use. Implementations differ from product to product, even within the Linksys product line, but that only makes things harder because when you're using WEP, you need to use the same keys on all your systems and access points.

Key Lengths

You may be confused at times by references to encryption being 40 bit, 64 bit, 104 bit, 128 bit, or even more. Without getting too deeply into the intricacies of cryptography, about which much larger books than this have been written, WEP uses what is called a 24-bit initialization vector in combination with a 40-bit or 104-bit key that you provide. So, $40 + 24 = 64$ and $104 + 24 = 128$, which is where all these numbers come from.

Some Linksys access points, such as the WAP54A Instant Wireless Access Point (an 802.11a product), implement a proprietary 152-bit WEP, in which the user-supplied key is a full 128 bits.

NOTE   *WEP works fine on ad hoc (peer to peer) wireless LANs.*

5

Using WEP

When using WEP on any system, you need to use a set of up to four keys that the user supplies. The keys are used to encrypt data, and all systems and access points that communicate with each other must be set with the same keys and WEP settings. As a rule, you should use the largest key your system supports. However, since every system and access point needs to use the same keys and settings, you can only use the strongest keys supported by the weakest system on your network.

Keys are usually displayed as a series of hexadecimal values (see the sidebar nearby on what hexadecimal is), and many WEP implementations actually make you type in literal hexadecimal sequences.

In some systems, including many Linksys systems, you can enter an English "passphrase," which is a essentially a password of up to a specified length. Usually, there is a button labeled "Generate" or something to that effect, which takes the passphrase and uses it to generate keys. Sometimes passphrase key generators will generate all four keys. Not all vendors' key generators are compatible, so don't assume that a passphrase used on one system will generate the same keys on another. (Windows XP needs to have the key entered manually. Linksys recommends using the passphrase generator on the access point, then copying whichever key you use into a Notepad document so you can enter the key into an XP station.)

Even though you can enter up to four keys, only one of them is used at any one time. There is always some mechanism—a set of radio buttons or arrows—to choose which is the key to use. In the case of a notebook computer, it's not hard to see how this could be useful, since you could have multiple keys for different wireless networks you connect to and switch between them when you move. It's less clear why storing multiple keys is useful for an access point, but they implement it as well.

Implementing WEP on Linksys Products

Even from one Linksys product to another you can see very different user interfaces for setting WEP, and it can be confusing. There are two basic configuration program types for setting WEP on client systems, so I will describe the approach in those two programs. I will also give two examples of access point implementations of WEP.

WEP on Some Routers, Including the BEFW11S4   Finally, there's a simple WEP configuration program. On some access points and routers such as the BEFW11S4, you configure WEP using the browser-based administration program.

What Is Hexadecimal?

You've seen several references in this book to hexadecimal values, which use numerical digits and characters between *A* and *F*. The more computer stuff you read, the more of this you'll see.

Hexadecimal originated as a convenient way to view data stored in computers. Computer data is organized into bytes, which are 8 bits long, and each bit can be on (1) or off (0). Because 2 to the 8th power is 256, an 8-bit byte can hold a number between 0 and 255.

If you're looking at a lot of this data, it would quickly become tiresome and error-prone to look at the actual 1's and 0's. But looking at the regular numerical equivalents—numbers between 0 and 255—is unappealing because these numbers don't obviously convey which bits are set and which aren't. That's what hexadecimal does.

One byte in hexadecimal is expressed as two digits that represent the first and second 4-bit halves of the byte. Each 4-bit value, sometimes called a "nibble," can hold a value between 0 and 15. To keep it in one digit, the letters *A* through *F* are used for 10 through 15. Thus, hexadecimal is base 16.

To figure out the value of a hex number in base 10, sometimes called "decimal" in the computer world, take the decimal value of the first nibble, multiply by 16, and add the value of the second nibble. For example, the value 7C is $(7 \times 16) + 12 = 124$.

Open a browser, go to *http://192.168.1.1/* and log in. On the Setup screen, click the WEP Key Setting button. You may be asked if you want to change the WEP enable setting to mandatory—select Yes. You should now see the WEP Key Setting window, as in Figure 5-10.

Select a key size, preferably the largest one available. In the Passphrase field, type in any phrase up to 31 characters. When you click the Generate button, a hexadecimal key will be filled into the Key field. Remember, not all passphrase generators are compatible, so you should copy all of the keys, making sure to keep each one separated into a Word or Notepad document. This is very helpful for setting up Windows XP, which does not support the passphrase. Click Apply to save the changes to the router.

The wireless LAN will now be unavailable until client systems have the same WEP key set.

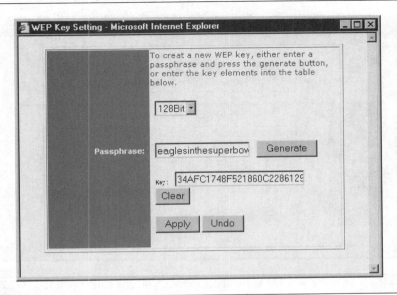

FIGURE 5-10   The BEFW11S4 has a simple WEP configuration window

WAP54A   Other access points and routers such as the WAP54A have different browser-based WEP configuration programs.

Open a browser, surf to *http://192.168.1.252/* or whichever address you have set the device to, and log in. On the Setup screen, click the WEP Key Setting button. You may be asked if you want to change the WEP enable setting to mandatory—select Yes. You should now see the Shared Keys Setting window, pictured in Figure 5-11.

You can enter up to four keys, but you probably need just one. Only the one selected with the radio button on the left is used. Select a key size from the list box on the right, then type in a hexadecimal key in the main field. For a 64-bit key, type in 10 characters (using 0 through 9 or A through F), and for a 128-bit key, type 26 hex characters. Make sure to copy the key you entered into a Word or a Notepad document to keep track of the key. This makes it extremely easy to set up WEP on other PCs.

Click the Apply button to save the changes.

Wireless Configuration Utility   The Linksys Wireless Configuration Utility comes with the WMP11 Instant Wireless PCI Card, the WPC11 Instant Wireless Network PC Card, and perhaps others. You can run it by double-clicking the icon in your

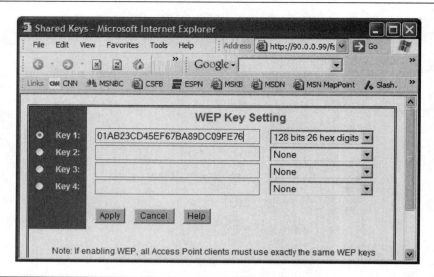

FIGURE 5-11   On the WAP54A, for some reason, you can enter up to four WEP keys

tray of a computer with an antenna. Click the Encryption tab (see Figure 5-12) to access the WEP features.

First, select a key size (64 bits or 128 bits) to match all the other equipment on the network. Try to choose 128 bit, which is better. Then you have the choice of selecting Create with Passphrase and simply typing in a phrase of up to 31 characters, in which case the program auto-fills the actual key fields, or manually typing hexadecimal characters in the key fields. If you type the hexadecimal in, for a 64-bit key, type in 10 characters (using 0 through 9 or A through F), and for a 128-bit key, type 26 hex characters.

Click the Apply Changes button to save the changes to the card. Note the keys you use, since you will need them for other equipment.

WLAN Monitor   The WLAN Monitor comes with the WUSB11 Instant Wireless USB Network Adapter - Version 2.6 and WPC54A Instant Wireless PC Card, and probably an increasing number of Linksys products. WEP is managed in this program on the Advanced Security Settings screen of the Profile Editor (see Figure 5-13).

To launch the program, double-click the icon in your tray of a computer with an antenna. Click Profile Setting on the right side of the window and click the Advanced button.

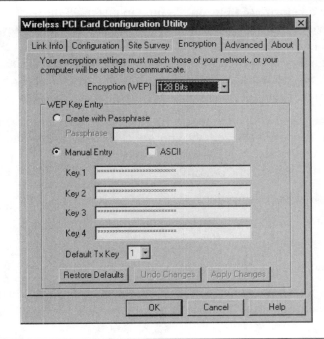

FIGURE 5-12   WEP is implemented in the Wireless Configuration Utility on the Encryption tab

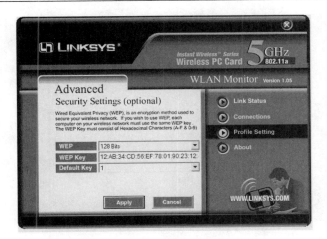

FIGURE 5-13   The WPC54A WEP configuration is slick-looking, but you have to enter your keys in hex

5

First, select a key size (64 bits or 128 bits) to match all the other equipment on the network. Try to choose 128 bit, which is better. For the actual key entry, you have to type in hexadecimal characters. For a 64-bit key, type in 10 characters (using 0 through 9 or A through F), and for a 128-bit key, type 26 hex characters.

Click the Apply button to save the changes to the card. Note the keys you use, since you will need them for other equipment.

Windows XP Integrated WEP   Windows XP integrates wireless network support, including WEP support. To access the appropriate screen, follow these steps:

1. Click Start and select Control Panel.

2. Select Network Connections.

3. Right-click on the icon corresponding to your wireless network connection and select Status.

4. Click the Wireless Network tab.

5. In the lower list of preferred networks, select the appropriate one and click the Properties button. You should see the window shown in Figure 5-14.

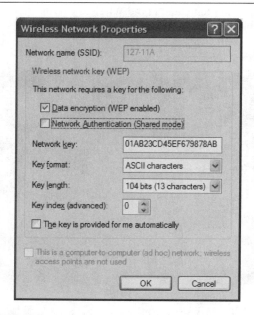

FIGURE 5-14   Windows has integrated WEP support

On the Wireless Network Properties window, make sure the Data Encryption (WEP Enabled) box is checked and that the Network Authentication (Shared Mode) and The Key Is Provided for Me Automatically boxes are unchecked.

Select a key length, preferably the longer one (104 bits, which is the same as what Linksys calls 128 bit). You can then select either ASCII characters or hexadecimal characters. Choose Hexadecimal characters and paste the first key that you generated (if you used passphrase) into the key area. Most of the time the first key (called 1 on most Linksys products but in XP called Key 0) is the correct one. So just copy the first one on the document and paste it. Click OK to save the changes.

802.11b (Wi-Fi) and 802.11a

Linksys makes two products—the WPC54A Instant Wireless PC Card and the WAP54A Instant Wireless Access Point—that use a different standard than Wi-Fi, 802.11a (the products themselves are discussed in further detail below). This standard is not interoperable with Wi-Fi and uses a different radio frequency, the 5-GHz band.

The 802.11a products operate at a much greater speed than Wi-Fi products. They can operate at up to 54 Mbps, and the Linksys products should be interoperable with other 802.11a products at this speed. Linksys products also have a proprietary Turbo mode that can boost network speeds up to 72 Mbps, so if you are considering 802.11a, it may make sense to stick with Linksys products.

NOTE   *At the time of this writing, Linksys only made a PC Card NIC for 802.11a. Keep this in mind; you may need to check what is currently being provided by Linksys for desktops.*

In general, 802.11a is at a stage where it is designed for high-end mobile users at larger businesses. Because only a PC Card is available, you really need a wired network into which to hook the access point. The products are much more expensive than Wi-Fi products and the speed difference is not a compelling advantage for most users.

However, if you're a high-end user with a notebook and the need for speed, 802.11a, especially the Linksys products in Turbo mode, can make a big difference.

The Linksys WAP54A Wireless Access Point

The WAP54A Wireless Access Point works only with the WPC54A Instant Wireless PC Card and other compatible hardware. Beware that interoperability may not be

5

in 802.11a as it is in 802.11b, so you may want to stay with Linksys equipment on both ends.

There are many advanced features in the WAP54A, but when you are initially setting it up, you may want to limit yourself to getting the network up and running before you implement any of the fancy stuff like WEP encryption or Turbo mode.

Setting Up the WAP54A

The WAP54A must be plugged into a wired network in order to function. Connect the power cord and then a cat-5 cable from the LAN port to a port on your hub or switch. There are three LED indicators on the front of the unit:

- Power is green to indicate that the access point is powered up.

- LINK flickers green when the access point is sending or receiving data.

- ACT flickers green when the access point is active.

The default IP address of the WAP54A will be 192.168.1.252, so plug it into a network, even just an empty hub, through which you can address it. (You may have to assign a static IP address to access the unit if you're not using a Linksys router.)

Open a Web browser and surf to *http://192.168.1.252/*. You will see a login screen. Leave the username blank and type **admin** for the password. The screen in Figure 5-15 comes up.

The Setup screen has the most basic important elements of access point configuration on it. The first line shows the firmware version. Firmware is the control program running in the access point itself. You can upgrade the firmware using a link on the Help tab, but don't do so unless you have a very good reason to. In general, only expert users should perform this function unless you are under the direction of Linksys Technical Support.

Next is the access point name. This name doesn't do much, although each access point must have a unique name.

The LAN settings—IP address, subnet mask and gateway—should be what is necessary for your network. If you are the network administrator, you'll know the right value to use. If you're not, you shouldn't be setting up an access point without consulting the network administrator.

Below that comes the Wireless section. Note that the MAC address of the access point is listed here; however, you shouldn't need to use it for anything.

The Turbo Mode button puts the access point into a proprietary mode that can reach 72 Mbps instead of the 802.11a-standard 54 Mbps. If Turbo mode works, great, but there are a few things you should know before pressing this button:

■ If you put the access point in Turbo mode, all the clients must also be in Turbo mode or they will not see the network. So don't set the mode on the access point unless you are sure you can do so on the clients. As I will point out in the next section, if you are using Windows XP, you can't use the built-in wireless support to invoke Turbo mode.

■ Turbo mode may not work on all 802.11a hardware. Do not set this mode unless you are sure your hardware supports it.

■ Turbo mode will decrease the range of the signal from your access point and cards.

Next is the SSID of the network. All cards and access points must use the same SSID and it's a good idea to change it from the default of "linksys."

Next is the channel setting. If you are experiencing signal problems, you can try changing the channel.

NOTE   *Access points will automatically assign channels to wireless equipment that are set to infrastructure.*

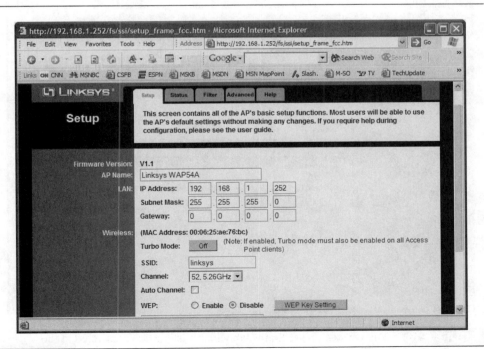

FIGURE 5-15   The Setup screen of the WAP54A lets you set basic communication features

WEP is a standard protocol for encrypting data on the wireless network. Click the WEP Key Setting button and the program will ask you whether you want to enable WEP. It's a good idea to implement WEP, but it's also a good idea to get your wireless network up and running before you implement such security measures. See the "Configuring Security" section earlier in this chapter for full treatment of WEP.

Next, you can set the access point password. It's a really good idea to change this password from the default, because otherwise anyone on the network can log into this administration program and reprogram the access point. Write down the password and keep it somewhere safe.

If you make any changes, you must click the Apply button to save them to the access point. When you do so, the access point may reboot, and there will be a period during which the wireless network will be inaccessible before clients have to reconnect to it.

The Status tab (see Figure 5-16) lists systems on the wireless network and their MAC addresses. Click the MAC address of one of them and you are brought to a

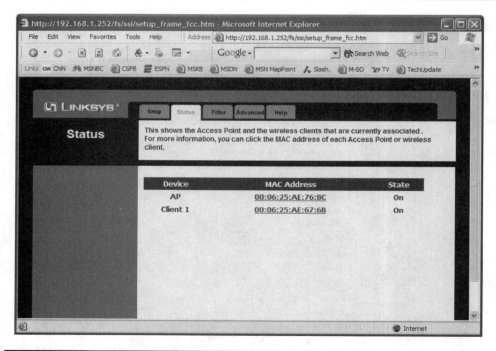

FIGURE 5-16   You can see on the Status tab which systems are connected to the wireless network

screen that lists data the access point tracks for each client, including information on errors and performance. This information is not useful in the normal course of events, although it may be helpful in tech support situations.

The Filter tab (see Figure 5-17) is where you can specify that certain adapters should or should not be allowed access to the access point. You need to know the MAC address of the adapter in order to implement these rules. If the adapter is connected, you can easily get the MAC address from the Status tab.

First, you need to enable the MAC Address feature by selecting Enable from the list box at the top of the page. Then, click the Add button to add an address to the filter. In the screen that follows, type the address of the adapter into the MAC Address field. MAC addresses are always in the format 12:AB:34:CD:56:EF, six hexadecimal byte values separated by colons. All the characters will be numerical digits or letters from A through F. Select Allow or Deny from the Type list below it and click Add to List.

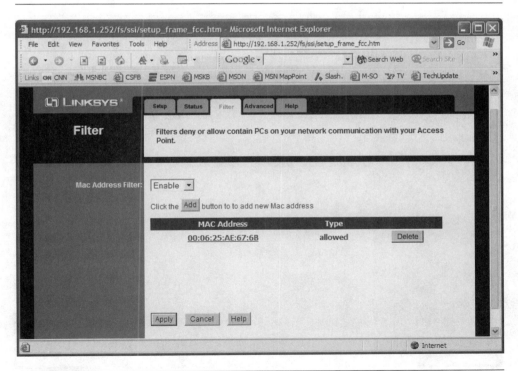

FIGURE 5-17   The MAC Address Filter feature lets you exclude or include specific adapters from the network

Back on the page with the list of addresses in the filter, either click Add to add more addresses, Apply to commit the filter list to the access point and implement it, or Cancel to abort the work.

On the Advanced tab (see Figure 5-18) are several communications settings that you are very unlikely to need to change. Be very careful changing some of these, as even small changes can have deleterious effects on the network's performance.

- The Beacon Interval field sets the frequency of a packet of data sent out by the access point to synchronize the wireless network.

- The 802.11 standard defines the RTS threshold as the packet size at which transmission is governed by the RTS/CTS transaction. Smaller packets need not employ these transactions, thus larger packets involve an added overhead. Each station can have a different RTS threshold. If you ever change this value, don't change it by much.

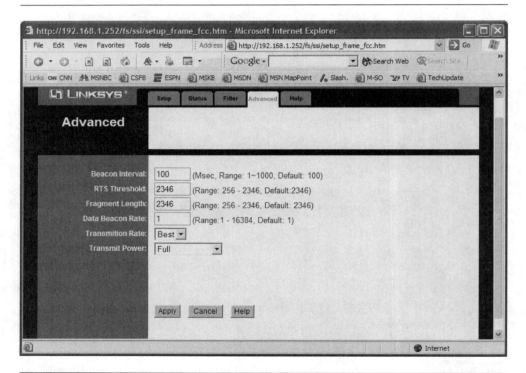

FIGURE 5-18   The values on the Advanced tab should rarely if ever be changed

■ Fragmentation length defines the size of a data packet at which the access point begins splitting the packets up for performance reasons.

■ The Data Beacon Rate field defines the DTIM interval, controlling the issuance of the DTIM, which is a timing packet sent on the network that helps clients to receive broadcast messages.

■ Transmission rate controls the speed of the network explicitly, but you probably want to keep the setting at Best and let the access point run as fast as it can.

■ Transmit power controls the power of the signal. Normally, this is set at Full to give you the best range, but you may want to limit the range for security purposes. Lowering the power can do that.

The Linksys WPC54A Instant Wireless PC Card

There's no point in installing the WPC54A until you have the WAP54A Access Point installed. Once you're ready, note that the procedures for Windows XP and all previous versions of Windows are different. Read carefully. Also, be sure that your notebook is Cardbus (32 bit). If it is not, the WPC54A will not work.

NOTE
Your portable computer will need a CD-ROM drive. If it doesn't have one, you'll need some way to get the files from the WPC54A CD-ROM onto some drive accessible to the notebook for the Plug and Play installation routine. If the laptop has an Ethernet port, you can also download the drivers from the Linksys Web site.

Installing Under Windows XP Like any PC Card, the WPC54A is a breeze to install. Plug it into the socket with the label side facing up. See Chapter 2 for more on PC Cards in general.

When the card is plugged in, or if you turn on the system after plugging it in while the system was off, the Windows Plug and Play feature will discover the wireless NIC. You will have to install the driver software for your wireless NIC. Put the CD-ROM that accompanies the WPC54A into the CD drive.

Windows XP automatically detects the new PC Card network adapter. First, a message appears above the notification area of the taskbar telling you that Windows has found new hardware. At this point, Windows XP launches the Found New Hardware Wizard so you can perform a driver installation. Follow these steps:

1. Select the option Install from a List or Specific Location (Advanced) and click Next.

2. In the next wizard window, select the option Search for the Best Driver in These Locations and clear the check box labeled Search Removable Media. In the field labeled Include This Location in the Search, type **d:\Drivers** (substitute the drive letter for your CD-ROM drive if it's not d:, or the appropriate location if you have put the drivers elsewhere).

3. If the wizard displays a window telling you that the driver is not tested for Windows, click Continue Anyway (don't worry, the driver is exactly what you need for Windows XP).

4. Click Finish in the next wizard window.

5. Windows XP may display a message above the notification area of the taskbar that a new network device is available and that you should click the notice to run the Network Setup Wizard. See Chapter 8 for more on the Network Setup Wizard.

Installing Under Windows 98

With versions of Windows prior to Windows XP, you want to go about things differently. Put the CD-ROM that accompanies the WPC54A into the CD drive.

NOTE *You need to install the Linksys WPC54A software before you install the card itself. Do not install the PC Card until instructed to do so.*

After you put the CD-ROM in the drive, Windows AutoPlay feature should load the Setup Wizard. If it does not, click Start, select Run, type **d:\setup.exe**, and press ENTER. Then, follow these steps:

1. Click on the Setup button to begin the Setup Wizard.

2. Click Next at the "Thank you for choosing a Linksys Wireless Adapter…" screen.

3. Click Yes to accept the license agreement.

4. If you wish to choose a different location for the wireless software than the one indicated on the next screen, click Browse and select it. Click Next when you are finished.

5. In the next screen, you have to choose between Infrastructure mode and Ad-Hoc mode. If you are using this card with a WAP54A Access Point, choose Infrastructure Mode. If you are setting up a peer-to-peer network, choose Ad-Hoc. Click Next when you are done.

6. Now enter the SSID of the network this card should connect to. The default value, "linksys," is also the default value for other Linksys cards and access points. Make sure to use the same value on all your equipment, and it's a good idea to change it from the default. Click Next to continue.

7. Now, prior to copying the files to the hard disk, the wizard will restate your settings for you. Click Next if they are correct.

8. Next, the wizard copies the files from the CD to the computer.

9. Then you may see a screen indicating that the software does not have a digital signature, and that there is no guarantee that it will work with Windows. Don't worry, it will work. Click Yes to indicate that you want to continue.

10. The wizard ends.

Now it's time to put the card in the computer. Plug it into the socket with the label side facing up. See Chapter 2 for more on PC Cards in general.

You may see some screens appear, but you should not need to provide any more input. The card installation should be finished.

Configuring the WPC54A

Configuring WPC54A is almost identical to configuring the 802.11b cards described above. In fact, for Windows XP it is identical. See the section "Configuring the Wireless Network" for instructions.

For versions of Windows prior to Windows XP, the WPC54A uses the WLAN Monitor program that you installed, along with the device driver software, prior to installing the card itself. You should have an icon in your system tray, a blue computer with an antenna on top (it's blue if the network is connected, red if not). Double-click on the icon. If you don't see the icon, run the program by clicking Start, selecting Programs, selecting the Instant 802.11a Wireless program group, then clicking on the Instant 802.11a Wireless LAN Monitor program. The opening screen is pictured in Figure 5-19.

This opening screen, which you can also reach by clicking Link Status on the right side of the window, shows you the state of the connection: the SSID of the network, whether it is Ad-hoc or Infrastructure; the speed; channel; and WEP status. The Signal Strength and Link Quality indicators will only display in Infrastructure mode. The set of numbers and letters after the SSID is called the BSSID, or Basic Service Set ID, which is a unique number identifying all the systems in the wireless network using the SSID.

Click Connections on the right to bring up a list of wireless networks that are in range (see Figure 5-20). You can connect to any one of them by selecting it and pressing the Connect button. Pressing the Refresh button will cause the program to

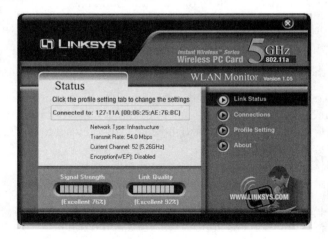

FIGURE 5-19   The Status screen tells you the state of the connection

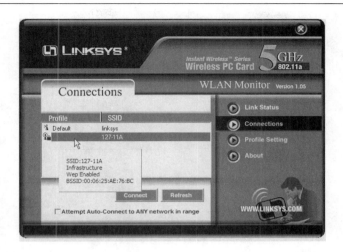

FIGURE 5-20   The Connections screen shows the available networks. Hovering over one shows some configuration information for it

rescan for available networks and repopulate the list. Selecting Attempt Auto Connect to ANY Network in Range will cause the program to connect to the closest network.

Clicking Profile Setting brings up a list of profiles (see Figure 5-21). You can have multiple profiles for multiple wireless networks. Type in a name and other information for the profile and press Apply.

Clicking the Advanced button brings up the WEP configuration screen. See the "Configuring Security" section for full treatment of security issues.

> NOTE   *It's essential to implement security on your network, including using WEP, but it's a good idea to get the network up and functioning first before implementing security.*

Finally, the About screen shows you the versions of the WLAN Monitor program, the device driver, and firmware.

The Linksys WAP51AB Dual-Band Wireless Access Point

Linksys recently shipped an access point that supports 802.11a and 802.11b simultaneously. Like the WAP54A, it supports proprietary extensions on 802.11a including 72 Mbps Turbo mode and 152-bit WEP (neither of which is presently accessible to Windows XP clients).

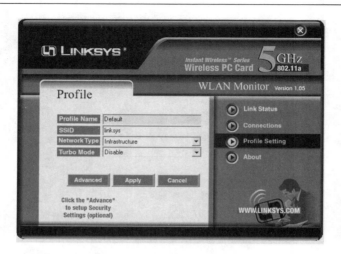

FIGURE 5-21   The Profile screen lets you define different groups of settings for the card

The WAP51AB lets you support both types of wireless devices while having just one access point to buy and manage. While you'll have one device through a single program to manage, the 802.11a and 802.11b networks are logically separate within the access point with, for example, their own WEP key settings.

You'll find the standard Linksys browser-based administration interface in the WAP51AB, which you can access through a browser at 192.168.1.250, with a few differences specific to the nature of the device. One difference includes two sets of SSID, channel, and WEP settings, one for the 802.11a and one for the 802.11b. Note, however, that if you can configure any of the other access points, you should be able to handle the WAP51AB.

Chapter 6

Using Telephone Lines

Wiring your home or office for Ethernet will probably be a pain, but you probably already have telephone lines that you can use for computer networking. Under normal circumstances, you can use your telephones for voice communications while simultaneously using the same lines for your computer network.

Like the other types of networking described in this book, phone line networking is based on an industry standard, this one maintained by an organization called the Home Phoneline Networking Alliance (*http://www.homepna.org/*), which gives the name HomePNA to the standard. An early version of the HomePNA standard operated at a stingy 1 Mbps, but the current standard can work at 10 Mbps. (Equipment written to the new specification switches down to 1Mpbs if any of the older equipment is on the network.) The 1Mbit equipment supports up to 25 computers with a distance of up to 500 feet of cabling. The 10Mbit equipment supports up to 30 computers with a distance of up to 1000 feet of cabling.

CAUTION   *Some houses have wiring problems that can prevent HomePNA networking from functioning properly. If your wiring is nonstandard in any way, you should at least confirm that you can return products you purchased for phone line networking before implementing them.*

HomePNA networking, like DSL, works on your phone lines while letting you use the lines for voice or fax communications, but HomePNA and DSL aren't the same thing. In fact, while you can probably use both on the same phone lines at the same time, the DSL connection and the HomePNA connection can't communicate with each other. You'll need a DSL modem and optionally other hardware, such as the Linksys HPRO200 HomeLink PhoneLine 10M Cable/DSL Router, to make the network connection between the two.

NOTE   *Synchronous DSL (SDSL) cannot coexist on the same phone line with either HomePNA or voice. Only Asynchronous DSL (ADSL) can work this way.*

Installing Phone Line Hardware

As with any other networking scheme, phone line networking requires a network adapter for each system on the network. Unlike some other networking schemes, you don't necessarily need a hub or hardware, although it can help at times.

After installing the adapter, you must configure Windows networking. See Chapter 8 for a full treatment of this topic.

Desktop Products

You probably have two choices for desktop PCs: a PCI adapter or a USB adapter. The advantages of the PCI adapter are that almost all desktop computers capable of running a modern version of Windows have PCI slots. PCI hardware also has potential performance advantages, but these are small compared to the convenience factor—which brings us to the downside: to install a PCI adapter, you must open up the computer.

> **NOTE** *You really ought to open up your computer before even buying a PCI adapter to make sure you have an available slot for it.*

6

USB hardware, found in all systems sold in the last few years, is much easier to work with. You can install it simply by plugging in a cable between the device and the system (see Chapter 2 for general instructions on installing USB hardware). Check to make sure you have an available USB plug on the system for the network adapter, but if you don't, you can buy a USB hub to expand the system.

PCI

The Linksys HPN200 HomeLink Phoneline 10M Network Card is a 1/10 Mbps phone line card that connects to the PCI bus. The backplane of the card (the metal plate exposed to the outside through the back of the system) has two plugs.

After installing the adapter in the system (see Chapter 2 for instructions on installing PCI hardware), turn on the computer and Windows will detect the presence of the new card.

If you have Windows XP, congratulations. It should just boot up and install the drivers for the HPN200 automatically.

If you have Windows 98, it's another story.

1. After you install the adapter and boot up the system, the Add New Hardware Wizard appears. If you have not already put the Phoneline 10M Network Card Driver CD into your CD drive, do so.

2. Click Next. On the next screen, the default selection will be Search For The Best Driver For Your Device (Recommended). Leave the default selection and click Next.

3. On the next screen, select CD-ROM from the list of drives and click Next again.

4. The next screen will say that Windows is ready to install the "Linksys Phoneline 10M Network Card" and specify the location. Click Next. Windows copies the driver from the CD to the computer. At this point, you may need to insert your Windows 98 CD-ROM, so have it ready. If you don't have a Windows 98 CD-ROM, you can usually specify c:\windows\options\cabs for any Windows files needed.

5. On the last screen, Windows tells you that it has finished installing the drivers for the card. Click Finish to end the wizard. You may be prompted at this point to reboot the computer.

If you are setting up a network, as opposed to adding one system to an existing one, you may be better off with the HPN200SK HomeLink Phoneline 10M Network In a Box, which basically has two HPN200 cards and two phone cables. Retailers often sell the HPN200SK at a small discount compared to the cost of two HPN200 cards.

USB

The USB200HA HomeLink Phoneline 10M USB Network Adapter is remarkably easy to set up. You plug the phone line into one of the two phone plugs, connect the USB cable from the device to the system, and there you are. You don't even need a power outlet, as this and many other USB devices draw their power directly from the system through the USB cable.

The USB200HA has the same speed and capabilities as the HPN200, although it's a slightly more expensive product. If you don't want to mess with the insides of your computer, or you want to move the adapter from system to system, USB is a better choice.

Four display lights appear on the USB200HA. The Power light indicates that the unit is drawing power from the system and is turned on. The Link light indicates that USB200HA is connected to a phone line network. The Tx light indicates that the device is transmitting data over a phone line network, and the Rx light indicates that it is receiving data from the network. In the normal course of operation of the USB200HA, the Power and Link lights should be on constantly, but the Tx and Rx lights should flash a lot.

The software installation for the USB device is similar to that of the PCI. If you have Windows XP, you should be able to plug the USB200HA into the system, and Windows will recognize it and install the device drivers for it automatically.

If you have Windows 98:

1. The Add New Hardware Wizard appears. If you have not already put the Phoneline 10M Network Card Driver floppy disk into your floppy drive, do so. Click Next.

2. On the next screen, the default selection will be Search for The Best Driver For Your Device (Recommended). Leave the default selection and click Next.

3. On the next screen, select Floppy Disk Drives from the list of drives (Figure 6-1) and click Next again.

4. The next screen will say that Windows is ready to install the "Linksys Phoneline 10M Network Card" and will specify the location. Click Next. Windows copies the driver from the floppy to the computer. You may at this point need to insert your Windows 98 CD-ROM, so have it ready. If you don't have a Windows 98 CD-ROM, you can usually specify c:\windows\options\cabs for any Windows files needed.

5. On the last screen, Windows tells you that it has finished installing the drivers for the card. Click Finish to end the wizard. You may be prompted at this point to reboot the computer.

Notebook Products

Most notebook computer users can also use USB devices, but almost all of them can use PC Cards (sometimes known as PCMCIA cards). See the preceding

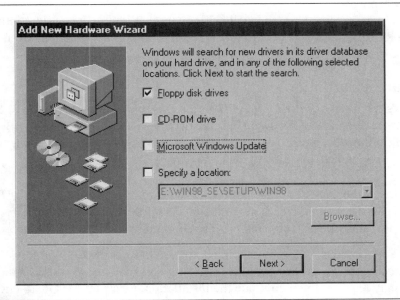

FIGURE 6-1   Make sure you have the driver disk in the appropriate drive and make the appropriate selection for the Add New Hardware Wizard

section, "Desktop Products," for a discussion of USB devices. Most notebook computer users will want to use a PC Card such as the PCM200HA HomeLink Phoneline 10M Integrated PC Card.

The PCM200HA requires a 32-bit CardBus slot, which some older notebooks will not have. See Chapter 2 for more information on PCMCIA hardware.

To install the PCM200HA, just insert it into one of the notebook's PC Card slots so that the three lights on the card are pointed up. Push the card until you can feel it seat inside. The two rows of pins at the inside of the PC Card slot need to slide into the two rows of holes in the card.

With a PC Card, as with USB, you don't have to turn off the system before adding or removing hardware. You can just plug it in, Windows will recognize it, and it will then begin the process of software installation, or it will just work.

Three display lights appear on the PCM200HA. The Link light indicates that PCM200HA is connected to a phone line network. The Tx light indicates that the device is transmitting data over a phone line network, and the Rx light indicates that it is receiving data from the network. In the normal course of operation of the PCM200HA, the Link light should be on constantly, but the Tx and Rx lights should flash a lot.

Insert a phone line from the wall or from another phone line system into one of the two RJ11 outlets on the PCM200HA. The two plugs are identical, even though one is labeled "Homelink" and the other "Phone."

Software Installation

Windows XP identifies the PCM200HA correctly, but take note that the opening screen of the Found New Hardware Wizard identifies the PCM200HA as a "Broadcom iLine10 Cardbus Network Adapter" (see Figure 6-2), which is a reference to the company that makes the chips in the card. This is OK.

1. Insert the CD-ROM that came with the card into the notebook's CD-ROM drive. Leave the default set to Install The Software Automatically (Recommended) and click Next to continue.

2. You may see a warning that the hardware has not passed Windows Logo testing to assure compatibility with Windows XP and that dreadful things may happen if you continue the installation. Fear not; it's OK to click Continue Anyway to install the device driver software, enabling the card.

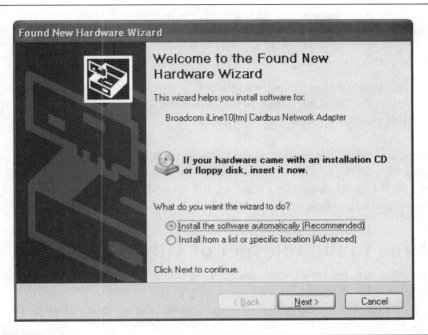

FIGURE 6-2   The PCM200HA is automatically recognized, but it's identified by its chipset, not as a Linksys adapter

3. The wizard will install the device driver files from the CD-ROM to the appropriate Windows directory. The installation should not require a Windows XP reboot.

If you have Windows 98, the Add New Hardware Wizard appears.

1. If you have not already done so, put the Phoneline 10M Network Card Driver CD into your CD drive. Click Next.

2. On the next screen, the default selection will be Search For The Best Driver For Your Device (Recommended). Leave the default selection and click Next.

3. Select the CD-ROM from the list of drives and click Next again.

4. The next screen will say that Windows is ready to install the Linksys Phoneline 10M Network Card and will specify the location. Click Next.

Windows copies the driver from the CD to the computer. You may at this point need to insert your Windows 98 CD-ROM, so have it ready. If you don't have a Windows 98 CD-ROM you can usually specify c:\windows\ options\cabs for any Windows files needed.

5. On the last screen, Windows tells you that it has finished installing the drivers for the card. Click Finish to end the wizard. You may be prompted at this point to reboot the computer.

At the end of the process, your card should be active. If you connect the phone cables to the rest of the network, you should be able to communicate with other systems on the network and, if it's set up, the Internet. See Chapter 8 for more details on how to configure Windows networking.

Connecting to the Internet or Other Networks

As with other network types, you connect your phone line network with the Internet in two ways. The cheaper, if not easier way, is to use Windows Internet Connection Sharing or a similar third-party program to connect the Internet connection with the phone line network. We explain how to do this in detail in Chapter 8. The second way is to use a router, such as the Linksys HPRO200 HomeLink Phoneline 10M Cable/DSL Router, which makes the Internet connection easy to set up.

The Linksys Phoneline Router

The Linksys HPRO200 (shown in Figure 6-3) provides dynamic Internet addresses for PCs on the network so that setting up client PCs is easy. The HPRO200 can also connect an Ethernet PC or other Ethernet device or even an Ethernet hub to your phone line network.

Finally, as opposed to Internet Connection Sharing, no single PC is responsible for keeping the Internet connection going, so you can shut off any PCs on the network if you want. The HPRO200 is set up for broadband routing though, such as that attained with a cable modem or DSL service. If your Internet connection is through a dial-up modem, you will need to use Internet Connection Sharing to share the connection with the rest of your phone line network.

Router Ports

All the connections start (or end, depending on your point of view) at the back of your router. I'll go over each connection on the router, moving from left to right, according to the unit shown in Figure 6-3.

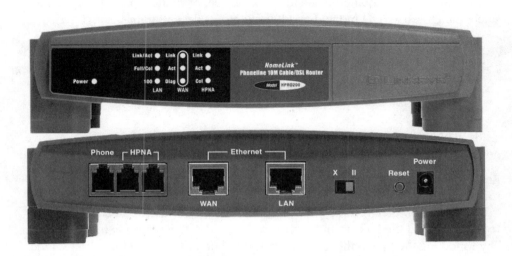

FIGURE 6-3 The Linksys HPRO200 HomeLink Phoneline 10M Cable/DSL Router connects to HomePNA, phone lines, a broadband connection, and a local Ethernet LAN

Phone   This port is meant for a telephone, fax, or some other conventional telephony device. The manual says that it has special filter hardware for telephones and that you should not use your phones in any other port.

HPNA   These two ports are for HomePNA network devices.

WAN Port   Use the WAN port to connect the router to your DSL/cable modem. WAN, for wide area network, is a term that's usually applied to a network that's spread across multiple locations. (See the sidebar "LAN, WAN, and MAN" if you're interested in learning more about the various types of networks that are used to connect computers.) While the router doesn't really create a WAN, it does provide a separation point (and a barricade) between two networks: your LAN and the Internet (the Internet is a network too—the largest network in the world).

LAN Port   Use this port to connect the router to a wired Ethernet PC or hub. If you plan to use this port, read the following section on the nearby crossover switch, which controls the wiring of this connection.

Crossover Switch (X/II)   This two-position switch sets the mode of the LAN port to either crossover (X) or straight-through (II). If you are connecting the LAN port directly to a computer, another stand-alone device, or to the Uplink port in a hub, select the crossover (X) mode. For anything else, select straight-through (II).

NOTE   *Remember that special crossover cables can do the same thing as the X mode in this switch. The preceding instructions presume that you are using a normal straight-through cable. If you are using a crossover cable, reverse the instructions.*

If you're confused about what selection to use or what kind of cable you have, no need to worry. Just plug it in and try both positions of the switch until it works.

Reset Button   Like the Reset button on your computer, the Reset button on the router clears data and restarts the device. To use it, press and hold the button for 2 to 3 seconds and then release it. Use this button only in case of an emergency, if for some reason the links to the router are jammed and communications are frozen. Try following the tips in the troubleshooting section of your router's User Guide before you press Reset.

It's possible, but unlikely, that the router could lock up like your computer sometimes locks up, to the degree that even the Reset button won't work. In these cases, remove the power cable from the router for 3 to 5 seconds and then reinsert it. There's a good chance that this procedure will retain network connections through the router, but if you leave the unit powered down much longer you may lose the connections.

Power   This connector accepts the power adapter, the other end of which is plugged into a wall outlet (or, preferably, a surge protector).

LAN, WAN, and MAN

The methods for interconnecting computers vary depending on the geographical circumstances. Each of the three basic types of networks, LAN, WAN, and MAN, has a variety of setup methods, but I'll stick to the basics here.

A LAN (Local Area Network) is a group of computers connected by a common communications line. That line is usually cable, but it can also be a noncable connection topology, such as telephone lines, power lines, or wireless technology. Most small business networks and all home networks are LANs.

A WAN (Wide Area Network) is a group of computers, widely geographically dispersed, that use public communication lines as the connection method. The public communication lines are telephone lines, usually special high-speed data communication lines.

A MAN (Metropolitan Area Network) is a group of computers that are geographically dispersed but in the same general area. The computers can be connected through public lines or through the use of fiber-optic cable that's capable of withstanding the elements. For example, the computers in a group of adjacent buildings might be connected in this manner. Many college campus networks are connected as MANs, providing network connections in classrooms, dormitories, and other buildings.

The Front Panel LEDs

You'll notice ten lights on the front panel of the HPRO200 (see Figure 3). At the far left, on its own, is the Power light, which is on when the router is powered up. To the right are three columns, each with three indicators, labeled LAN, WAN, and HPNA.

> **NOTE**   *To power up the HPRO200, simply plug it in.*

The LAN indicators show the status of the connection to the LAN port:

- Link/Act, the top indicator, is on continuously when a successful connection exists to a device on the LAN port. The LED flashes when the data is being sent or received through the port.

- If the Full/Col LED is on continuously, the LAN connection is full-duplex, which means that it is running at full speed both sending and receiving data. When it flashes, collisions on the connection are occurring, which means that the traffic load is heavy.

- The LED labeled 100 turns orange when the router is connected to the LAN at 100 Mbps.

The WAN indicators show the status of the connection to the WAN port:

- The top indicator, Link, is lit continuously when a successful connection to a device, such as a cable or DSL modem, exists on the WAN port.

- The Act LED flashes when data is sent or received on the WAN port.

- The Diag LED turns on during the router's self-diagnostic stage while starting up. It turns off if the test is successful. If it is on for a long period of time, there is a problem with the unit. You need help. See Appendix C for information on obtaining support from Linksys.

The HPNA indicators show the status of connections through the HPNA ports:

- The top indicator, Link, is on continuously when a successful connection to a HomePNA Phoneline adapter is made on one of the HPNA ports or the Phone port.

- The Act LED flashes when data is sent or received on the HPNA or Phone ports.

- The Col LED flashes when collisions on the connection occur, which means that the traffic load is heavy. Heavy flashing may indicate a problem. See Appendix C for information on obtaining support from Linksys.

Making the Connections

You need to start by physically connecting your router to your DSL/cable modem and to the computers on your network. Depending on your current network topology (if a network is in place), making the physical connections can be merely a matter of moving some cable, or you may need to install the cable from scratch, or you may have to do a little of both.

NOTE *Linksys advises that all nodes on the network be powered off while you make your connections.*

Attaching an Existing Hub/Switch to the Router If you'd already set up a wired Ethernet network before deciding to add a HomePNA router, you don't have to abandon the hub or switch you're using (see Figure 6-4).

At first, this might seem a strange thing to do: if you have a wired Ethernet network, why would you need a HomePNA network? But there are good reasons for doing this. For instance, I have a wired Ethernet network in my office, with wires simply laying on the floor between systems and my Ethernet hub. But if I wanted to include computers elsewhere in the house on that network, I would have to run wires through the walls or perhaps down the stairs. No way is my wife going to let me do that. Instead, I can use the HPRO200 to connect my office network to a HomePNA network, and then I can network any PC within reach of a phone plug.

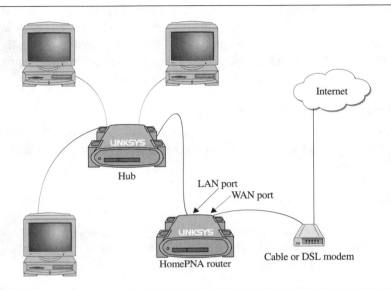

 You can connect an existing hub to the router

6

To make this connection, connect a regular port on the hub to the LAN port on the router. Make sure to switch the Crossover switch to the X position. If you have an Uplink port on your hub, you can connect from it to the LAN port on the router, but make sure that you switch the Crossover switch to the II position.

If you had been connecting a DSL or cable modem through the hub, it should be connected through the WAN port on the router, which might open up a port on your hub.

CAUTION   *If you have an existing network, and you're using any form of Internet connection sharing, you must disable it. The router takes care of sharing the connection.*

Configuring the Computers

You need to configure your computers to access the Internet through the router. (See Chapter 8 to learn how to access the TCP/IP settings for your NICs.) You must configure the computers to obtain an IP address automatically (the router takes care of issuing the IP addresses). Nothing else is enabled—no gateway, no DNS, no WINS, nothing.

If one of the computers on your network had been connected to the DSL/cable modem and its NIC is configured for your ISP settings, that NIC must be reconfigured as a client to obtain an address and other TCP/IP information automatically (matching the settings for the other computers on the network). The original settings from the ISP are used to configure the router.

Configuring the Router Connection

You configure your router by accessing it from one of the connected computers. No special software has to be installed on that computer; the router is accessed through the browser.

NOTE *When you open the browser to begin configuration of the router, you may receive an error message. That's because the browser can't get to the home page you configured (because until you finish configuring the router, you don't have access to the Internet). If your browser home page is set for About:Blank, however, you won't see an error message.*

Follow these steps to begin configuring your router:

1. In the browser Address Bar, enter **http://192.168.1.1/** and press ENTER to open the Enter Network Password dialog (it may take a few seconds for the dialog to appear).

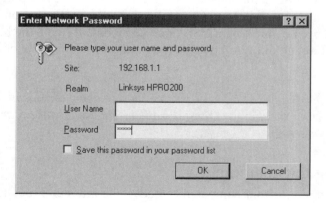

NOTE *This dialog may look slightly different if you're not doing this on a Windows 98 computer.*

> **TIP** *Add the URL for the router to your Favorites list to make it easy to open the window later, in case you want to add or modify the features.*

2. Leave the User Name field blank, and in the Password field type **admin** (in lowercase characters). Then click OK.

3. The Linksys Setup window appears with the Setup tab selected, as shown in Figure 6-5.

> **NOTE** *The Setup window has multiple tabs for setting up all the features offered by your Linksys HomePNA router. I'll discuss the other tabs in the sections that follow.*

In the Setup tab, you specify the basic options for your Internet connection. You must configure this tab and restart your DSL/cable modem and also restart the

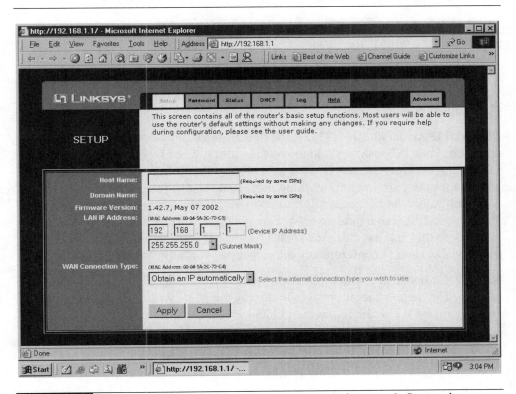

FIGURE 6-5   Configure your Internet connection through the router's Setup tab

computers on the network to provide Internet access for your network, before you set configuration options on the other tabs in the Setup window.

- **Host Name and Domain Name** These fields can usually remain blank, but if your ISP requires this information, fill in the data as instructed.

- **Firmware Version** This is the version number for the router's firmware, as well as the release date for the version. Firmware is programming code that is inserted into the read-only memory of a device. This technology provides a way to enhance the capabilities of hardware devices. When new firmware is available, you can download it from the Linksys Web site, along with instructions on how to insert the new code into the device's memory; however, Linksys does not recommend upgrading your firmware unless you're having trouble with the router.

- **Device IP Address and Subnet Mask** The default values for the router's IP address and subnet mask are preset and should not be altered.

- **WAN Connection Type** Click the arrow to the right of the text box and select a connection type.

The WAN connection specifications must match the instructions from your ISP. The Linksys HomePNA router supports five connection types, which are discussed next.

Obtain an IP Automatically This is the default selection, because it's the most common. Your ISP instructs you to use this setting when DHCP (Dynamic Host Configuration Protocol) services are provided by the ISP. If this is the correct setting for your ISP, you have nothing more to do in the Setup tab.

Click Apply, and then click Continue to save your settings. Close the browser. Power your DSL/cable modem off and on again. Restart all the computers on the network so they can establish the router's settings. You can return to this Setup utility at any time to configure any other features you want to use.

Static IP Choose this option if the instructions from your ISP require a static IP address. The Setup window changes to display the fields you need for configuration (see Figure 6-6). Use the following guidelines to supply data in the fields:

- **Specify WAN IP Address** Enter the IP address for the router as seen from the WAN (Internet).

■ **Subnet Mask**   Enter the subnet mask as seen by the Internet and the ISP.

■ **Default Gateway Address**   Enter the IP address for the gateway.

■ **DNS (Required)**   Enter the IP address of the DNS server your ISP wants you to use. Your ISP provides at least one DNS IP address. Many ISPs provide a secondary DNS IP address. The Setup window also has a field for a third DNS IP address if your ISP provided one.

Click Apply and then click Continue to save your settings. Close the browser. Power your DSL/cable modem off and on again. Restart all the computers on the network so they can establish the router's settings. You can return to this Setup utility at any time to configure any other features you want to use.

6

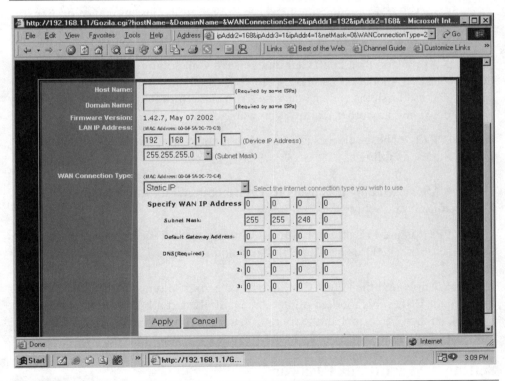

FIGURE 6-6   Use the information from your ISP to configure a static IP address

PPPoE   If your DSL provider uses Point-to-Point Protocol over Ethernet (PPPoE), select this option to enable the protocol (see Figure 6-7). Then configure your connection, using the following guidelines:

- **User Name and Password**   Enter the data provided by your DSL ISP.

- **Connect on Demand: Max Idle Time**   You can configure the router to disconnect from your ISP after a specified amount of inactivity. Then, whenever you're disconnected as a result of inactivity, the connection is re-established as soon as a user attempts to access the Internet (by opening a browser or an e-mail application). Enter the number of minutes of inactivity that must elapse to cause the router to disconnect from your DSL ISP.

- **Keep Alive: Redial Period**   Select this option to have the router periodically check the state of your Internet connection and reconnect to your ISP if the connection has been broken. Enter an amount of time that must elapse to cause the router to reconnect.

Click Apply and then click Continue to save your settings. Close the browser. Power your DSL modem off and on again. Restart all the computers on the network so they can establish the router's settings. You can return to this Setup utility at any time to configure any other features you want to use.

RAS and PPTP   These services are less common and are used only outside the United States, as follows:

- RAS is used only in Singapore. Contact Singtel for information on the appropriate settings.

- PPTP is used mostly in Europe. Contact your ISP for information on settings. (PPTP is also used in Israel and Australia.)

Click Apply and then click Continue to save your settings. Close the browser. Power your DSL/cable modem off and on again. Restart all the computers on the network so they can establish the router's settings. You can return to this Setup utility at any time to configure any other features you want to use.

Setting a New Router Password

The default router password is the same for all Linksys routers, so it's easy for someone to guess. Any user on the local network could connect to the router and

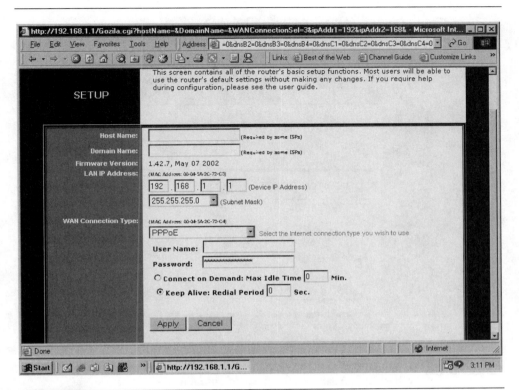

FIGURE 6-7   Enter your connection settings for PPPoE

change the configuration settings, and all they have to do is read the manual or this book to know that the default IP address is 192.168.1.1 and the default password is *admin*. Bottom line: one of the first things you should do is to change the default password (see Figure 6-8).

On the Password tab, delete the dots that currently appear in the Router Password text box and enter a new password. Then, delete the dots in the next text box and enter the new password again to confirm it. You can use up to 63 characters for your password, but you can't use a space.

CAUTION   *For added password security, don't enable the option to save the password and automatically log in when you open the router's configuration feature.*

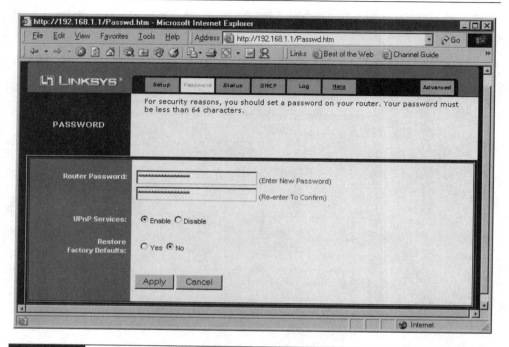

FIGURE 6-8   It's important that you change the default password on the unit so that others can't easily change the configuration

UPnP Services

This is a Windows XP–only feature, and unless all the computers on your network are running Windows XP, you should select Disable. Even if all the computers on your network are running Windows XP, you may want to disable this option. It means that the Windows XP Universal Plug and Play service can automatically reconfigure the router if somebody on the network tries to use certain interactive Internet applications. A great many security problems have been reported as the result of using UPnP, and although Microsoft provides fixes and patches rather quickly, if you don't keep up with the patches and install them, you could compromise the security of your network. (WinME also has UPnP compatibilities.)

Restoring the Router to Factory Default

This is a selection that you must consider as a last ditch; life as you know it has changed for the worse, send up a flare for rescue. If you select Yes and then click Apply, all of your router's settings are cleared and you have to start all over again.

It's rare that an occasion would arise for such a drastic move, and don't even think about this unless you've exhausted all troubleshooting suggestions from Linksys technical support and they've told you that this is the only solution. You can also hold the Reset button for 30 seconds to restore the factory defaults if you're unable to access the router.

Checking the Current Status of the Router

The Status tab (Figure 6-9) displays the current status of the Router and its configuration. Most of the entries are self-explanatory, but the Login status may not be—it refers to whether or not Login is enabled for PPPoE, RAS, or PPTP connection types. If you're not using one of those connection methods, the Login status is marked Disabled.

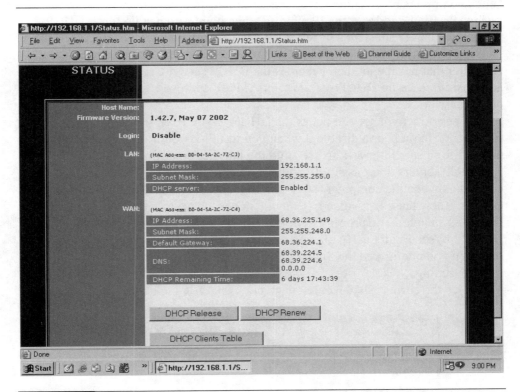

FIGURE 6-9   The Status tab displays network information and includes some buttons for managing DHCP functions

You cannot make changes on this page to the values displayed here; it's only reporting your setup configuration. When you make changes to the Setup tab, those changes are reflected in the Status tab.

At the bottom of the Status page are three buttons related to DHCP management. The first two come into play if your router is a DHCP client on your ISP's network—in other words, if your router obtains an IP address automatically from the ISP's network. Clicking DHCP Release releases that address back to the ISP network. Click it and you will see all the WAN settings on the Status page revert to zeros. Click DHCP Renew and the router will request a new address from the network.

The third button, DHCP Clients Table, is the same as the button of the same name on the DHCP page. See the discussion of it in the next section, "Managing DHCP."

Managing DHCP

When computers receive their IP addresses automatically, instead of using an assigned static IP address, the IP address assignments are handled by a DHCP server. You can create a DHCP server on any network, using any computer—in fact, if you run Internet Connection Sharing (ICS) instead of using a router, the computer that has the modem becomes the DHCP server. Corporate network administrators set up DHCP servers to provide IP addresses for all the computers on the network.

It's best to let your router act as the DHCP server. Even if you had been running ICS, you had to disable it when you installed your router, so it would be unusual for a small network to use anything but the router for DHCP services.

DHCP servers don't assign IP addresses permanently; they're leased to computers when the computers start up and request an IP address. When the lease expires, a new lease is assigned. (Computers don't have to reboot to request a new lease; it's an automatic process.) The default length of the lease appears on the DHCP tab (see Figure 6-10) along with other DHCP settings (some of which you set when you configured the Setup tab). There's no particular reason to change any of these settings.

To see the current DHCP client data, click the DHCP Clients Table button.

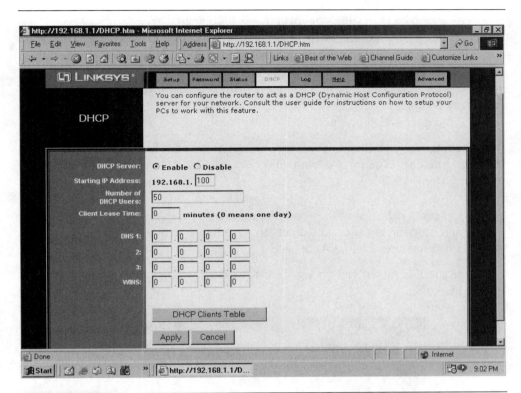

FIGURE 6-10   Configuration settings for your router-based DHCP server are displayed on the DHCP tab

Logging Events and Warnings

Use the Log tab to enable logging and to view logs. By default, logging is disabled. You can enable logging simply by clicking Enable on the Log page. You can view the information being collected by opening the logs. The Incoming Access Log button displays incoming Internet traffic, and the Outgoing Access Log button displays the URLs and IP addresses of Internet sites that users on the network accessed.

Saving Logs with LogViewer

If a computer on your network has a fixed IP address (admittedly, unlikely), you can save log data permanently. Using the logs to keep an eye on the system is usually sufficient. However, if you think your network is in some serious danger from an Internet attack, you may want to store logged information in files. This gives you a chance to examine the data to see if you can discern any patterns, especially attempts from the same IP address to enter your network. Even if you're not suspicious about attacks, you may want to track activities for some period of time by saving logged information in permanent files. To accomplish this, you need LogViewer software, which you can download from Linksys and install on one of the computers on your network, and then you can configure the router to send the log data to that computer.

Downloading and Installing LogViewer   The LogViewer software is available from Linksys at no cost. You must download the software and then install it, using the following steps:

1. Open the browser on the computer that will install the viewer software and hold the log files, and enter **ftp://ftp.linksys.com/pub/befsr41/LogViewer.exe** in the Address bar.

2. In the File Download dialog, choose Save This Program To Disk and click OK.

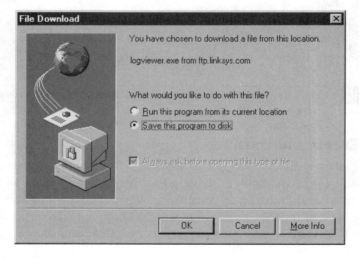

3. Select a folder to hold the downloaded file and click Save to save the file.

4. Close the browser and open My Computer or Windows Explorer to navigate to the folder where you saved the file (LogViewer.exe).

5. Double-click the file's listing to launch the LogViewer installation process. This is a wizard, so you click Next to move through each window.

6. Select a folder for the software, or accept the default location (C:\Program Files\Linksys\LogViewer), and click Next.

7. The installation wizard displays the Programs menu item it will add to your system. Click Next.

8. Click Finish to complete the installation.

Configuring the Router to Save the Logs

On the Log tab of the router's Setup utility, as depicted in Figure 6-11, use the Send Log To field to specify the IP address of the computer that has the LogViewer software. Remove the default number (255) that appears for the last section of the IP address, and replace it with the last section of the IP address for the computer that's running LogViewer. Use the Active IP table, accessible via the DHCP Clients Table button on the DHCP tab (see the preceding section, "Managing DHCP," for

6

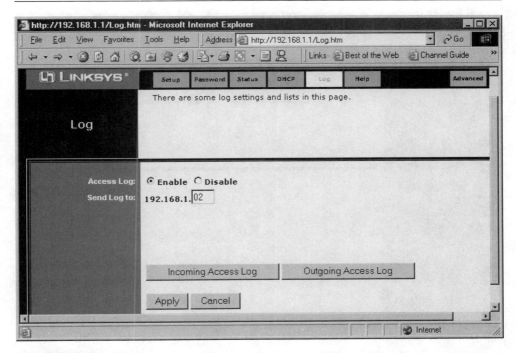

FIGURE 6-11   The router can send logs directly to one of the client systems specified by IP address

an explanation) to determine the correct number if you have not assigned that computer a static IP.

Click Apply and then click Continue to save your new settings.

Viewing the Permanent Logs   You can view the logs by opening LogViewer from the Programs menu. The logs continue to grow—unlike operating system logs, they don't have a finite size and use a First In First Out algorithm to get rid of older entries. Therefore, you must periodically clear them out or risk running out of disk space.

Getting Help

Use the Help tab to travel to specific support pages on the Linksys Web site (see Figure 6-12). In addition to finding answers to your questions, you can download a copy of the user guide, and you can even check to see whether a new firmware upgrade is available for your router.

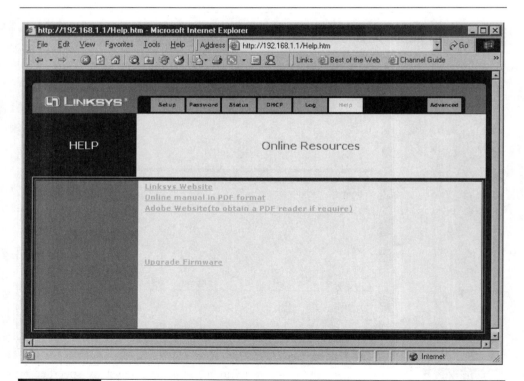

FIGURE 6-12   Click the appropriate link to get to the Linksys support pages

NOTE *Appendix C has detailed information about the support options offered by Linksys.*

Advanced Setup Configuration Options

Clicking the Advanced tab opens a whole new set of tabs you can use to tweak your router's settings. (To return to the original window, and the original tabs, click the Setup tab.) Most of the options available in these tabs are unnecessary for home and small business networks, but I'm going to offer brief descriptions of them because that gives you a better understanding about the way Internet communications work. (I believe that the more information you have about the way things work, the better off you are.) In addition, you may find a few options that are appealing to you as a way to enhance the security of your network, or as a way to control network users.

Filtering Internet Traffic   The Filters tab (see Figure 6-13) offers options you can use to enhance the security of traffic moving through your router. The Packet Filter

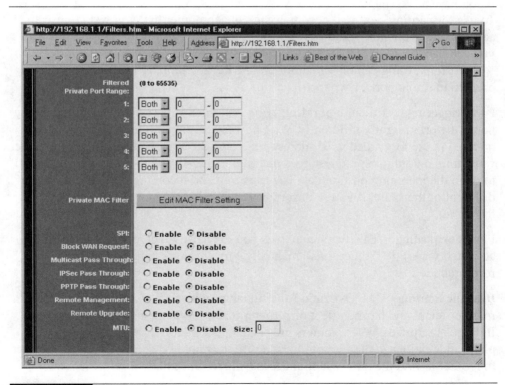

FIGURE 6-13   Tweak the router's settings with advanced options

option lets you deny access to certain types of traffic for specific computers. For example, you could establish a blockade against using certain protocols, such as FTP (File Transfer Protocol), so that a particular computer on your network can't download files from Internet servers. You can also establish blockades against certain Internet services in the other direction—forbidding computers on the Internet from sending particular types of data to a computer on the network.

Even though I've only briefly described the way packet filtering can work, you can probably come up with several ways in which it would be helpful to use this technology to secure your network and control your network users. It's actually quite an attractive idea. However, implementation requires a clear understanding of data types and the ramifications of restricting them—for home and small business networks this is a job for a consultant rather than a do-it-yourself task.

Forwarding Data Packets   The Forwarding tab provides options that let you forward Internet traffic so that data intended for certain ports is intercepted and then forwarded to certain computers. These settings are useful if one of the computers on your network is actually running on the Internet, which is highly unlikely for any small network—if you have a Web page, it's probably located on a server at a Web hosting company. To use forwarding, you will need to assign the computer that you wish to use an address that is outside of the DHCP scope (normally this is 100–149); this means you can use the addresses 2–99 and 150–254.

Port forwarding can only be used on one PC at a time. If you wish to forward ports to multiple ports, try port triggering.

Port Triggering   Although port triggering is similar to port forwarding in opening ports, it works slightly differently. With port forwarding, all incoming packets on port 12345 are forwarded to IP address 192.168.1.20. With port triggering, the router waits until an outgoing request goes out on port 12345 and the router is "triggered" to open the incoming port range. (The triggered and incoming port ranges can be different or the same; if you're unsure which should be which, simply make them the same).

UPnP Forwarding   This feature enables you to check which ports have been activated via UPnP. You can also manually forward ports here; however, it is not recommended.

Dynamic Routing   The Dynamic Routing tab provides a way to make routing more efficient and has no effect on a router that's servicing a self-contained LAN. In large enterprises, where routers move data packets to remote servers in other physical locations, dynamic routing is a nifty technology, because you can instruct the router to find the quickest or cheapest way to move data.

Static Routing   The Static Routing tab lets you set options that force routers to access other routers on your network in a specific way. Small networks don't use multiple routers, so you have no reason to use these options.

DMZ Host   You can use the options on the DMZ Host tab to establish one of the computers on your network as a DMZ host.

A DMZ (Demilitarized Zone) is exposed to the Internet without any of the filtering and other protections the router may provide. For small networks, the DMZ can be useful for letting users perform actions that the router might normally prevent, such as playing certain interactive Internet games or participating in Internet conferences.

DMZ is also a useful feature for a machine that is running multiple services such as HTTP and FTP. Using DMZ you do not have to forward multiple ports to that machine; simply put it into DMZ. Note, however, that DMZ will override port forwarding, so please do not run the same services at once.

NOTE   *DMZ does not disable the firewall completely. A computer in DMZ will still be under NAT (Network Address Translation). If you try to use a service that does not support NAT, it will not work through DMZ.*

MAC Address Clone   The MAC Addr. Clone tab lets you change the MAC address of the router. A MAC (Media Access Control) address is a hardware-level ID number that uniquely identifies a hardware device. Some ISPs require you to register the MAC address of the device that's connected to the ISP. Before you installed your router, if you had a NIC in a computer to connect that computer to your DSL/cable modem—and therefore, to your ISP—the NIC's MAC address was registered with the ISP. After you installed your router, that router became the only connection your ISP sees, and its MAC address is not the one you originally registered with your ISP. Rather than go through a new MAC registration process with your ISP (not fun, unless you enjoy being transferred from technician to technician and spending a lot of time on hold), you can clone the original NIC's MAC address to your router. Your ISP will never know you changed the connection device.

To accomplish this, select the User Defined option and then enter the MAC address of the NIC that was originally connected to the DSL/cable modem. The tab displays the MAC address of the computer you're working on, so it's easiest to perform this task by accessing the router's Setup program (one of the CDs you received with the router) from the computer that was originally connected to the DSL/cable modem. Otherwise, check the Active IP Table, accessible using the DHCP Client Table button on the DHCP tab to ascertain the MAC address of the computer that was originally connected to the ISP.

Connecting to Jacks

Almost any HomePNA adapter will have two RJ-11 phone plugs. On some adapters they will be labeled, as on a conventional modem, for "Line" and "Phone", however, these plugs are interchangeable.

You have many options for how to wire a home phone line network, but basically there has to be a path through the phone wire from every system on the network to every other system on the network. This path can be in the phone wires through the walls (see Figure 6-14) or it can just be a long a wire that extends from one system to another (this is "daisy-chaining"; see Figure 6-15). Once you accomplish this, you can use any free plugs to connect telephones, faxes, answering machines, or any other telephony device. You may also find it convenient to buy some phone line splitter devices so you can run multiple phone wires.

Although it doesn't matter what rooms or floors the different phone outlets are in, they must be on the same phone line. This means that they have a common junction at some point, at least at the point where the line enters the house.

NOTE   *These phone lines must be conventional analog phone lines, not ISDN phone lines or digital PBX phone lines.*

Potential Interference Problems

Some very old telephone equipment creates noise in frequency ranges reserved for HomePNA equipment, preventing a reliable network connection. Some older home

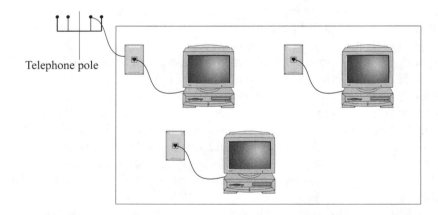

Telephone pole

FIGURE 6-14   HomePNA adapters can use phone plugs in the same building if they are all on the same phone line

FIGURE 6-15   You can also daisy-chain HomePNA systems together directly

6

phone wiring cannot meet the signal requirements of HomePNA. If, after you install your HomePNA network equipment, you have connection problems with either the network equipment or your telephone equipment, you could be experiencing this problem.

If you are having problems with your telephone equipment, the easy test is to unplug all the HomePNA equipment from the phone system and try the phones again. If the problem goes away, it was probably caused by the networking equipment.

If you are having problems with the HomePNA networking equipment, you should try unplugging telephone equipment from the lines, especially older telephone equipment, if you have any. Removing the phone lines from your walls is a bit much to ask.

See Chapter 10 for more on such troubleshooting techniques.

Sharing Jacks with Modems

Most users have a modem to connect with the Internet, and one of the main goals of most home networks is to share an Internet connection. But it's not all that uncommon for a user of a HomePNA network to also need to use a modem.

The situation is a simple one: Modems are just like telephones and faxes, and you can connect your phone lines through your HomePNA adapters to modems, or from the Phone jack on your modem, into a HomePNA adapter.

Chapter 7

Plugging In to Electric Wires

I f you're loath to run cable through your home or office, an easy alternative is to connect your network by means of your existing power lines. It's a safe bet that every room in your house or office has at least one electrical outlet, and that convenience is certainly one of the attractions for choosing this network topology. The Linksys PowerLine Series provides networking that is incredibly easy to install. Two PowerLine products are available:

- **Instant PowerLine USB Adapter (PLUSB10)**, which can be installed on any computer that contains a USB Port (including a laptop computer)

- **Instant PowerLine EtherFast 10/100 Bridge (PLEBR10)**, which you can use to connect your PowerLine network to a DSL/cable modem or router, to share the broadband access across the network. It can also connect to a computer with an existing Ethernet port on it. Most new computers have Ethernet ports built in, so this is a convenient way of not having to install additional drivers. It's also handy for Windows 95 and NT computers that aren't USB compatible.

Installing the Network Adapter

The nifty thing about USB connections is that you don't have to open your computer to install them, and, in fact, you don't even have to turn off your computer. (They will not work, however, with Windows 95 or NT because they do not support USB.) As soon as you connect a device to a USB port, Windows Plug and Play wakes up and announces, "I've found new hardware on your computer."

When Plug and Play finds hardware, it wants to install the drivers immediately. Therefore, you need to have the drivers available, and you do that by installing them to your hard drive before you connect the adapter to the USB port.

Installing the Software

You must install the software for your USB adapter before connecting the hardware to your computer. The software is on the CD that is in your USB adapter package. The software has two components: drivers and a security program. (See the Section "Securing Your PowerLine Network" later in this chapter.)

Insert the CD into your CD-ROM drive, and the installation program should launch automatically. If you've disabled the AutoRun feature that manages automatic startup of CD programs, you can start the installation program manually with either of the following actions:

- Choose Start | Run and enter **D:\setup.exe** in the text box (substitute the drive letter for your CD-ROM if it isn't D:).

- Open Windows Explorer or My Computer and display the contents of your CD-ROM drive; then double-click setup.exe.

The installation program is a wizard, which means you must click Next to move through the wizard's windows. The opening window displays a welcoming message, so click Next to get started with the installation program.

In the next window, enter your name and optionally enter your company name. If you're installing the USB adapter in Windows 2000 or Windows XP, you must also specify whether you want to make the adapter's drivers available to anyone who uses this computer or only to you whenever you log on to the computer. It would be rather unusual to limit the use of a network device to a single individual, so you should select the default option, which is to let anyone who logs on to the computer have access to the network.

The next wizard window displays the configuration settings you entered (your name and company name), as well as the location of the drivers on your hard drive (see Figure 7-1). You can click the Back button to change the user information, but you cannot change the destination folder for the software.

Click Install to begin the installation process. If you're running Windows 2000 or Windows XP, the system displays a message telling you there's a problem with the software, but there really isn't. Take the following action to indicate that you want to continue with installation:

- In Windows 2000, click Yes.

- In Windows XP, click Continue Anyway.

The wizard displays a progress bar as the software is installed to your hard drive (see Figure 7-2).

Check your taskbar to see if another window has opened while you're performing the installation. I found that sometimes the Windows message window about the uncertified driver didn't pop into the foreground to place itself in front of the installation progress window. A button appeared on the taskbar (because every open window gets a taskbar button), but the first time this happened, I didn't notice the button on the taskbar. However, I did notice that the progress bar on the installation progress window didn't move all the way to the right, and after a few minutes I realized something was wrong. Finally, I noticed the taskbar button, clicked it to display the message from Windows, clicked the Continue Anyway

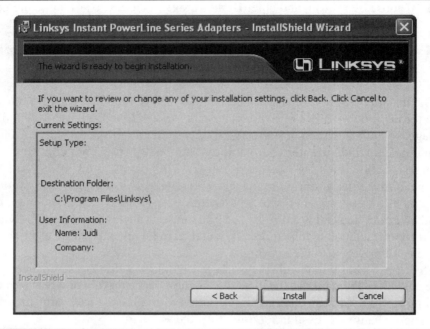

FIGURE 7-1   Your settings are displayed for your approval before the software is installed

button, and immediately the progress bar moved on, and the installation program finished transferring files to the hard drive.

After the files are copied, the wizard displays a message telling you that installation is complete. Click Finish. When the wizard displays a message telling you that you must restart the computer, click Yes.

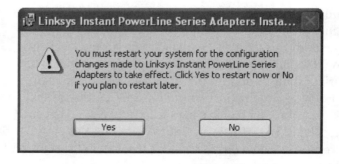

While Windows shuts down and restarts, you can prepare the hardware for the next step—the physical installation of your adapter.

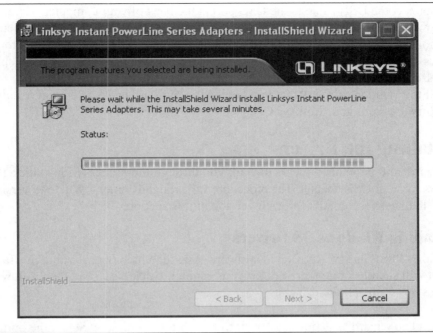

FIGURE 7-2   It takes only a minute or so to install the files on your hard drive

Connecting the USB Adapter

Your Linksys USB adapter has three components:

- The adapter itself
- A power cord
- A USB cable

The adapter has a connector at each end—one for the power cord and the other for the USB cable. Start by connecting the power cord and the USB cable to the adapter.

NOTE
USB cable has different connectors at each end. The Type A connector is a male rectangle, and it goes into the USB port on your computer (which is a female rectangle). The Type B connector is a small square, and it connects to the USB device—in this case, an adapter.

Connect the USB cable to the USB port at the back of your computer. Then, plug the power cord into a wall outlet. (The USB adapter contains its own surge protection technology, so you don't have to worry about plugging it into a surge protector.)

As soon as the cord is inserted into the outlet, Windows Plug and Play displays a message that the system has discovered new hardware. Now you're ready to install the Windows drivers that you copied to your hard drive when you installed the software from your Linksys CD.

Installing the Drivers

A wizard automatically appears to walk you through the process of installing the drivers for your USB adapter. The procedure varies slightly among Windows versions, and I'll discuss the details for each version in this section.

Installing Windows 98 Drivers

Windows 98SE has an Add New Hardware Wizard, which opens with a message that it will search for new drivers for your adapter. Click Next, and then follow these steps to install the drivers:

1. The wizard asks how you want to search for the drivers. Select the option Search For The Best Driver For Your Device (Recommended) and click Next.

2. Select the option Specify A Location. Then enter **c:\program files\linksys\ usb drivers** in the location text box, or click the Browse button and navigate through the folders to reach that location (if you prefer clicking to typing). Then click Next.

3. The wizard displays a message telling you it has found the drivers and is ready to install them. Click Next.

4. The wizard asks you to insert your Windows 98 CD in the CD-ROM drive. After you insert the CD, click OK. (If you do not have the Windows 98 disk, then try c:\widows\options\cabs.)

5. When the wizard announces it has completed its task, click Finish.

6. Windows displays a message telling you that you have to restart your computer to complete the installation. Click Yes.

When Windows restarts, you can configure the adapter's settings (IP address and other settings), which is covered in Chapter 8. After your adapter is set up, you must set up the security features (see "Securing Your PowerLine Network" later in this chapter).

Installing Windows Me Drivers

As soon as you plug in your new adapter, Plug and Play detects its presence. The New Hardware Found dialog box appears, asking for the location of the driver files. Enter **c:\program files\linksys\usb drivers** in the text box, or click Browse and then select that subfolder. Click OK, and when the drivers are installed, restart your computer.

When Windows restarts, you can configure the adapter's settings (IP address and other settings), which is covered in Chapter 8. After your adapter is set up, you must set up the security features (see "Securing Your PowerLine Network" later in this chapter).

Installing Windows 2000 Drivers

Windows 2000 Plug and Play automatically senses the presence of the adapter and also automatically finds the drivers. The operating system displays a message telling you that the driver lacks a proper digital signature. This isn't a real problem, so click Yes to install the drivers, and then restart the computer.

When Windows restarts, you can configure the adapter's settings (IP address and other settings), which is covered in Chapter 8. After your adapter is set up, you must set up the security features (see "Securing Your PowerLine Network" later in this chapter).

Installing Windows XP Drivers

Windows XP Plug and Play automatically senses the presence of the adapter and launches the Found New Hardware Wizard. The opening wizard window says you need the Linksys Installation CD, but you really don't (because you've already installed the drivers to your hard drive). Click Next to begin using the wizard, following these steps:

1. Select the option Search For The Best Driver In These Locations, and also select the check box labeled Include This Location In The Search. Then

enter **c:\program files\linksys\usb drivers**. Alternatively, you can click the Browse button and locate that folder (if you prefer clicking to typing). Click Next.

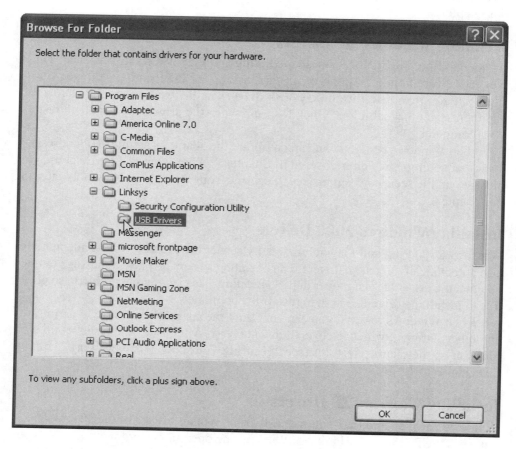

2. Windows displays a message telling you the driver isn't certified for the Windows Logo (don't worry—the driver is fine). Click Continue Anyway.

3. When the wizard announces the drivers have been installed, click Finish.

4. Restart the computer.

When Windows restarts, you can configure the adapter's settings (IP address and other settings), which is covered in Chapter 8. After your adapter is set up, you must set up the security features (see the next section, "Securing Your PowerLine Network").

Securing Your PowerLine Network

When you use power lines as your connection medium, you're sort of on a large peer-to-peer network that's centered at the transformer that supplies electricity to your home or office. Of course, that transformer also supplies electricity to other homes and offices. If anyone else in the neighborhood is using power lines for networking, it's possible that one network could access data that's being transmitted across a different network. To prevent this, Linksys encrypts the data that's being transmitted on your network.

Understanding Encryption

Linksys uses Data Encryption Standard (DES) to encrypt your network data. DES is a popular encryption scheme that uses secret keys that both the sending and receiving computers must know in order to decrypt data. A new key is created for each 64 bits of data, and DES technology chooses each key at random, from a pool of 72,000,000,000,000,000 (72 quadrillion) possible keys. This makes it statistically impossible for another set of computers to have the same keys at the same moment those 64 bits of data are traveling through your network.

Running the Security Configuration Utility

The CD you used to install the Linksys PowerLine hardware drivers also installed a Security Configuration Utility. In fact, the installation process puts an icon for the security software on your desktop in addition to the listing on the Programs menu. You can configure the security features for each adapter on your network as soon as the following conditions are met:

- All the adapters are physically installed and plugged in.
- Drivers have been installed on each computer in the network.
- The adapters have been configured for IP addresses (see Chapter 8).

In fact, once these tasks are accomplished, you have a working network—it's just not secure, and you shouldn't begin sharing resources and transmitting data among your computers until you've guaranteed the security of those transmissions. To add encryption to your network communications, follow these steps:

1. Double-click the Security Configuration Utility icon on your desktop (or choose the utility from the Programs menu). The Security Configuration Utility wizard opens with a welcoming message. Click Next to get started.

2. In the Network Password field, enter a password (it's not a good idea to keep the default password, which is seen in Figure 7-3). Your password must be between 4 and 24 characters (using any keyboard character except the space), and it's case sensitive.

NOTE   *You don't have to install the software on each computer—you can configure each adapter individually, which is easier, especially if you're using the PLEBR10.*

3. Click Next to see the MAC address of the adapter that is now password-protected. When you move to the next computer and run the Security Configuration Utility, that computer's adapter is added to the list. The last computer you configure shows all the computers on your network that are protected with this password. (There's nothing you need to do with this data, it's just for your information.)

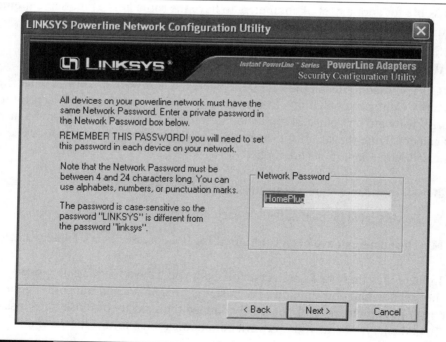

FIGURE 7-3   Enter the password you want to use for all the computers on your network

4. Click Next to see a congratulatory message on having successfully protected this adapter.

5. Click Finish.

6. Repeat these steps on every computer in your network, using the same password.

You now have a working, secure network. Congratulations!

7

Renew now and get two years of PC Magazine for less than the one-year basic price!

That's like getting more than one year FREE!

2 for 1

✓ YES!

I want to receive
2 years of
PC Magazine
for just $39.97.

Name	(please print)
Company	
Address	
City/State/Zip	
E-mail	

5SR77

☐ **Payment enclosed.** ☐ **Bill me later.**

Basic one-year price is $44.97. Non-U.S. add US$40.31 per term; Canadian GST included. Allow 3-6 weeks delivery. PC Magazine is published semimonthly, with occasional exceptions. A special issue may count as a subscription issue, a combined issue counts as two subscription issues, and there may sometimes be an extra issue. Your subscription will continue for as long as you wish, unless you instruct otherwise. We will notify and bill you at the discounted renewal rate in effect prior to each subscription term.

☐ Check box to sign up as a new subscriber and get 2 years for $39.97.

Chapter 8

Configuring Network Settings

After you've physically installed your networking equipment, and you've installed the drivers, you still have several tasks in front of you. This chapter covers the following tasks, which you need to perform to complete your network configuration:

■ Configure the settings for the network adapters.

■ Configure the settings for sharing your Internet connection device (telephone/DSL/cable modem).

The network adapter you installed in each computer must be configured to make sure all the computers have the appropriate settings; otherwise, they can't communicate.

NOTE   *You also must configure the computers to share their resources (folders, drives, and printers), which is covered in Chapter 12.*

Configuring the Host Computer

If all the computers on your network are going to use Internet connection sharing, one computer will become the *host*, and this is the computer that should be configured first. A host computer has the following characteristics:

■ The Internet connection device (telephone/DSL/cable modem) is physically attached to this computer.

■ The other computers (called *clients*) access the Internet through this host computer.

■ It contains two adapters: one for the network and the other for the Internet connection. If the Internet connection device is a telephone modem, you don't have a physical second adapter in the computer, but the dial-up connection you create has configuration settings just like those found on an adapter that's connected to a DSL/cable modem.

> NOTE
>
> *If all the computers on your network are going to use Internet connection sharing, you're not using a router. If you're using a router, see the upcoming section "Using a Router."*

Using the Windows XP Network Wizard

If your host computer is running Windows XP, you can use the Network Setup Wizard to configure your network settings and your shared Internet connection. The wizard also creates a program for configuring the client computers, and offers to copy the program to a floppy disk that you can run on the client computers. If you don't have a blank floppy disk, you can run the same program on the client computers from the Windows XP CD.

> NOTE
>
> *If your host computer is running Windows Me, you'll also find a Network Setup Wizard, but my experience has been that this wizard has some problems. Go to www.microsoft.com and follow the links to the Windows Me section of the Knowledge Base. Enter Network Wizard in the search box to find all the articles on bugs, problems, and workarounds. Print the articles and use the information to solve any problems that occur.*

8

If all the computers on your network are running Windows 98SE, see the section "Configuring Windows 98SE Networks," later in this chapter.

Configuring the Windows XP Host

In this section, I'll go over the steps for setting up your network by using the wizard on the Windows XP computer that has the modem. I'm assuming the settings for the telephone/DSL/cable modem are already established, following the instructions from your ISP. Now, follow these steps to have the wizard set up your network and share the Internet connection:

1. Choose Start | All Programs | Accessories | Communications | Network Setup Wizard to launch the wizard, which opens with a welcome message. Click Next.

2. The next wizard window presents a checklist for the tasks you should have completed before running this wizard (installing hardware and setting up the modem on this computer or on another computer on the network). Click Next.

3. Select the option that establishes this computer as the Internet connection host (see Figure 8-1). Click Next.

4. Select the device that connects this computer to the Internet, which is either a NIC attached to a DSL/cable modem or a dial-up connection you created to access your ISP with a dial-up modem. Click Next to set up the network.

5. Name the computer (it's best to use the current name, unless you have some reason to change it), and optionally enter a description (see Figure 8-2). The name must be unique on the network. Click Next.

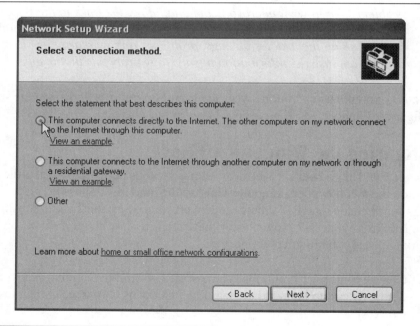

FIGURE 8-1   For the computer that has the modem, select the option that establishes this computer as the host

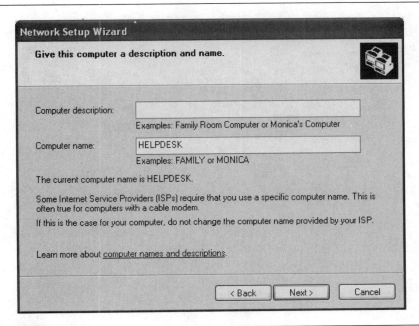

FIGURE 8-2   Every computer on a network must have a unique name

6. Name the workgroup, which is the name you're giving your network (see Figure 8-3). All the computers on the network must use the same workgroup name. You can use the name Windows suggests (MSHOME) or type in a different name. Click Next.

7. The wizard displays a summary of all your selections. Click Back if you want to return to one of the previous windows and change an option. Otherwise, click Next to install the network and Internet connection settings. Follow the wizard prompts to complete the setup process.

The wizard sets up the files and settings, which takes a few moments, and then asks if you want to create a floppy disk copy of the setup program, which you can

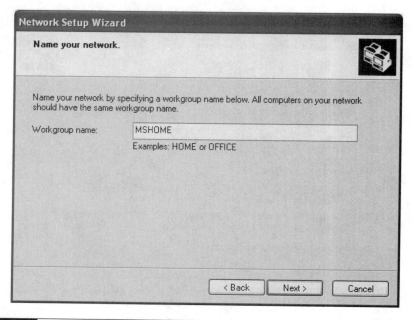

FIGURE 8-3   The network itself (which is called a workgroup in a peer-to-peer network) must have a name

use on the other computers on your network (see Figure 8-4). Select the appropriate option and click Next. If you don't have a floppy disk, you can also use the Windows XP/Me CD, which has a copy of this program.

Understanding TCP/IP Settings on the Host Computer

When you run the Network Setup Wizard on the host computer, you establish that computer as the DHCP server for your internal network. DHCP stands for Dynamic Host Configuration Protocol, which is a method of automatically managing IP addresses on a network. The host computer gets its own IP address (an assigned address, which is called a *static* IP address), and it then provides the client computers with their IP addresses. These IP addresses are used only for your network, and they're called *private IP addresses*, which means they're assigned a number range that isn't accepted on the Internet. The settings for the private IP address are established on the network adapter.

However, when a computer is accessing the Internet, it must have an IP address that is accepted as an Internet IP address, which is called a *public IP address*.

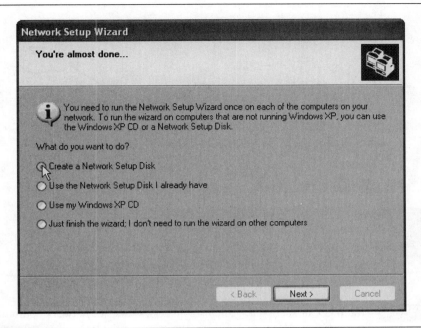

FIGURE 8-4   Select an option for setting up the client computers on your network

Unless you've purchased a special plan from your ISP that lets you set public IP addresses for all the computers on your network, your ISP is the DHCP server for those addresses. The settings for the Internet connection are established on the adapter for your Internet connection device (a DSL or cable modem) or in the dial-up connection you create for a telephone modem.

NOTE   *If your ISP sold you a range of public IP addresses, it changes the way you set up your network and your Internet connection. See the section "Configuring Static IP Address" later in this chapter.*

To make sure you have both private and public IP addresses, you must set up two sets of IP addresses for the host computer—one set for your network (also called a LAN, which stands for Local Area Network) and the other set for Internet use. Figure 8-5 shows the connection scheme for a network that's using Internet Connection Sharing.

It's important that you understand the way IP addresses are configured to enable Internet Connection Sharing, as illustrated in Figure 8-5. The host computer

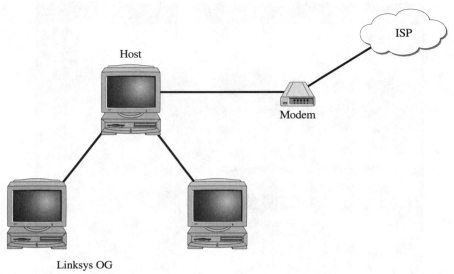

Linksys OG

FIGURE 8-5 Internet Connection Sharing establishes two sets of network configuration settings—one for your LAN and the other for the Internet

has the following two network connections, both of which contain configuration settings for IP addresses:

■ The LAN connection, which is the network adapter that communicates with the computers on your internal network.

■ The Internet connection, which is either another network adapter (for a DSL or cable modem) or a software dial-up connection (for a telephone modem).

To check the IP address for the LAN on the host computer, right-click the icon for the Local Area Network connection and choose Properties from the shortcut menu. Then, select the listing for Internet Protocol (TCP/IP) and click the Properties button. As you can see in Figure 8-6, the Network Setup Wizard automatically assigns the host computer a private IP address.

The settings for the Internet connection are established on your Internet connection device, which is either another physical adapter or a dial-up connection you created.

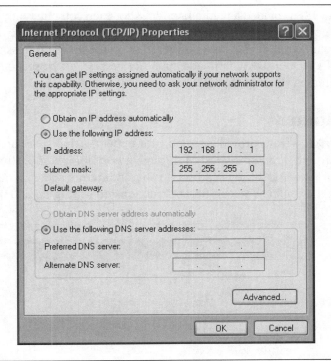

FIGURE 8-6   For the internal network (the LAN), the host computer is assigned an IP address

To check the settings of your Internet connection, right-click the icon for the Internet connection and choose Properties. Then open the Properties dialog for TCP/IP as follows:

- For an adapter (DSL/cable modem connection), select the listing for Internet Protocol (TCP/IP) and click the Properties button.

- For a dial-up connection, take either of the following steps:

    - In Windows XP, go to the Networking tab, select the Internet Protocol (TCP/IP) listing, and click Properties.

    - In Windows 98SE/Me, go to the Server Type tab and click the TCP/IP Settings button.

Unless your ISP provided a public IP address for each computer on your network, even the host computer gets its public IP address from an ISP, so the settings for the Internet connection device are configured to obtain an IP address automatically (see Figure 8-7). If your ISP did provide public addresses, see the section "Configuring Static IP Addresses" later in this chapter.

Using a Router

The Windows XP wizard provides support for networks that share an Internet connection through a router instead of through a host computer. Before you can configure your network settings and set up shared Internet access, you must install and configure the router. You can find instructions on setting up and using Linksys

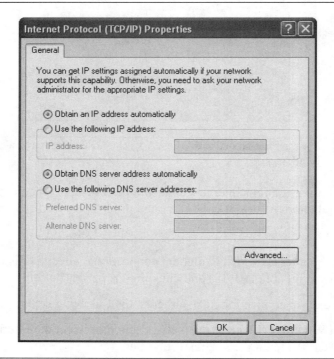

FIGURE 8-7   For this shared Internet connection, the ISP provides the public IP addresses for the host computer and all the client computers

routers throughout this book—the specific instructions you need are found in the chapter that discusses the type of network topology (Ethernet, wireless, and so on) you choose for your network.

To configure your connection via a router, launch the wizard as described earlier in this chapter. When you get to the Select The Connection Method window, choose the option This Computer Connects To The Internet Through Another Computer On My Network Or Through A Residential Gateway.

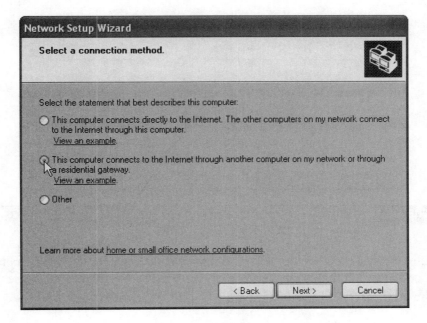

NOTE   *The Windows XP Internet Connection Wizard uses the term residential gateway instead of router.*

Click Next, and in the wizard windows that follow, provide a computer name, an optional description of the computer, and the name of your workgroup (by default, MSHOME). In the last wizard window, your settings are summarized (see Figure 8-8). Click Next to have Windows configure your network and your Internet connection.

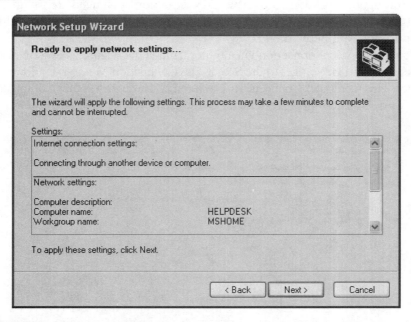

FIGURE 8-8 After you've selected the options you need, Windows is ready to configure your network settings and your Internet settings

After the system is set up, create a floppy disk program for the other computers as described earlier in this chapter (or skip the floppy disk if you want to use the Windows XP CD).

Configuring the Client Computers

After you've set up the host computer to share its Internet device, you need to set up all the other computers (the clients). Make sure the original Windows CD for each computer is handy, because you may be asked to insert it so the system can copy files for setting up network services. Launch the wizard in one of the following ways, and then follow the prompts to install the network files and configure the system.

■ If you created a floppy disk for this purpose, insert the disk in the floppy drive, open Windows Explorer or My Computer to access Drive A, and then double-click the file (netsetup.exe).

■ If you're using the Windows XP CD, insert it in the CD drive. When the opening window appears, choose Perform Additional Tasks, and then choose Set Up Home Or Small Office Networking.

> **NOTE** *If you use the Windows XP CD and the opening window doesn't appear automatically, you must start the wizard manually. From My Computer, right-click the icon for the CD drive, and choose Open from the shortcut menu. Then double-click Setup.exe.*

Disabling Internet Connection Firewall

When you use the Windows XP Network Setup Wizard to establish your network and Internet connection settings, the wizard usually turns on the built-in firewall automatically. (To learn what a firewall is, and how it works, turn to Chapter 9.) The built-in firewall is a Windows XP feature called Internet Connection Firewall (ICF).

You do not want to run ICF. It doesn't work on networks because it blocks network traffic coming in to any Windows XP computer. Windows XP offers a workaround by suggesting you run your network on a protocol other than TCP/IP— but you don't need a workaround, you need a better firewall. My recommendation is that you choose one of the following options:

■ Buy and install a Linksys firewall router if you have a DSL/cable modem (see Chapter 9 to learn how to set up the firewall router).

■ Download the popular software firewall, ZoneAlarm, from *http://www.zonealarm.com* (it's free).

To turn off ICF after the wizard has finished its work, take these steps:

1. Choose Start | Control Panel to display the Control Panel window.

2. Click the Network And Internet Connections link.

3. Click Network Connections.

4. Right-click the icon for your Local Area Connection, and choose Properties from the shortcut window.

5. Go to the Advanced tab and clear the check box to disable ICF.

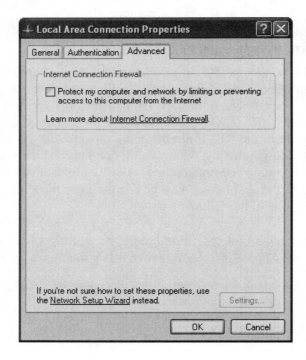

Configuring Windows 98SE Networks

If your network is made up of computers running Windows 98SE, you have to set up a host computer for the shared Internet connection, and you have to configure the other network settings. Windows 98SE does not have a wizard to set up the network, but it does have a wizard to set up Internet Connection Sharing (ICS). In this section, I'll cover the following topics:

■ How to run the ICS Wizard on the host computer

■ How to set up the client computers to share the Internet connection on the host

■ How to set up the other network components on Windows 98SE computers

Even if you have a Windows XP computer on your network, you need to configure a Windows 98SE computer as the Internet connection host if your telephone/DSL/cable modem is connected to a Windows 98SE computer.

8

NOTE *You must configure the host computer first, regardless of whether the client computers are running Windows 98SE or Windows XP.*

Installing ICS

Windows 98SE ICS isn't installed by default when you install the operating system, so you must add it by following these steps:

1. Put the Windows 98SE CD in the CD drive, and if it automatically starts the Setup program, click Cancel. You aren't installing Windows 98SE; you just need to install some files from the CD.

2. Choose Start | Settings | Control Panel to open the Control Panel window.

3. Double-click Add/Remove Programs.

4. Select the Windows Setup tab.

5. Scroll through the list and select Internet Tools.

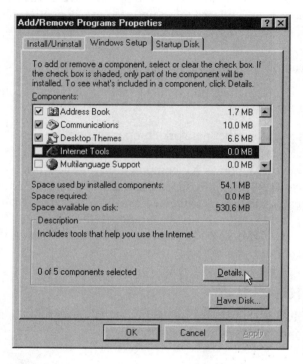

6. Click the Details button.

7. Place a check mark in the check box next to Internet Connection Sharing and click OK.

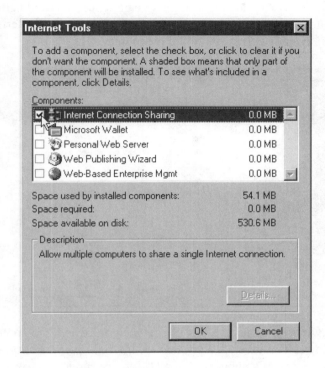

Windows transfers the necessary files, and when the installation process is complete, the system automatically launches the ICS wizard (which is actually called the Internet Sharing Setup Wizard).

Running ICS on the Host Computer

The ICS wizard opens with a welcoming message; click Next to begin setting up the host computer. In the first wizard window, select the type of Internet connection device that's connected to the computer.

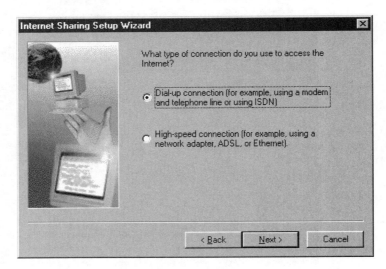

In the next window, select the specific device you're using to connect to the Internet. The device could be a telephone modem dial-up connection you created or a network adapter that's connected to a DSL/cable modem.

If you're using a dial-up connection, the wizard offers the option Automatically Dial When Accessing The Internet, which is enabled by default. This means that when anyone opens browser or e-mail software on any computer, the dial-up connection automatically opens and dials out to reach your ISP. If you disable this option, when anyone on the network wants to connect to the Internet, somebody has to be at this computer to launch the dial-up connection manually.

The wizard offers to create a client setup program on a floppy disk, so you can set up the Internet connection on the client computers. Put a blank floppy disk in the floppy drive and follow the prompts to create the client program. (If you don't have a floppy disk, you can set up the client computers manually—see the section "Configuring Windows 98SE Network Components.")

Click Finish in the last wizard window. The wizard displays a message telling you to restart your computer—click Yes to restart.

Checking IP Addresses on the Windows 98SE Host

After your computer restarts, open the Network applet in Control Panel to see the changes ICS made to your setup. You'll see additional entries in the list of components, and they're all related to your ICS settings. For example, Figure 8-9 shows the new entries for a Windows 98SE host computer that connects to the Internet with a telephone modem. If your computer has a second adapter connected to a DSL/cable modem, you'll see entries for that adapter.

CAUTION   *When you're viewing properties in Windows 98SE, always click Cancel instead of OK to close the windows. Windows 98SE isn't as intelligent an operating system as Windows XP, and it always tries to install files when you click OK (even if you haven't made any configuration changes).*

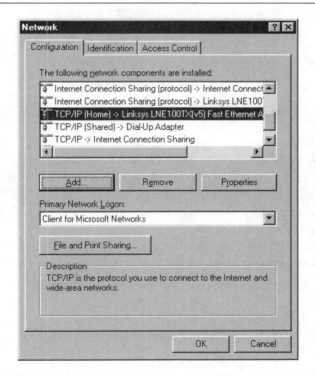

FIGURE 8-9   ICS adds network components to your system

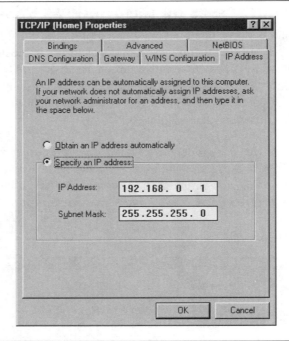

The IP address for the network adapter on the host computer is a
static address

Check the IP address for the network by selecting the TCP/IP component for
the network adapter for the network and clicking Properties. As you can see in
Figure 8-10, the host computer has a static IP address. For your LAN, the host
computer becomes the DHCP server, and the client computers will get their
network IP addresses from the host.

If you check the TCP/IP Properties for the Internet/dial-up adapter, you'll see that
no IP address is assigned. Instead, you get your Internet IP address from your ISP.

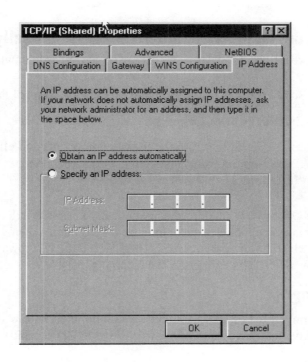

Configuring IP Addresses for the Client Computers

You can use the floppy disk you created with the ICS wizard to configure IP addresses for the client computers that are running Windows 98SE (or Windows Me). Put the floppy disk in the floppy drive and open Windows Explorer. Select the floppy drive and double-click the file listing for icsclset.exe. Then, follow the prompts to set up the client computer.

For Windows XP client computers, you can use the Windows XP Network Setup Wizard and choose the option This Computer Connects To The Internet Through Another Computer On The Network. Then, follow the prompts to finish setting up the Internet connection.

8

Configuring the Clients Dynamic IP Address Manually

If you didn't make a floppy disk, you can set the IP addresses manually, as follows:

1. Choose Start | Settings | Control Panel to open the Control Panel window.

2. Double-click the Network icon.

3. Select the TCP/IP listing from the list of components and click Properties. (If TCP/IP isn't on the list of installed network components, see the next section, "Installing TCP/IP.")

If the option Obtain An IP Address Automatically is already selected, you don't have to do anything except click Cancel to close the Properties dialog. If that option is not selected, select it now and click OK. Then, wait until Windows copies files from the Windows 98SE CD and restart the computer.

Installing TCP/IP

If TCP/IP isn't on the list of installed network components, follow these steps to install it (you'll need to have your Windows 98SE/Me CD at hand):

1. Click Add to open the Select Network Component Type dialog.

2. Select Protocol and click Add.

3. In the Manufacturers pane, select Microsoft; then select TCP/IP from the Network Protocols pane.

4. Click OK and follow the prompts to close the dialogs and transfer the files from the Windows CD.

Configuring Other Windows 98SE Network Components

Windows 98SE doesn't offer a network setup wizard—only an ICS wizard. As a result, you must configure the other network components manually. After you finish running ICS on the host and clients, return to each Windows 98SE computer to complete the configuration tasks.

Put your Windows 98SE/Me CD in the CD drive. (If it automatically starts the Setup program, close the window, because you're not setting up the operating system—you only need to fetch some files from the CD.) Then, begin installing and configuring network components as described in this section.

Enable File and Print Sharing

To participate in a network, a computer must be configured to share its resources. (To learn how to select the specific resources you want to share, read Chapter 12.) Click the File And Print Sharing button to display the File And Print Sharing dialog, and enable the file sharing feature. If the computer has a printer attached, also enable the printer sharing feature.

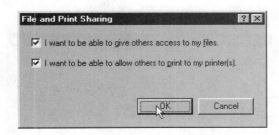

Click OK to return to the Network Properties dialog.

Enable Network Logon

In the Primary Network Logon drop-down list, select Client For Microsoft Networks as the logon option for this computer. (The other choice on the list, Windows Logon, refers to logging on to this computer when you start Windows, instead of logging on to the network.) The choice is available only if Client For Microsoft Networks is listed as an installed component. If you don't see Client For Microsoft Networks in the list of installed network components, you'll have to add it, as follows:

1. Click Add to open the Select Network Component Type dialog.

2. Select Client and click Add.

3. In the Manufacturers pane, select Microsoft; then select Client for Microsoft Networks from the Network Clients pane.

8

4. Click OK and then follow the prompts to return to the Network Properties dialog.

5. Click OK to let Windows copy the appropriate files from the Windows 98SE CD.

6. Restart the computer.

Identify the Computer on the Network

Click the Identification tab to make sure the computer's name, and the name of your network/workgroup, is accurately entered. You can also optionally enter a description of the computer, which users on other computers will see when they open Network Neighborhood or My Network Places.

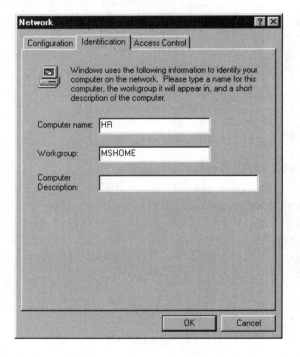

> NOTE
>
> *The Access Control tab enables password protection for shared folders and other resources. See Chapter 12 to learn about creating and protecting shared resources.*

Configuring Static IP Addresses

If your ISP service includes a range of static IP addresses, you must enter those addresses manually. You also have a router or a DSL/cable modem that is connected to the same hub as your networked computers; all the computers access the Internet through the same device (instead of through a host computer). This is why each computer requires a public IP address.

Entering the IP Address and Other Network Settings

To enter static IP addresses, open the Properties dialog for your LAN connection using the appropriate steps:

- In Windows XP, right-click the Local Area Connection icon and choose Properties from the shortcut menu.

- In Windows 98SE, double-click the Network applet in Control Panel.

Then, take the following steps to configure your network adapter for a static IP address:

1. Select TCP/IP and click Properties.

2. Select the option Use The Following IP Address.

3. Enter one of the IP addresses you received from your ISP.

4. Enter the Subnet Mask settings, using the information you received from your ISP.

5. Enter the DNS server addresses supplied by your ISP (in Windows 98SE, first select the DNS tab).

6. Enter the IP address for the Gateway as follows:

   - In Windows 98SE, click the Gateway tab, enter the IP address of the Gateway, and click Add.

   - In Windows XP, click the Advanced button on the TCP/IP Properties dialog, and click Add in the Default Gateways section of the Advanced TCP/IP Settings dialog. Enter the IP address of the Gateway.

8

7. Click OK.

8. If Windows prompts you to restart the computer, do so.

Repeat this process on each computer, making sure you don't use an IP address twice. Each IP address must be unique on the network.

Static IP Addresses and the Windows XP Network Wizard

When you set up your Windows XP computer for assigned IP addresses, you'll probably see the Network Setup Wizard, even though you want to do a manual configuration. The wizard just pops up—it's impossible to suppress it. On the third wizard window (the window that asks for your connection type), select Other and click Next. In the next window (see Figure 8-11), select the first option (which describes a scenario in which all computers connect to the Internet through a hub) and click Next.

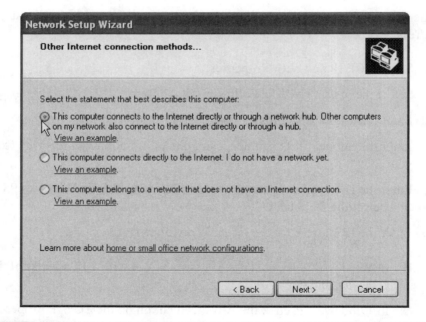

FIGURE 8-11   The wizard offers an option that describes a system with assigned IP address

In the next window, select the network adapter as your Internet connection. Because your adapter is connected to a DSL router or a hub, and it has a static IP address, your adapter is also an Internet connection device. Click Next.

The wizard displays displeasure, issuing a stern warning about security threats and advising you that the Windows XP Internet Connection Firewall must be enabled on your adapter.

Continue to respond to the wizard's prompts, clicking Next to move through the wizard windows. When you finish the wizard, open the Properties for the LAN connection using the steps outlined in the previous section, and manually set up the IP address. Then, disable ICF as described earlier in this chapter.

8

Part III

Advanced Networking

Chapter 9

Security

Your network is running, users are sharing printers and files, and everybody can be on the Internet simultaneously. Sorry, but you're not finished.

You have to protect your network from evil-doers who want to get into your computers over the Internet. You also have to know how to check and troubleshoot network performance problems. And, you may want to integrate the laptop computer you use at work with your home network. Of course, you have to know how to share the resources of each computer on your network with the other computers.

Instructions for setting up and using all of these features and functions await you in the chapters in Part III.

Beware of evil-doers who want to attack your computers. They have two ways to get to you: they sneak into your computers while you're connected to the Internet to perform dastardly deeds, and they use e-mail to deliver viruses. The only way to thwart their attacks is to protect your computers with a firewall and protect your e-mail with anti-virus software.

In this chapter, I'll discuss how firewalls work and explain how you can use a Linksys firewall router with your DSL/cable modem hardware to protect all the computers on your network. (For telephone modem Internet connections, you can use only software firewalls.) I'll also explain viruses and how to use anti-virus software to protect yourself against them.

Understanding Firewalls

A computer firewall provides a blockade between your computers and the Internet, preventing the unauthorized exchange of data. To understand how a firewall works, and to be able to configure a firewall for maximum protection, you have to understand the components of Internet communication: IP addresses, data packets, and ports.

IP Addresses

When a computer is connected to the Internet, it has a public IP address, which is also called an Internet IP address. The same computer may have a private IP address that's used to facilitate TCP/IP communication within the network, but that private IP address doesn't work on the Internet. Several ranges of numbers have been assigned for private IP addresses, and they're not recognized as true Internet IP addresses:

- 10.0.0.0 to 10.255.255.255

- 169.254.0.0 to 169.254.255.255

- 172.16.0.0 to 172.31.255.255

- 192.168.0.0 to 192.168.255.255

If your computer has an assigned IP address, it probably falls into one of these private ranges. However, when your computer connects to the Internet, it must have a public IP address, and frequently this address is assigned to your DSL/cable modem (for always-on connections) or by your ISP at the time of connection. Today, some DSL services are not always-on connections, so you may have to reconnect to your DSL provider when you want to use the Internet; you'll receive an IP address each time you connect. All telephone modem connections are assigned an IP address each time they dial out and connect to the ISP. (Chapter 8 covers the configuration of computers on your network, including the options for assigning IP addresses.)

NOTE *Some small networks have public IP addresses assigned to each computer, because the ISP provides those addresses (for a fee). Business DSL and cable modem services sell public IP addresses as part of the package, and if you use public IP addresses for each computer, you can enter those addresses in the TCP/IP options when you're configuring your connection, because they're valid on the Internet.*

When you're on the Internet with your public IP address, that address is a doorway between you and every other computer on the Internet. Data communication packets flow through that doorway in both directions. It's possible that a malicious hacker can access your computer through that IP address doorway, unless you've prevented that with a firewall.

Internet intruders work by selecting an Internet IP address and then trying to connect to that IP address. They usually don't pick an IP address themselves, they're not specifically looking for your computer (even if you have the secret Swiss bank account numbers of famous people in a document on your hard drive). They usually use software that selects an IP address at random and then tries to access the computer that's using that address on the Internet. If the attempt fails, either because the IP address is not currently on the Internet or because a firewall blocked the attempt, the software selects another IP address and tries again.

9

If your IP address comes up and you're not protected by a firewall, the attempt to access your computer succeeds, and the intruders have access to your computer and its contents. You won't know that anything is going on, even if you're working at the computer, because all of this occurs in the background without interfering with anything you're doing.

Here are some of the common nefarious acts that are known to be performed by intruders:

- Send viruses to your computer

- Rename or remove important system files

- Copy your documents back to their own systems to gain personal and sensitive information

- Send an enormous number of files just for the fun of filling up your drive

- Bombard your computer with data in a way that overwhelms the computer, which is called a *Denial of Service* (DoS) attack. A variety of methods are available for DoS attacks, and they can do harm well beyond merely freezing the computer.

NOTE   *Don't think that using passwords on folders or setting up restricted access via the NTFS file system protects you. Intruders who gain access to your computer have tools to assist them in getting past those security blocks, which are really designed for security within the network.*

Data Packets

The Internet uses the communications protocol TCP/IP, which operates with two layers:

- TCP (the higher layer)

- IP (the lower layer)

The TCP layer breaks data transmissions into small packets of information, called data *packets*. The TCP layer on the sending computer disassembles the original data into these packets and sends them across the Internet. The travel route across the Internet may not be the same for each packet, and some packets may hop across one set of servers, while other packets may use a different set of servers. In the end, when all the packets arrive at their destination, the TCP layer at the receiving computer reassembles the packets to put the data into the right order.

The IP layer keeps track of the IP addresses involved in the data transmission, to ensure that each packet gets to the right recipient computer. Even if packets are routed through different Internet servers, all the packets land at the correct recipient because the IP layer knows the recipient's IP address. If a packet is damaged or lost during its travels, the IP layer knows the sender's IP address and can request a resend of that packet.

A firewall checks every data packet passing through your computer. It checks the data in the IP layer to determine whether or not an IP address is approved or unapproved. An unapproved IP address is one that you haven't specifically configured as an IP address from which you're willing to receive data. (The IP addresses of other computers on your network, or the range of IP addresses included in your DHCP configuration, are configured as those from which your computer will accept data.)

Data Ports

Computers send and receive data through ports, which you already know because you've probably attached a printer to a parallel port, a modem to a serial port, and some sort of device to a USB port. What you probably don't realize is that your computer has thousands of invisible, nonphysical ports. They run as software services, and they're called *virtual* ports. Just like physical ports, virtual ports accept and send data.

All communication processes use ports, and most types of communication are programmed to use specific ports. Virtual ports are numbered from 0 to 65536, and the port numbers between 0 and 1024 are reserved for specific data communication services. (For example, HTTP, the protocol you use when you're viewing a Web page, uses port number 80.) Ports work by listening for data and will usually automatically accept data if it's the right type of data for that port. A port that is listening is open, waiting to accept data, and because it's open, it's vulnerable.

Internet hackers need to use ports if they want to communicate between their computers and your computer. Lots of software is available to aid these folks in testing whether a port on a remote computer is listening. Frequently, the software tests only certain ports, by pretending to send data of the type that's supported by that port. This technique is called *port scanning*, and it's a popular method of testing whether a computer is vulnerable to attack. It enables Internet hooligans to scan the ports on computers, see which services are currently listening for connections, and determine the ports they are listening on. Then, their software uses that information to create a data stream that masquerades the appropriate type of data for the listening port.

A good firewall checks the virtual ports to see whether data passing through each port is of the correct data type. This process is called *stateful packet inspection* (SPI). SPI checks the actual content of the data passing through ports, which enables the firewall to catch data packets that identify themselves as being appropriate for the port; but when the data is examined closely, the firewall discovers that the data type has been faked. At that point, the firewall blocks communication. This procedure is performed in addition to the IP address check, making the firewall more effective. The Linksys firewall router performs stateful inspections.

Linksys Firewall Router

The advantage of a hardware firewall over a software solution is that it's always there; it doesn't produce loading errors when a computer is low on RAM or resources; and users can't accidentally delete a hardware firewall, remove it from the Startup folder, or "exit" a hardware firewall. The Linksys EtherFast Cable/DSL Firewall Router (Model BEFSX41) is not just a firewall—it has plenty of extras, including a Virtual Private Network (VPN) feature.

Router Ports

All the connections start (or end, depending on your point of view) at the back of your router. I'll go over each connection on the router, moving from left to right.

Reset Button

Like the Reset button on your computer, the Reset button on the router clears data and restarts the device. To use it, hold the button for 2 or 3 seconds and then release it. Use this button only in case of an emergency, if for some reason the links to the router are jammed and communications are frozen. Try following the tips in the troubleshooting section of your router's User Guide before you press Reset.

WAN Port

Use the WAN port to connect the router to your DSL/cable modem. WAN means Wide Area Network, which is a term that's usually applied to a network that's spread across multiple locations and connected via telephone lines. (See the sidebar "LAN, WAN, and MAN" if you're interested in learning more about the various types of networks that are used to connect computers.) While the router doesn't really create a WAN, it does provide a separation point (and a barricade) between two networks: your LAN and the Internet (the Internet is a network too—the largest network in the world).

Ports Numbered 1, 2, and 3

Use these ports to connect your network devices to the router. Usually, this means computers, so if your network is made up of three (or fewer) computers, the router becomes your hub. However, you can also use these ports to connect hubs or switches to which you've already connected multiple PCs, or any other type of node (for example, a stand-alone print server).

Port 4/DMZ

This port is capable of playing either of two roles:

- Providing the same connection as the ports numbered 1 through 3
- Providing a DMZ

A DMZ is a Demilitarized Zone, and it's "firewall-neutral" (just as an army general would describe a wartime DMZ as "neutral"). If you set up a DMZ (covered later in this chapter in the sections on advanced configuration of the router), the computer you connect to this port becomes the DMZ node. Also, all four ports will automatically detect if you're connected to another hub or switch and will use the proper setting, so you won't need a crossover cable.

Power

This connector accepts the power adapter, the other end of which is plugged into a wall outlet (or, preferably, a surge protector). The router lacks an On/Off switch, so the power connector is the only way to turn the router on and off.

LAN, WAN, and MAN

The methods for interconnecting computers vary depending on the geographical circumstances. Three basic types of networks exist (each of which has a variety of setup methods, but I'll stick to the basics): LAN, WAN, and MAN.

A LAN (Local Area Network) is a group of computers connected by a common communications line. That line is usually cable, but it can also be a noncable connection topology, such as telephone lines, power lines, or wireless technology. Most small business networks and all home networks are LANs.

A WAN (Wide Area Network) is a group of computers, widely geographically dispersed, that use public communication lines as the connection method. The public communication lines are telephone lines, usually special high-speed data communication lines.

A MAN (Metropolitan Area Network) is a group of computers that are geographically dispersed but in the same general area. The computers can be connected through public lines or through the use of fiber-optic cable that's capable of withstanding the elements. For example, the computers in a group of adjacent buildings might be connected in this manner. Many college campus networks are connected as MANs, providing network connections in classrooms, dormitories, and other buildings.

Making the Connections

You need to start by physically connecting your router to your DSL/cable modem, and to the computers on your network. Depending on your current network topology (if a network is already in place), making the physical connections can be merely a matter of moving some cable, or you may need to install the cabling from scratch, or you may have to do a little of both.

NOTE   *Linksys advises that all nodes on the network be powered off while you make your connections.*

Using the Router as Your Hub

If you have a network consisting of four or fewer computers, you can build your network around the router, which is perfectly capable of acting as a hub (actually, it's a switch). (See Figure 9-1.)

■ Run cable from the NIC in each computer to one of the numbered ports on the router.

■ Connect the Ethernet cable from your DSL/cable modem to the WAN port on the router. (Be sure to use the same cable that came with the modem. If you're unsure which cable to use, just pull the cable from computer that the modem was connected to and connect it to the WAN port of the router.) The other end of your DSL/cable modem, of course, remains attached to the outside world—-to your DSL phone wire or to your cable company's cable.

If your DSL/cable modem was already installed on a stand-alone computer, and connected to a NIC in that computer, move the cable connector from the NIC

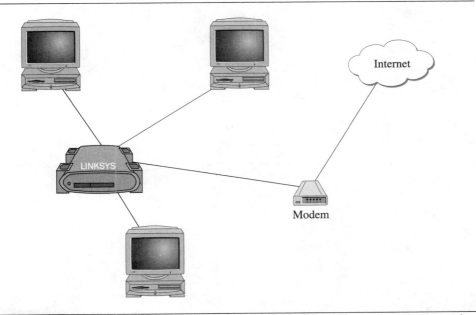

FIGURE 9-1   The router can also act as a hub, connecting all the nodes on the network

to the router. The NIC in the computer becomes the network NIC and will have to be reconfigured for the network settings. (See Chapter 8 for information about configuring NICs.)

Attaching an Existing Hub/Switch to the Router

If you'd already set up your network before deciding to add a firewall router, you don't have to abandon the hub or switch you're using. You can connect the hub or switch to the router (see Figure 9-2).

- Connect a regular port on the hub to one of the numbered ports on the router. If all the ports on the hub are used, move one of the computer connections from the hub to a numbered port on the router to free up the hub port for the connection to the router.

- Connect the Ethernet cable from your DSL/cable modem to the WAN port on the router.

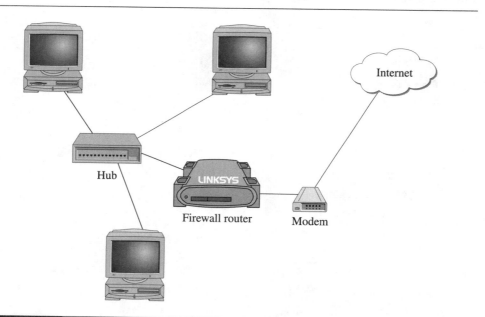

FIGURE 9-2   You can connect an existing hub to the router

 *If you have an existing network and you're using any kind of Internet connection sharing, you must disable it. You must also disable any software firewall applications. The router takes care of sharing the connection and running a firewall.*

However, if your network consists of four or less computers, you may want to consider using the router and selling the hub to a friend or neighbor who has voiced an interest in creating a home network (or sell it on an online auction). The advantage of keeping the hub (outside of the obvious advantage of saving yourself the work of moving cable) is that it makes it easier to "grow" your network. When you want to add computers to your network, you can use the router for the new machines instead of buying a larger hub or buying another hub and linking it to the existing hub.

Configuring the Computers

You need to configure your computers to access the Internet through the router. (See Chapter 8 to learn how to access the TCP/IP settings for your NICs.) You must configure the computers to obtain an IP address automatically (the router takes care of issuing the IP addresses). Nothing else is enabled—no gateway, no DNS, no WINS, nothing.

If one of the computers on your network had been connected to the DSL/cable modem and its NIC is configured for the ISP settings, that NIC must be reconfigured as a client (matching the settings for the other computers on the network). The original settings from the ISP are used to configure the router.

Power Up the Firewall Router

After you've configured the NICs on the network computers, power up the router by plugging it in. The LED lights in the front of the router should respond as follows:

- **Power** light is green as soon as the router is plugged in.

- **Diag** light is red after power-up while the router runs a self-diagnostic procedure, and then it turns off. If the light remains red for more than a minute or so, the router may have a problem. Check the User Guide that came with the router, or call Linksys for service. (See Appendix C for information about Linksys support.)

- **DMZ** is green if you've enabled the DMZ function.

- **Link/Act** is green for each port that has a network device (such as a computer) connected. If the light flickers, it indicates that communication is in progress between the network device and the router.

- **Full/Col** is green for each port connection that is operating in Full Duplex mode.

- **100** is yellow if the port connection is operating at 100 Mbps (otherwise, the connection is operating at 10 Mbps, and no light appears).

Configuring the Router Connection

You configure your router by accessing it from one of the connected computers. No special software has to be installed on that computer, as the router is accessed through the browser.

NOTE *When you open the browser to begin configuration of the router, you may receive an error message. That's because the browser can't get to the home page you configured (because until you finish configuring the router, you don't have access to the Internet). If your browser home page is set for About: Blank, you won't see an error message.*

Follow these steps to begin configuring your router:

1. In the browser Address Bar, enter **http://192.168.1.1/**, and press ENTER to open the Connect To dialog (it may take a few seconds for the dialog to appear).

NOTE *This dialog looks slightly different if you're not doing this on a Windows XP computer.*

TIP *Put the URL for the router on your Favorites list to make it easy to open the window later, in case you want to add or modify the features.*

2. Leave the User Name field blank, go to the Password field and enter **admin** (in lowercase). Then click OK.

3. The Linksys Setup window appears with the Setup tab selected, as seen in Figure 9-3.

NOTE *The Setup window has multiple tabs for setting up all the features offered by your Linksys firewall router. I'll discuss the other tabs later in this chapter.*

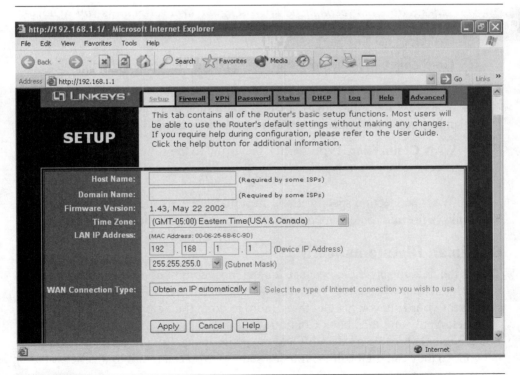

9

FIGURE 9-3 Configure your Internet connection through the router's Setup tab

The Setup tab is where you specify the basic options for your Internet connection. You must configure this tab and restart your DSL/cable modem, and you may need to restart the computers on the network to provide Internet access for your network and before you set configuration options on the other tabs in the Setup window.

- **Host Name and Domain Name**   These fields can usually remain blank, but if your ISP requires this information, fill in the data as instructed.

- **Firmware Version**   This is the version number for the router's firmware, as well as the release date for the version. Firmware is programming code that is inserted into the read-only memory of a device. This technology provides a way to enhance the capabilities of hardware devices. When new firmware is available, you can download it from the Linksys Web site, along with instructions on how to insert the new code into the device's memory.

NOTE   *Linksys does not recommend upgrading the firmware unless you're having problems with the router.*

- **Time Zone**   Use the drop-down menu to select your local time zone.

- **Device IP Address and Subnet Mask**   The default values for the router's IP address and subnet mask are preset and should not need to be altered unless you have a special configuration that is needed (such as VPN).

- **WAN Connection Type**   Click the arrow to the right of the text box and select a connection type.

The WAN connection specifications must match the instructions from your ISP. The Linksys firewall router supports six connection types, which are discussed next.

Obtain an IP Automatically

This is the default selection, because it's the most common. Your ISP instructs you to use this setting when DHCP services are provided by the ISP. If this is the correct setting for your ISP, you have nothing more to do in the Setup tab.

Click Apply and then click Continue to save your settings. Close the browser. Power your DSL/cable modem off and on again. Restart all the computers on the network so they can establish the router's settings. You can return to this Setup utility at any time to configure any other features you want to use.

Static IP

Choose this option if the instructions from your ISP require a static IP address. The Setup window changes to display the fields you need for configuration (see Figure 9-4). Use the following guidelines to supply data in the fields:

- **Specify WAN IP Address** Enter the IP address for the router as seen from the WAN (Internet).

- **Subnet Mask** Enter the subnet mask as seen by the Internet and the ISP.

- **Default Gateway Address** Enter the IP address for the Gateway.

- **DNS (Required)** Enter the IP address of the DNS server your ISP wants you to use. Your ISP provides at least one DNS IP address. Many ISP's provide a secondary DNS IP address. The Setup window also has a field for a third DNS IP address if your ISP provided one (which is unusual).

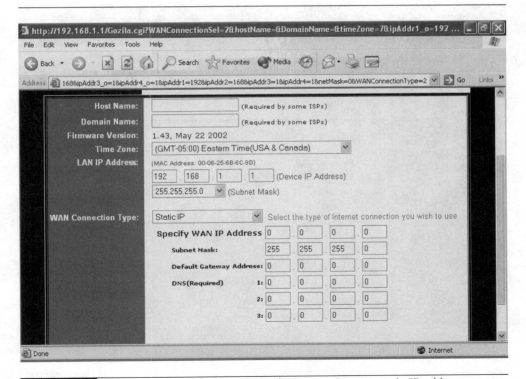

FIGURE 9-4 Use the information from your ISP to configure a static IP address

Click Apply and then click Continue to save your settings. Close the browser. Power your DSL/cable modem off and on again. Restart all the computers on the network so they can establish the router's settings. You can return to this Setup utility at any time to configure any other features you want to use.

PPPoE

If your DSL provider uses Point-to-Point Protocol over Ethernet, select this option to enable the protocol (see Figure 9-5). Then, configure your connection using the following guidelines:

- **User Name and Password**   Enter the data provided by your DSL ISP.

- **Connect on Demand: Max Idle Time -** You can configure the router to disconnect from your ISP after a specified amount of inactivity. Then,

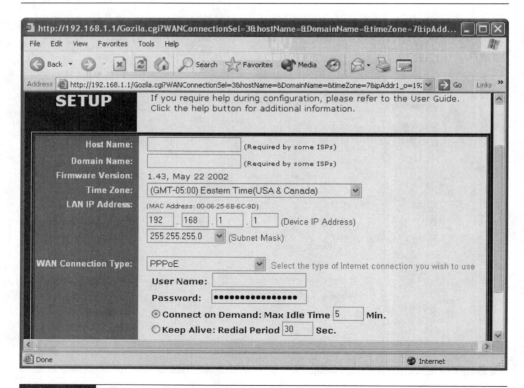

FIGURE 9-5   Enter your connection settings for PPPoE

whenever you're disconnected as a result of inactivity, the connection is re-established as soon as a user attempts to access the Internet (by opening a browser or an e-mail application). Enter the number of minutes of inactivity that must elapse to cause the router to disconnect from your DSL ISP.

■ **Keep Alive: Redial Period** Select this option to have the router periodically check the state of your Internet connection and reconnect to your ISP if the connection has been broken. Enter an amount of time that must elapse to cause the router to reconnect.

Click Apply and then click Continue to save your settings. Close the browser. Power your DSL/cable modem off and on again. Restart all the computers on the network so they can establish the router's settings. You can return to this Setup utility at any time to configure any other features you want to use.

RAS, PPTP, and HBS

These services are less common and are used only outside the United States, as follows:

■ RAS is used only in Singapore. Contact Singtel for information on the appropriate settings.

■ PPTP is used only in Europe. Contact your ISP for information on settings.

■ HBS is used only in Australia. Contact your ISP for information on settings.

Click Apply and then click Continue to save your settings. Close the browser. Power your DSL/cable modem off and on again. Restart all the computers on the network so they can establish the router's settings. You can return to this Setup utility at any time to configure any other features you want to use.

Configuring the Firewall

Select the Firewall tab of the router's Setup utility to establish your firewall and configure its settings. In this section, I'll go over the options available to you in the Firewall tab.

Advanced Firewall Protection

This option, which is enabled by default, adds the following technologies to the basic firewall services that come with your Linksys firewall router:

- Stateful packet inspection

- DoS protection

Both of these subjects are discussed earlier in this chapter. I can't think of any reason to disable these advanced protections.

Web Filter

You can disable any of the following security filtering methods by changing the Allow default option to Deny:

- **Proxy**   Select Deny to disable access to any WAN (ISP) proxy servers if they compromise the security available through your router. To make the decision about enabling or disabling this filtering method, check the documentation on your ISP's Web site, or discuss this issue with support personnel.

- **Java**   Many Web sites, especially sites with a lot of interactive content, use Java programming. If you deny Java, the router strips Java files from Web pages, and you may not be able to use the functions on those sites.

- **ActiveX**   ActiveX controls are used on many Web site programs, and if you disable this technology, the router strips ActiveX files from Web pages and you won't be able to use those features.

- **Cookie**   If you deny cookies, the router permits Web sites to write cookies to computers but denies access when the site attempts to retrieve the cookie. This means you won't be able to save passwords or save any customized settings on Web sites.

Blocked URL Contents

You can deny access to specific Web sites, to Web pages with certain text in the site's content, and to file types. You have ten fields in which to enter the specific blockades you want to impose. In each of the ten fields, you can enter any of the following:

- A URL (the address of a specific Web page)

- Text you want the firewall to discriminate against by stripping files that contain that text from Web pages

- A file extension (such as *.bmp) to block files of that type

Time Filter

You can use the Time Filter feature to block access to your network, from your network to the Internet, or both for specific periods of time. The default setting is Disable, which means your network has access to the Internet all the time. Click the arrow to the right of the Time Filter text box to select one of the following options:

- **Block Incoming Traffic**, which prevents data packets from entering the computers on your network.

- **Block Outgoing Traffic,** which prevents access to the Internet.

- **Block Bidirectional Traffic**, which stops all data from moving between your network and the Internet in either direction.

Once you enable any of these options, the window on the Firewall tab displays the fields necessary to configure the time periods (see Figure 9-6). Even though the option uses the word *block*, you enter the time periods for which you'll *allow* Internet traffic—all other times are blocked.

NOTE *The Time Filter feature uses a 24-hour clock (military time).*

Firewall Report and View Logs

Click these buttons to view the logs your router keeps. The same logs are available on the Log tab, and you must enable logging in the Log tab before you can view logs. See "Logging Events and Warnings" later in this section.

When you finish configuring the Firewall tab, click Apply, and then click Continue. Move to another tab to continue configuring your router, or close the browser.

VPN Tab

This tab is for configuring Virtual Private Networks, a complicated technology adopted mostly by corporations with branch offices or headquarters in various geographical locations. If you're interested in setting up a VPN you can purchase the Linksys VPN router model BEFVP41, and I advise you use a consultant who understands the security issues involved.

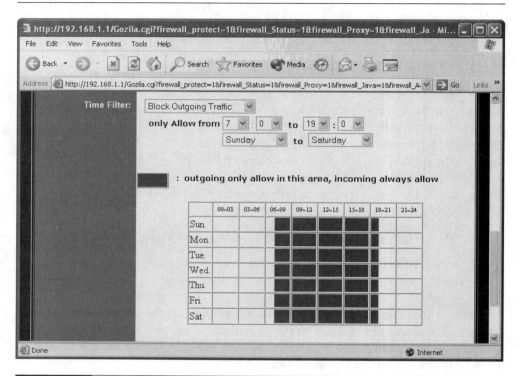

FIGURE 9-6 Users on this network can't generate outgoing data packets during overnight hours

Managing Configuration Security

Use the Passwords tab to set security for the router configuration functions (see Figure 9-7). Anyone can access the router configuration windows from any computer on the network by entering its address (http://192.168.1.1/). You need to make sure that network users can't make wholesale changes that could mess up your ability to connect to the Internet. Just as important, you need to make sure nobody can undo the firewall protections you've configured.

Router Password

You should create a new password to replace the default password (admin), to prevent the immediate world from accessing the router's configuration. Delete the dots that currently appear in the Router Password text box and enter a new password. Then do the same thing in the next text box to confirm the new password. You can use up to 63 characters for your password, but you can't use a space.

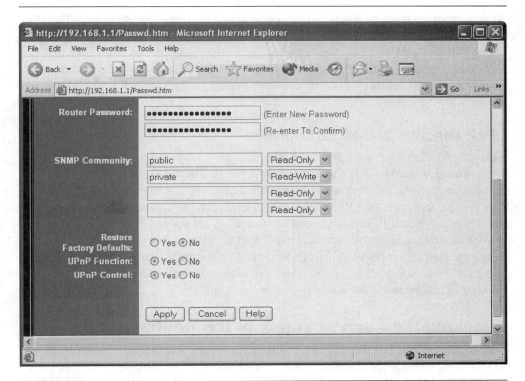

FIGURE 9-7   Protect the settings you carefully configured from inadvertent (or purposeful) modifications

CAUTION   *For added password security, don't enable the option to save the password and automatically log in when you open the router's configuration feature.*

SNMP Community

Simple Network Management Protocol (SNMP) is a protocol that's used to manage computers, routers, and lots of other devices. Network administrators use a management information base (MIB) to track the objects they're controlling. The options offered in this section of the Password page mean that the Linksys router supports the MIBs. This is well beyond the scope of any management tasks needed for a small network, so you can just skip the SNMP options and leave the default settings intact.

Restore Factory Defaults

This is a selection that you must consider as a last ditch; life as you know it has changed for the worse, send up a flare for rescue. If you select Yes, and then click

Apply, all of your router's settings are cleared and you have to start all over again. It's rare that an occasion would arise for such a drastic move, and don't even think about it unless you've exhausted all troubleshooting suggestions from Linksys technical support and they've told you that this is the only solution. You can also restore factory defaults by holding the reset button on the router for 30 seconds or more.

UPnP Function and UPnP Control

This is a Windows XP–only feature, and unless all the computers on your network are running Windows XP, you must select No to disable it. Even if all the computers on your network are running Windows XP, you may want to disable this option. It means that the Windows XP Universal Plug and Play service can automatically reconfigure the router if somebody on the network tries to use certain interactive Internet applications. A great many security problems have been reported as the result of using UPnP, and although Microsoft provides fixes and patches rather quickly, if you don't keep up with the patches and install them, you could compromise the security of your network.

Checking the Current Status of the Router

The Status tab displays the current status of the router and its configuration. Most of the entries are self-explanatory, but the Login status may not be—it refers to whether or not Login is enabled for PPPoE, RAS, PPTP, or HBS connection types. If you're not using one of those connection methods, the Login status is marked Disabled.

   You cannot make changes on this page; it's a report of your setup configuration. When you make changes to the Setup tab, those changes are reflected in the Status tab. When you make changes to the DHCP tab (covered next), those changes are reflected in the CHCP Clients Table.

Managing DHCP

When computers receive their IP addresses automatically, instead of using an assigned static IP address, the IP address assignments are handled by a Dynamic Host Configuration Protocol (DHCP) server. You can create a DHCP server on any network, using any computer—in fact, if you run Internet Connection Sharing (ICS) instead of using a router, the computer that has the modem becomes the DHCP server. Corporate network administrators set up DHCP servers to provide IP addresses for all the computers on the network.

It's best to let your router act as the DHCP server. Even if you had been running ICS, you had to disable it when you installed your router, so it would be unusual for a small network to use anything but the router for DHCP services.

DHCP servers don't assign IP addresses permanently; instead, they're leased to computers when the computers start up and request an IP address. When the lease expires, a new lease is assigned. (Computers don't have to reboot to request a new lease, because it's an automatic process.) The default length of the lease appears on the DHCP tab (see Figure 9-8) along with other DHCP settings (some of which you set when you configured the Setup tab). There's no particular reason to change any of these settings.

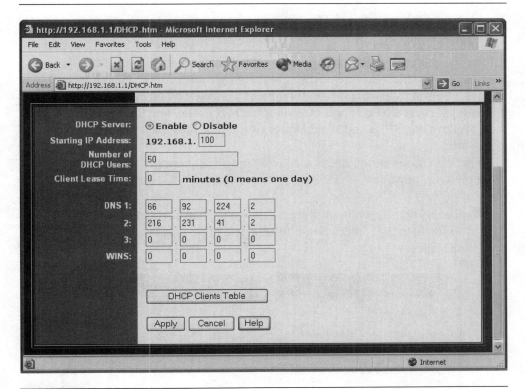

FIGURE 9-8   Configuration settings for your router-based DHCP server are displayed on the DHCP tab

To see the current DHCP client data, click the DHCP Clients Table button.

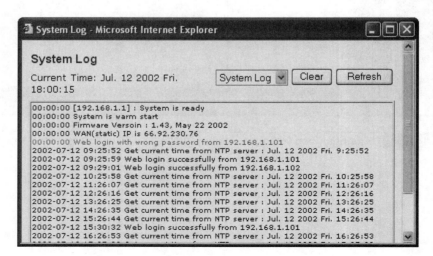

Logging Events and Warnings

Use the Log tab to enable logging and to view logs. By default, logging is enabled, telling the router to collect information, but the information is in memory, not written to a log file. (See the next section on LogViewer to learn about storing logs in files.) You can view the information being collected by opening the logs. The Incoming Access Log displays incoming Internet traffic, and the Outgoing Access Log displays the URLs and IP addresses of Internet sites that users on the network accessed.

The View Logs button opens a window in which you can select any of the logs from the drop-down list:

■ The System Log shows system activity, such as computer restarts, attempts to log in to the router's Setup feature, and other system activity connected to the router.

■ The Access Log displays incoming and outgoing traffic through the router.

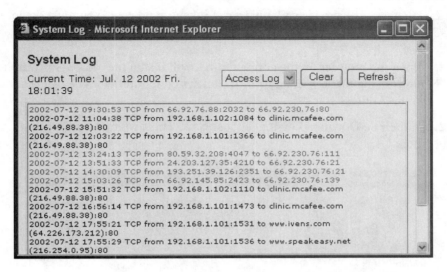

■ The Firewall Log displays the actions of the firewall to prevent DoS attacks, and it displays results of the URL and Time filters you configured.

■ The VPN Log displays information about connections over the VPN.

Saving Logs with LogViewer

If you have a computer on your network with a fixed IP address (admittedly unlikely), you can save log data permanently. Using the logs to keep an eye on the system, and to make sure the router's firewall feature is doing its job, is usually sufficient. However, if you think your network is in some serious danger from an Internet attack, you may want to store logged information in files. This gives you a chance to examine the data to see whether you can discern any patterns, especially attempts from the same IP address to enter your network. Even if you're not suspicious about attacks, you may want to track activities for some period of time by saving logged information in permanent files. To accomplish this, you need LogViewer software, which you can download from Linksys, install on one of the computers on your network, and configure the router to send the log data to that computer.

Downloading and Installing LogViewer

The LogViewer software is available from Linksys at no cost. You must download the software and then install it, using the following steps:

1. Open the browser on the computer that will install the viewer software and hold the log files and enter **ftp://ftp.linksys.com/pub/befsr41/LogViewer.exe** in the Address Bar.

2. In the File Download dialog, choose Save This Program To Disk and click OK.

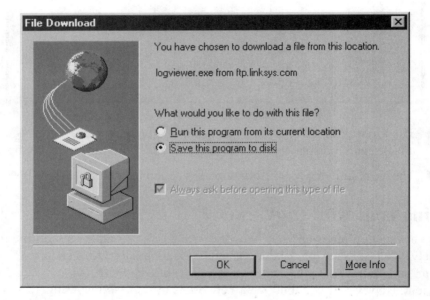

3. Select a folder to hold the downloaded file and click Save to save the file.

4. Close the browser and open My Computer or Windows Explorer to navigate to the folder where you saved the file (LogViewer.exe).

5. Double-click the file's listing to launch the LogViewer installation process. This is a wizard, so you click Next to move through each window.

6. Select a folder for the software, or accept the default location (C:\Program Files\Linksys\LogViewer), and click Next.

7. The installation wizard displays the Programs menu item it will add to your system. Click Next.

8. Click Finish to complete the installation.

Configuring the Router to Save the Logs

On the Log tab of the router's Setup utility, use the Send Log To field to specify the IP address of the computer that has the LogViewer software. Remove the default number (255) that appears for the last section of the IP address, and replace it with the last section of the IP address for the computer that's running LogViewer. Use the DHCP Clients Table in the DHCP tab to determine the correct number if you have not assigned that computer a static IP.

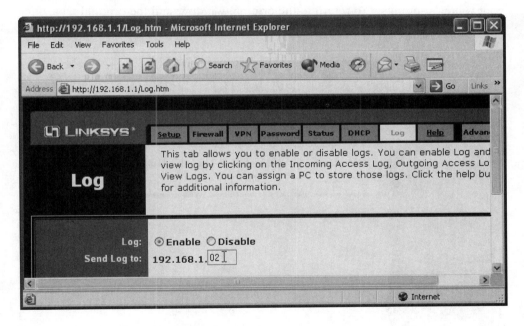

Click Apply and then click Continue to save your new settings.

Viewing the Permanent Logs

You can view the logs by opening LogViewer from the Programs menu. The logs continue to grow—unlike operating system logs, they don't have a finite size and use a First In First Out algorithm to get rid of older entries. Therefore, you must periodically clear them out or risk running out of disk space.

Getting Help

Use the Help tab to travel to specific support pages on the Linksys Web site (see Figure 9-9). In addition to finding answers to your questions, you can download a copy of the user guide, and you can even check to see whether a new firmware upgrade is available for your router.

NOTE *Appendix C has detailed information about the support options offered by Linksys.*

Advanced Setup Configuration Options

Clicking the Advanced tab opens a whole new set of tabs you can use to tweak your router's settings. (To return to the original window, and the original tabs, click the Setup tab.) Most of the options available in these tabs are unnecessary for

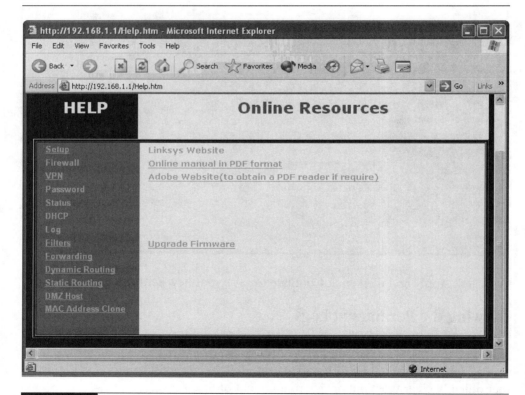

FIGURE 9-9   Click the appropriate link to get to the Linksys support pages

home and small business networks, but I'm going to offer brief descriptions of them because that gives you a better understanding about the way Internet communications work. (I believe that the more information you have about the way things work, the better off you are.) In addition, you may find a few options that are appealing to you as a way to enhance the security of your network, or as a way to control network users.

Filtering Internet Traffic

The Filters tab (see Figure 9-10) offers options you can use to enhance the security of traffic moving through your router. The Packet Filter option lets you deny access to certain types of traffic for specific computers. For example, you could establish a blockade against using certain protocols, such as FTP (File Transfer Protocol), so that a particular computer on your network can't download files from Internet servers. You can also establish blockades against certain Internet services in the other direction—forbidding computers on the Internet from sending particular types of data to a computer on the network.

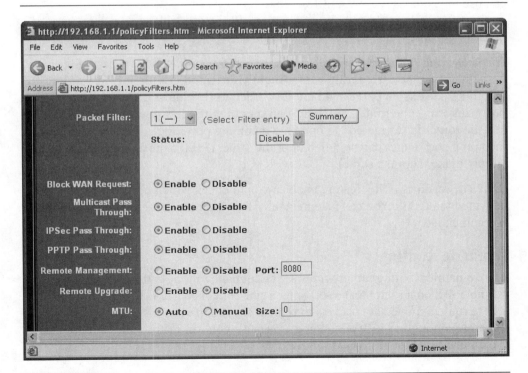

FIGURE 9-10   Tweak the router's settings with advanced options

Even though I've only briefly described the way packet filtering can work, you can probably think of several ways in which it would be helpful to use this technology to secure your network and control your network users. It's actually quite an attractive idea. However, implementation requires a clear understanding of data types and the ramifications of restricting them—for home and small business networks, this is a job for a consultant rather than a do-it-yourself task.

The other options on the Filters tab control the security settings for traffic through your VPN.

Forwarding Data Packets

The Forwarding tab provides options that let you forward Internet traffic so that data intended for certain ports is intercepted and then forwarded to certain computers. These settings are useful if one of the computers on your network is actually running on the Internet, which is highly unlikely for any small network; if you have a Web page, it's probably located on a server at a Web-hosting company. To use forwarding, you will need to assign the computer that you wish to use an address that is outside of the DHCP scope (normally 100–149), so this means you can use the addresses 2–99 and 150–254.

Port forwarding can only be used on one PC at a time. If you wish to forward ports to multiple ports, try port triggering.

Port Triggering   Port triggering is similar to port forwarding in the aspect of opening ports; however, port triggering works slightly differently. With port forwarding, all incoming packets on port 12345 are forwarded to IP address 192.168.1.20. With port triggering, the router waits until an outgoing request goes out on port 12345 and the router is "triggered" to open the incoming port range (The triggered and incoming port ranges can be different or the same. If you're unsure which is which, simply make them the same).

UPnP Forwarding   This feature enables you to check which ports have been activated via UPnP. You can also manually forward ports here; however, it is not recommended.

Dynamic Routing

The Dynamic Routing tab provides a way to make routing more efficient, and it has no effect on a router that's servicing a self-contained LAN. In large enterprises, where routers move data packets to remote servers in other physical locations, dynamic routing is a nifty technology, because you can instruct the router to find the quickest or cheapest way to move data.

Static Routing

The Static Routing tab lets you set options that force routers to access other routers on your network in a specific way. Small networks don't use multiple routers, so you have no reason to use these options.

DMZ Host

You can use the options on the DMZ Host tab to establish one of the computers on your network as a DMZ host. As explained earlier in this chapter, that computer must be connected to port 4 of your router.

A DMZ host ignores the firewall (it may be more accurate to say that the firewall ignores the DMZ host). DMZ hosts can send data packets back and forth between the two networks (your LAN and the Internet) without obeying any rules. The other nodes (your network computers) continue to be protected by the firewall, and they use the DMZ node as the "sacrificial lamb" that sends and receives data from the outside network. In large corporate networks, a DMZ is normally used to gain access to the company servers that are exposed to the Internet, while keeping the internal network secure from users who are visiting the company Web site. (That's why, when you visit a Web site such as *www.linksys.com*, you can't issue commands that would let you access data on the Linksys internal servers or the employees' computers, even if you know the commands that would permit such access.) DMZ is also a useful feature for a machine that is running multiple services such as HTTP and FTP. You do not have to forward multiple ports to that machine; simply put it into DMZ.

NOTE   *DMZ will override port forwarding, so do not run the same services at once.*

For small networks, the DMZ can be useful for letting users perform actions that the firewall would usually prevent, such as playing certain interactive Internet games or participating in Internet conferences. However, establishing a network node that is unprotected by the firewall is dangerous, and you should call a consultant to help you set this up.

NOTE   *DMZ does not disable the firewall completely. The computer that is in DMZ will still be under NAT (Network Address Translation). If you try to use a service that does not support NAT, it will not work through DMZ.*

9

MAC Address Clone

The MAC Addr. Clone tab lets you change the MAC address of the router. A MAC (Media Access Control) address is a hardware-level ID number that uniquely identifies a hardware device. Some ISP's require you to register the MAC address of the device that's connected to the ISP. Before you installed your router, if you had a NIC in a computer to connect that computer to your DSL/cable modem—and therefore, to your ISP—the NICs MAC address was registered with the ISP. After you installed your router, that router became the only connection your ISP sees, and its MAC address is not the one you originally registered with your ISP. Rather than go through a new MAC registration process with your ISP (not fun, unless you enjoy being transferred from technician to technician and spending a lot of time on hold), you can clone the original NIC's MAC address to your router. Your ISP will never know you changed the connection device.

To accomplish this, select the User Defined option and then enter the MAC address of the NIC that was originally connected to the DSL/cable modem. The tab displays the MAC address of the computer you're working on, so it's easiest to perform this task by accessing the router's Setup program from the computer that was originally connected to the DSL/cable modem. Otherwise, check the DHCP Client Table on the DHCP tab to ascertain the MAC address of the computer that was originally connected to the ISP.

Viruses

Computer viruses have become an enormous problem, and the spread of a variety of forms of this rogue programming code has grown to epidemic proportions. Viruses erase data, change program files, change system files, or damage operating system files so the computer can't boot.

You should be running an anti-virus program all the time. Two of the popular applications are McAfee (*http://www.mcafee.com*) and Symantec's Norton Anti-Virus (*http://www.symantec.com*). You can also check reviews of anti-virus products in computer publications.

Understanding Viruses

A virus is a program, even though it may be disguised as something else (including something as seemingly benign as a screen saver). The programming code of a virus is designed to cause harm, sometimes causing annoying damage, and sometimes inflicting utter disaster. Viruses are always designed to replicate themselves to other computers, either over a network or through e-mail.

The fact that part of the definition of a virus is that it's a program confuses some people, because they know they can get a virus through a document prepared in Microsoft Word or Microsoft Excel (there has certainly been plenty of press coverage of that fact). However, the virus you may get from an e-mail attachment of a Word or Excel document is indeed from a program, because the virus travels in a macro that's linked to (and essentially, part of) the document. Microsoft uses Visual Basic Script (VBS) programming code for macros, and VBS produces executable code just like any other programming language. Therefore, Word and Excel macros qualify as programs.

> **TIP** *If you don't use VBS and don't need to run .vbs files, change the file association for .vbs files to Notepad. Then, if you accidentally open a file containing a virus in the VBS code, the file opens as a text file in Notepad. Check your Windows help files to learn how to change file associations.*

Types of Viruses

Viruses arrive in many forms and categories, and within each category are many subcategories. Covering all of these variants and explaining what they do would take forever (and fill a thick book). Therefore, I'll present a brief, albeit somewhat simplified, overview of some of the basic types of viruses.

File Infector Viruses

File infector viruses are the oldest type of virus, and they've been around as long as the PC has existed (although in those early days viruses were transmitted by infected floppy disks, as nobody was surfing the Internet back then).

A file infector virus attaches itself to an existing program file, perhaps a file you open frequently. When you launch the program you launch the virus, which then does its damage and plants itself somewhere on your drive so it can spread itself to other computers. These viruses can use any executable file type, although they most commonly use .com and .exe files. However, other executable file types, including .sys, .mnu, and others, can also be targets of their parasite behavior.

> **NOTE** *Some file infector viruses arrive as fully contained programs (frequently as scripts) instead of attaching themselves to other programs.*

When I tell people who have been victimized that the virus was linked to an executable file, they're usually surprised (or tell me I'm wrong). They point out that they examined the filenames of e-mail attachments, looking for a file extension that indicates an executable file. They saw an attachment with the file extension .txt and assumed the attachment was safe.

Sigh! Unfortunately, they didn't see the actual, full, filename. For reasons I will never understand, Microsoft decided that the default behavior of Windows is to hide the display of file extensions that are associated with programs. This means a file that displays its name as readme.txt could actually be named readme.txt.exe. You should change that behavior immediately, which you can do by taking the following steps:

1. Open any system folder such as Windows Explorer, My Computer, or Control Panel.

2. Choose Tools | Folder Options (or View | Folder Options in Windows 98).

3. Click the View tab, and locate the item Hide File Extensions for Known File Types. Click the check box to remove the check mark.

4. Click OK.

Macro Viruses

Macro viruses are programmed to do the same type of damage as file infector viruses, but they use a different method of transportation. Instead of being attached to a program file, they're linked to a macro in a Word or Excel document. They're launched when the document file to which they're attached is opened, carry out their nefarious tasks, and replicate themselves into other documents.

Boot Sector Viruses

A boot sector virus places its code in the Master Boot Record of a hard drive (or the boot sector of a floppy disk). As the computer boots, during the time the computer reads and executes the programs in the boot sector, the virus launches itself into memory. Once it's in memory, it can control computer operations and replicate itself to other drives on the computer or to other computers on the network. Some boot sector viruses are programmed to destroy the computer's ability to boot, while others let the computer boot normally and then perform their ugly tasks.

Worms

A worm is a self-contained program that doesn't need to attach itself to another program to do damage. A worm counts on users opening the rogue file manually, at which point it performs whatever damage it's programmed to do and replicates itself. Worms commonly replicate themselves by mailing themselves to all the recipients in an Outlook or Outlook Express address book, and by installing themselves on hard drives, including across a network.

Because they don't have to attach themselves to other programs, worms propagate themselves faster and easier than the proverbial rabbit. They just lay down anywhere they feel like it and clone themselves all over your drives. Sometimes their propagation scheme is designed in a way that gives each clone a different assignment, so when all of them go into action, they can do incredible damage.

Trojan Horses

A Trojan horse performs the same type of evil tasks as a virus does, but it's technically not a virus because it doesn't replicate itself. Since replication is part of the strict definition of a virus, the term Trojan horse was invented to create a distinction between this type of rogue code and true viruses. If you've been victimized by a Trojan horse, however, you don't care much about those technical niceties.

One serious challenge in dealing with Trojan horses is that even if your anti-virus software can remove the file, the attendant damage to your system may not be easy to remove. You should always contact your anti-virus software vendor to get instructions. You may have to undo changes to the registry or replace system files to rid your system of the damage. You can obtain software that's dedicated to managing Trojan horses; two companies that offer these products are PestPatrol (*http://www.safersite.com*) and Tauscan (*http://www.agnitum.com*).

Understanding Anti-virus Software

Anti-virus software is complicated and powerful, because it operates in multiple ways, using multiple components. The software contains two main components: the engine and the virus information data files.

The engine, which is responsible for running all the processes, has two different programs:

- An on-access component that automatically checks files for viruses as you open them

- A scanning component, which performs a scan of the files on your computer to check for viruses

The virus information data files contain information about known viruses, which makes it possible for the software to spot them.

The software works by intercepting operations such as reading files or opening e-mail messages to check the file for viruses before permitting the operation to continue. Checking the file involves several steps:

- Comparing the data with the information in the virus data information files, looking for a string of characters or bytes that's found in a particular virus (called a virus *signature*).

- Checking for a change in a file's attributes since the last time the file was checked—for example, looking for a change in the size of an executable file.

- Using heuristic scanning to check for suspicious data (see the sidebar "Heuristic Scanning").

When the software detects a virus in a file, it displays a message asking you what you want to do. The choices vary depending on the software, but usually you have the following options:

- *Clean the file.* This choice is available when a virus has infected an existing file. The software tries to clean the virus out of the file to put the file back in its original condition. If cleaning fails (it frequently does), the software usually suggests that you delete the file, using the Delete option in the anti-virus software window.

- *Delete the file.* The file is permanently deleted, and it is not sent to the Recycle bin.

- *Isolate the file.* The file is placed in a special folder that's created and managed by the anti-virus software (to prevent the virus from launching). Later, you can delete the files in that folder or send them to the anti-virus software company (if you're participating in a program for that purpose).

The software names the viruses it finds, and it's a good idea to go to the software company's Web site to learn more about that virus. You'll find instructions for taking additional steps to rid your system of the effects of the virus.

Heuristic Scanning

Heuristic scanning is a behavior-based method for analyzing an executable file to try to identify whether it may be a threat. Anti-virus software uses heuristic scanning to try to catch viruses that are new and haven't yet been analyzed to determine their signatures (which would permit the software company to add the information about the virus to its virus information data file). Heuristic scanning is similar to a guessing game, but the guesses are educated, based on expertise in virus behavior.

You can turn off the option to perform a heuristic scan, and some people do so because the process has some minor side effects on your system. (Personally, I don't think the side effects are serious enough to turn off the feature.) Heuristic scanning slows down the scanning process, and it occasionally produces false alarms (sometimes an innocent program may contain programming code that seems to behave the way a virus might behave).

9

Chapter 10

Tips and Tricks for Networking

After you've created a network, you automatically earn the title "Network Administrator." The administrator is the person in charge, and in most home and small business networks that title belongs to the person who took time to read books, read the documentation that came with the equipment, and then moved on to install the hardware.

In this chapter, you'll learn about the things you should do to make sure your network runs smoothly all the time. In the process, you'll pick up some of the tricks used by network administrators of large corporate networks.

Document Everything

You need to keep a record of everything you do. You won't remember the details of all the steps you took to set up your network, even if your network consists of only two computers. Create a file in your word processor (call it Network or something similar), back it up to a floppy disk, put a copy on another computer on the network, and print a copy for filing. Every time you make changes to your network, document those changes in your file, update the copies, and print out the new file. Make the first line of the file the current date, so if you find duplicates you know which is the latest copy.

The reason for doing this is, of course, that at some point, each of these computers will die, or some important component (the hard drive or the network adapter) will die. When you replace it, you'll know the settings you need.

Track Your ISP Settings

Your Internet service provider (ISP) provided instructions about setting up your Internet connection. Those instructions include the way the computers on your network get their IP addresses, whether or not you have to specify a DNS server, and other important information. Copy the important settings into the file you're creating to document your network's setup.

Track Hardware Settings

Some devices require specific settings, such as interrupt request (IRQ) levels and I/O addresses. (It doesn't matter whether you understand what they are; it just matters that you can find them if you need technical support or you have to replace a device.) Windows has a feature called Device Manager that tracks this information, and you should copy the information. (If your computer or drive dies, you won't be able to get to Device Manager.) To open Device Manager, right-click My Computer—located on the Desktop or on the Start menu—and choose Properties from the shortcut menu. Click the Hardware tab, and then click the Device Manager button. (In Windows 98 and ME, there's a Device Manager tab, so you save yourself a mouse click.)

When Device Manager opens, it displays each type of hardware component in your computer. When you expand a component type by clicking the plus sign (+) next to its listing, you see the specific device of the type that's installed in your computer. Figure 10-1 shows the Network Adapter expanded in Device Manager to display the specific adapter in this computer.

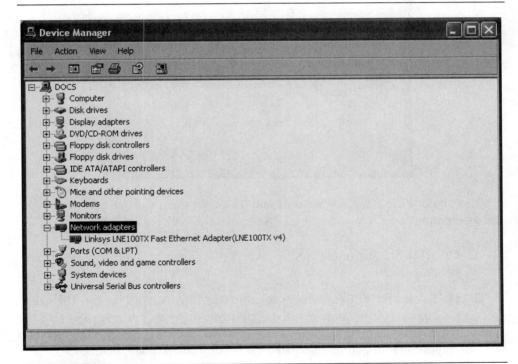

FIGURE 10-1   Expand a device type to see the specific component that's installed in your computer

10

Right-click the device (not the device type) and choose Properties from the shortcut menu. The General tab, the Resources tab, and the Driver tab all provide information about the device and its settings.

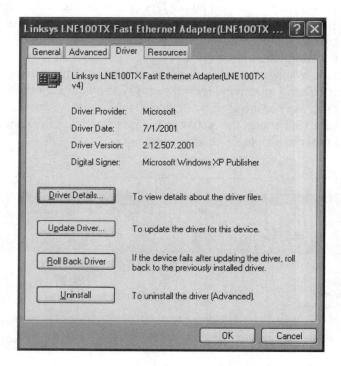

You could write down the settings and then type them in your network documentation file. Or you could take a shortcut, as follows:

1. Click the title bar on the device's Properties dialog to make sure that the window is active.

2. Hold down the ALT key while you press the PRINT SCREEN button. This puts a picture of the window into the clipboard's memory. (The ALT key tells the clipboard to capture only the active window; otherwise, everything you see on your monitor is put into memory, which is more than you need.)

3. Choose Start | Programs | Accessories | Paint to open the Paint program.

4. Choose Edit | Paste from the Paint menu bar.

5. The graphic is pasted from the clipboard into the Paint window.

6. Choose File | Save and save the file (use a filename that reminds you of the contents, such as Kit-NIC-Drivers for the Drivers tab of the NIC in the computer named Kitchen).

7. Repeat for each set of information you want to keep about devices.

If you save the file on the local computer, copy it to the computer on which you're saving your network documentation file. Or, better still, when you save the file, navigate across the network to that computer. (See Chapter 12 to learn how to access folders on other computers.)

You can save each of these graphic files separately—put each of them, along with your documentation file, in its own folder. Or, you can import each graphic file into your documentation file. (In Microsoft Word, choose Insert | Picture | From File, and then choose the file you saved.) Your network documentation file will grow large, but everything is in one place.

Track NIC Configuration Settings

To capture the information about the NIC's network configuration, open the Properties dialog for the NIC and either write down the information or capture a graphic.

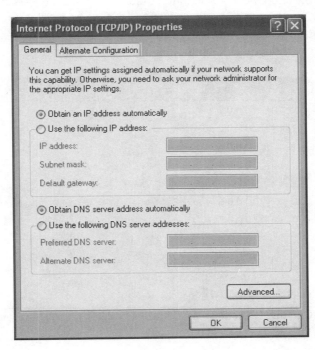

If all your NICs get IP addresses from a DHCP Server (either the host computer for a shared Internet connection or a hardware device such as a router), you don't have to track each computer—they're all the same. However, if you're using internal IP addresses, or if you're buying public IP addresses from your ISP, you must keep track of each computer's configuration. The easy way to accomplish this is to create a table in your word processor, with an entry for each IP address you plan to use (including extra addresses for network growth), an example of which is shown in Table 10-1.

Track Cable Connections

If you're using Ethernet cable, it's a good idea to label the connectors so you know which cable is attached to each computer. This makes troubleshooting easier if a computer has a problem when it attempts to join the network (the cable connection is always the first suspect). Tape a paper label to each end of the cable, near the RJ-45 connector (don't put tape on any part of the connector), or use a permanent marker to write the computer name on the cable.

In fact, it's a good idea to label all connections for a computer. The back of every one of my computers is filled with notes that I wrote with a thick marker (which makes it so much easier to find everything if I have to open the computer—reattaching all those connections is much quicker). I have a big *M* and *K* next to each of the PS/2 ports that connect my mouse and keyboard. I wrote *CAM* next to the serial port to which I attach my camera, and *MOD* next to the serial port to which I attach my modem. (I keep a modem for faxing and for a backup Internet

Computer Name	IP Address
AcctsPay	10.0.0.1
AcctsRec	10.0.0.2
FrontDesk	10.0.0.3
Docs	10.0.0.4
HelpDesk	10.0.0.5
Apps	10.0.0.6
Server-2	10.0.0.7
	10.0.0.8
	10.0.09
DNS Server-ISP	216.231.41.2
Router	216.231.41.5

TABLE 10-1   Charting IP Addresses Eliminates Problems with Duplicate Numbers

connection in case my broadband connection goes down.) I have an arrow pointing to the jack that accepts the speakers on my sound card (I got tired of plugging the speakers into the microphone jack and then having to go back to move the plug).

Expanding Your Network

Most networks grow, and even though you're sure at the moment that your household won't need more than two computers, you'll change your mind. If you're putting your network in a small business environment, growth is expected (and hoped for). As businesses grow, new employees arrive, and each new employee needs a computer.

Expanding Ethernet Networks

If you have a cabled network and your hub runs out of ports, you can connect a hub to another hub, which is called *uplinking*. Linksys hubs are built to let you perform this task easily, but you do have to pay attention to the documentation for your specific hub model.

Adding Hubs

The number of ports on your hub depends on the Linksys model you purchased. Linksys hubs come in 5-, 8-, 16-, and 24-port configurations, and most people buy a hub that has more ports than the number of computers they're planning to install on the network (they know that networks almost always grow). In fact, the Linksys Network In a Box kit contains two NICs and a 5-port hub, because even small home networks eventually gain at least one additional computer beyond the two computers that motivated the move to a network. The Linksys 5-port hubs include a port that's clearly marked as a Uplink port, which means the port isn't used to connect a computer; it's used only to connect another hub.

The other, larger, Linksys hubs have one port (the highest number) that can be used for either a computer connection or for a connection to another hub. To uplink the hub, connect the cable from the Uplink port to any port on the next hub. Figure 10-2 shows a multiple-hub solution for managing an expanding network.

10

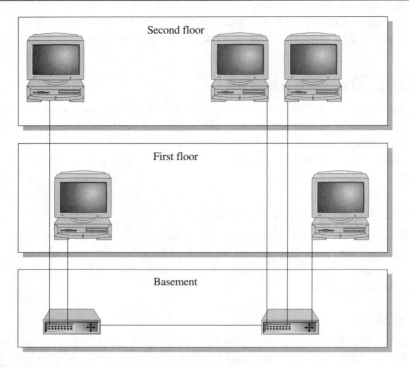

FIGURE 10-2   Cable the computers to multiple hubs, and then link the hubs

Using Multiple Hubs for Difficult Cabling Environments

Figure 10-2 is also a good illustration of using multiple hubs to solve difficult cabling problems, even if you don't have more computers than ports. If the physical layout of your home or office is such that there's no easy-to-reach midpoint at which to logically locate a single hub, you can split your network between two sets of cable runs. One set of cables can connect to one hub, and the other set can connect to another hub. Then you connect the hubs to create one network.

Technical Specs for Linked Hubs

The nature of the Ethernet topology means you cannot link 100BaseT hubs if they're further apart than 16.4 feet (5 meters). If you're using multiple hubs to connect groups of computers that are difficult to cable to a single hub, this distance maximum can be inconvenient or even fatal to your cabling plan. However, Linksys sells a nifty device called a *distance extender*, which lets you connect those hubs even if they're as far apart as 328 feet (100 meters). The distance extender is installed inside the hub and occupies a port. (The specifics differ by the models of the equipment involved, so check with the Linksys specifications on the Web site to make sure you're marrying the right pieces of equipment.)

Also, the Fast Ethernet technology limits you to linking a maximum of two hubs if both hubs are straight 100 Mbps hubs (the limit doesn't apply to 10/100 autosensing hubs). The solution is to link the 100 Mbps hub to a switch, which is a more intelligent, and faster, connection device. (See Chapter 4 to learn about the difference between a hub and switch.)

For business networks that keep growing, either by adding more computers or by adding office space on a different floor (or a different section of the same floor), consider stackable hubs or rack-mounted hubs, which are built for easy linking. This is a good solution for bringing together multiple groups of computers that are rather isolated, or just for continuing to add computers as your business grows.

Expanding Wireless LANS

Wireless communication has some distance limits, so the computers on your wireless network may have to be located in a manner that enhances communication. This is not always the most efficient way to position computers, especially in a business environment. Additionally, the further apart the wireless nodes, the slower the communication. While the distance limitations vary, depending on the number of walls (and whether metal pipes or ducts are in those walls) and other possible impediments to wireless communication, you can generally expect the following standards for speed:

10

- 11 Mbps up to 100 feet

- 5.5 Mbps up to 165 feet

- 2 Mbps up to 230 feet

- 1 Mbps up to 300 feet

If you need to place computers more than 300 feet apart, or if you want more speed, or both, you need a wireless *access point*. Access points push the communication limits for both distance and speed. You can also use a wireless access point as a bridge to merge a wireless LAN with a wired LAN (see the next section on mixing connection types). Chapter 5 has instructions for installing access points in wireless LANs.

Mixing Connection Types

Sometimes, growth is easier to manage by mixing topologies and combining your original topology with new connection types. For example, you may have started with two computers connected by wireless adapters, phone lines, or power lines. Then you add two more computers that are physically near each other and easy to connect via Ethernet cable. Now you have two LAN segments: one Ethernet, one not Ethernet.

Or, it works the other way around—you started with a couple of computers that are connected through an Ethernet hub, and the new computers are far removed, or on a different floor, and there's no easy method of joining each of them to a cabled network. You decide to use wireless, phone line, or power line connections.

Perhaps you need only one non-Ethernet LAN segment, and you have no need to connect computers via Ethernet. However, you've installed a DSL/cable modem, which requires an Ethernet connection, and you need to be able to connect your non-Ethernet computers to the modem so everybody can get to the Internet.

You can merge these diverse setups into a single network, thanks to a clever device called a *bridge*. A bridge is a connection point where two topologies meet. (Actually, bridges can perform a number of useful functions, but for this discussion, I'm covering only their ability to link Ethernet LAN segments with other LAN segments that are using a different topology.)

Linksys provides a bridge for each combination of Ethernet and non-Ethernet connection types.

- Wireless/Ethernet

- Phone line/Ethernet

- Power line/Ethernet

Installing a bridge is easy (and logical), because the device has multiple connector types (that match the technologies it's bridging). Plug an Ethernet cable into the Ethernet port, and then attach the other technology through the appropriate port. Some bridges may require a setup program; if so, the package includes a CD.

Troubleshooting and Tweaking Network Communication

On a day-to-day basis, networks run smoothly and efficiently without any help from human beings. In fact, some networks run for years without a single problem. However, sometimes communications break down, and one computer can't access the rest of the network.

NOTE   *A computer must have at least one shared resource (usually a folder) to be seen on the network. Until a share is created, the computer cannot be accessed by other computers on the network. See Chapter 12 to learn how to create a network share on a computer.*

When you need to troubleshoot a network problem, there's a pecking order for your investigative efforts. Luckily, the things you look for first are also the easiest tasks to accomplish: start with the connectors, move to the cable, then to the adapters, and finally to the software settings.

Checking Network Connections

The first thing to check is the connection. Is everything attached as it should be? Are all the components working properly? Following are some guidelines to follow as you check your network for problems.

Troubleshooting Ethernet Connections

For an Ethernet network, make sure the RJ-45 connector is plugged into both the NIC and the hub properly—fully inserted. Windows XP displays a pop-up message to announce the fact that a connection seems to be unplugged, and then displays a red *X* over the icon. (Of course, to see these indicators, you must enable the option to display the network connection icon on the taskbar, which is not the default setting. Open the Properties dialog of your network connection and choose the option to put an icon on the taskbar.)

If you extended the length of any cable segment by using a coupler to combine two cable lengths, check the connectors in the coupler. Disconnect the RJ-45 connectors and use canned air to clean the port. Then order a patch cable of the appropriate length so you can get rid of the coupler.

10

Check to make sure the cable isn't passing close to anything that could cause interference, such as fluorescent lights, uninterruptible power supplies, or other sources of strong electromagnetic signals.

Make sure the adapter is connected to the computer properly. If you're using an Internal NIC, open the computer and make sure the card is seated firmly in the bus. If you're using a USB connector, make sure the connector is inserted firmly.

CAUTION *You cannot assume that the USB port on the back of your computer is working. I've run into a number of computers in which the USB port is not activated by default and must be turned on by entering the BIOS Setup program that's available while the computer is booting. Check the documentation for your computer to see whether this could be your problem.*

Check the cable for any of the following problems:

- Be sure the cable isn't coiled tightly (some people do this when the cable is longer than is necessary). Coiled cable can create electromagnetic fields that may disrupt data communication. If you must coil, try to keep the cable fairly slack, about 5–6 inches in diameter.

- Be sure your computer is within 328 feet of the hub, which is the maximum distance for an Ethernet connection.

- Test the cable by replacing it with cable that is currently connected to a computer that is working properly.

Troubleshooting Phoneline Connectors

For a phone line network, check the RJ-11 connectors at both ends of the telephone cable to make sure they're fully engaged. If your home has more than one telephone line, make sure all the RJ-11 connectors are plugged into wall jacks for the same telephone line. You cannot "cross" telephone lines for phone line networking, in the same way you cannot pick up an instrument that's attached to one line and join a conversation taking place on the other line. Swap your cable for a new cable that you know is working.

TIP *Even though your phone line network adapter has two RJ-11 ports, one marked for the network and the other marked for a phone or fax, it really doesn't matter which port you use—they're identical.*

Troubleshooting Power line Connectors

For a power line network, make sure the adapter is securely attached to the USB port. (See the earlier note on making sure the USB port is activated on the computer.) Make sure the plug from the adapter is fully inserted in the electrical outlet.

If the outlet is switched (controlled by an On/Off switch on the wall), be sure the wall switch is in the On position. (It's not really a good idea to plug anything related to computers or networks into a switched outlet.)

If the adapter is plugged into a surge protector strip (or any other type of strip), be sure the strip's On/Off switch is set to On. In case the strip is damaged, remove the adapter from the strip and plug it into a wall outlet. (The power line adapter has its own surge protector built in, so you don't need to plug it into a surge protector; in fact, some strips may have circuitry that may interfere with your power line adapter, so it's best to use a wall outlet.)

Be sure you've run the Security Configuration Utility on every computer on the network, using the same network password. You cannot enable security on some computers and omit security on other computers. However, if you can't set up security on one computer, then configure the unit on another computer and set up the encryption that way.

10

Troubleshooting Wireless Connections

For a wireless network, although there are no connectors, you should check the antenna (which is the equivalent of a connector). Make sure the antenna doesn't have something on it. (I've seen books, purses, and backpacks on antennas.) Make sure the computer, and therefore the antenna, isn't under a metal desk or in a location that puts metal between it and the rest of the network. For example, if a metal file cabinet sits next to the computer, it's probably interfering with your ability to transmit or receive data.

NOTE   *Don't forget to check the antenna on your access point if you're using one.*

Make sure you're not having a problem with distances, because you really have no way of knowing the maximum range of your wireless network until you test it. Too many factors can interfere with the range, such as leaded glass, metal, reinforced concrete floors, and walls with pipes or ducts. Bring two computers (or a computer and an access point) into the same room and see if they can communicate. Then move them further apart and test again—repeating this until you determine whether distance is the problem.

Be sure other RadioFrequency (RF) devices aren't interfering with the signal. (Portable telephones are frequently a problem; check the frequency range to make sure you're not overlapping.)

See Chapter 5 for more details on wireless networks.

Checking Network Configuration Settings

If the configuration and condition of the physical components of your network seem to be okay, you must investigate the software side: drivers and settings.

Device Manager

Start with Device Manager, which can reveal problems with drivers, hardware resource conflicts, and other settings. To open Device Manager, take the appropriate steps, as follows:

- In Windows XP and Windows 2000, right-click My Computer and choose Properties from the shortcut menu. Click the Hardware tab, and then click the Device Manager button.

- In Windows 98 and Windows Me, right-click My Computer and choose Properties from the shortcut menu. Click the Device Manager tab.

Device Manager displays all hardware devices by category, and to see a specific device, you must click the plus sign (+) next to its category to expand the display to include the specific device(s) of that category that are installed on your computer. However, if a device has a problem, the Device Manager display changes in the following ways:

- The device category is automatically expanded to show the troublesome device.

- The device's listing has a yellow icon with an exclamation point.

For example, in Figure 10-3, my Windows 98SE Device Manager opened with the SCSI controller category expanded and displayed a SCSI device with an exclamation point.

To investigate further, right-click the device listing (not the category) and choose Properties. The tabs and information that appear on the Properties dialog

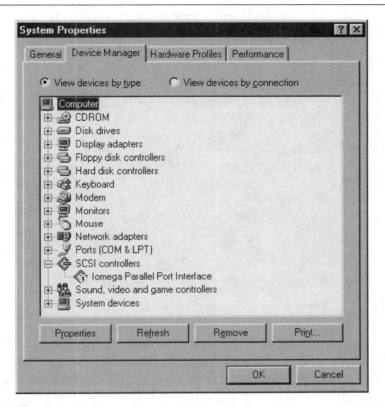

FIGURE 10-3   Device Manager knows that Windows can't communicate with the device, which means something is wrong

depend on the type of device and the operating system. All device Properties dialogs open to the General tab, which isn't always terribly specific about the problem affecting a device that isn't working (see Figure 10-4). However, sometimes Device Manager knows exactly what's wrong. (For example, if you never installed the driver for the device, the General tab will display "No Driver Installed.")

Check the Resources tab to see if any conflicts exist between this device and any other device in your system. A conflict means that basic computer resources that are supposed to belong to one device at a time are being shared by two devices, which just doesn't work. If a conflict exists, a message appears on the Resources tab to inform you of that fact. You must find the other device that's grabbing the same resource, and the way to do that is to change the way Device

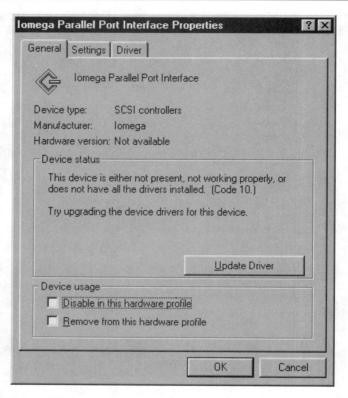

FIGURE 10-4 Device Manager isn't specific about the cause of this problem (I'd disconnected the device from the port to move it to another computer)

Manager displays devices, which you can do in Windows XP and Windows 2000 only. Choose View | Resources By Connection to display the system resources. Then, expand each resource listing to determine whether two devices are assigned the same resource.

Figure 10-5 shows a display of resources, sorted by connection, with the Interrupt Request (IRQ) resource expanded. If you see two devices on the same IRQ, it's not a conflict as long as the devices are on a PCI bus, because PCI manages resource allocation. However, if two devices are on the same IRQ on an ISA bus, you have a problem—one of those devices isn't working. You have to change the IRQ assignment for one of the devices, and to accomplish this, you must check the documentation that came with the device or call the manufacturer for technical support.

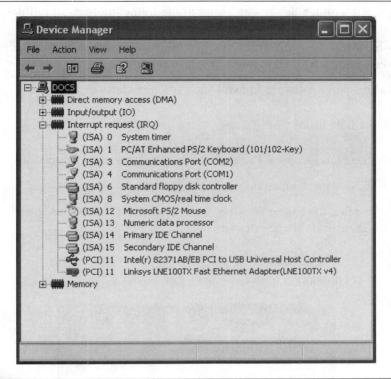

FIGURE 10-5   It looks as if two devices are sharing IRQ 11, but it's okay because the devices are on a PCI bus

Network Adapter Configuration

All the configuration settings for your network adapters must follow the same pattern. The protocol you're using for network communication (usually TCP/IP) must be installed for every adapter. File and printer sharing must be enabled. If there's a configuration problem, it's most likely to be in the TCP/IP settings. Read Chapter 8 to learn about the permutations and combinations of IP addresses and make sure the settings on each computer are correct.

Turn Off Internet Connection Firewall in Windows XP

During the network setup on Windows XP, the system usually enables the Internet Connection Firewall (ICF) automatically. ICF is a primitive firewall that doesn't let you configure it to allow incoming network traffic. This means no computer on your network can access a Windows XP computer that's running ICF.

Disable ICF and replace it with either of the following firewall utilities:

■ A hardware firewall, which you can use with DSL/cable modem devices (see Chapter 9 to learn about firewall routers)

■ A third-party software firewall such as ZoneAlarm or BlackIce

To disable ICF, follow these steps:

1. Choose Start | Control Panel | Network And Internet Connections.

2. Click Network Connections.

3. Right-click the listing for your Local Area Connection and choose Properties from the shortcut menu.

4. Select the Advanced tab.

5. Deselect the option to use ICF, and then click OK.

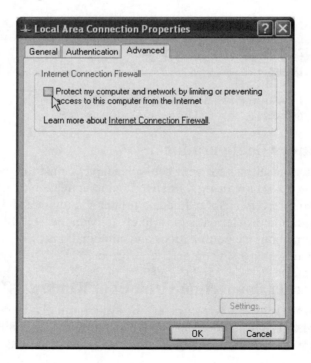

Using a Router to Connect Your Network to the Internet

If you're using a DSL/cable modem for Internet access, you should think about installing a router instead of running Internet Connection Sharing (ICS). A router is a device that ties your Internet connection to your local network. Routers also provide a number of functions that benefit small networks and make network administration easy, the most important being Dynamic Host Configuration Protocol (DHCP) and Network Address Translation (NAT). (See the sidebars on DHCP and NAT.) A computer running ICS also provides DHCP and NAT, but a router provides better protection against Internet-based attacks because none of your computers are seen on the Internet; only the router is exposed.

NOTE   *Network Address Translation (NAT) devices such as routers are often called firewalls; however, they are only basic firewalls and do not offer the extensive protection that the Linksys BEFSX41 Instant Broadband EtherFast Cable/DSL Firewall Router with 4-Port Switch/VPN EndPoint offers. See Chapter 9 for more information on firewalls and the BEFSX41.*

10

DHCP for Assigning IP Addresses

When you use TCP/IP as your network protocol, every computer needs an IP address. You can use DHCP to provide automatic IP address assignments, which is easier than setting up all your computers with their own unique addresses. DHCP is a service that runs on a host device (either the computer hosting the Internet connection device or a router). When they first start, the other nodes of the network (computers and other network devices that require an IP address) find the DHCP server and retrieve an IP address. When the nodes shut down, the address they retrieved is released back to a pool of addresses maintained by the DHCP server and can be reused by the next computer to ask for one.

NAT

When you share an Internet connection, one device is actually connected to the Internet and the other devices are connected only to the local network. Devices that aren't directly connected to the Internet don't need real Internet addresses. Instead, they have special IP addresses (such as 192.168.1.1, which is not recognized on the Internet). These special IP addresses are Network Address Translation addresses.

NAT addresses are in ranges that are designated as *nonroutable* by the rules of IP networking, which means that they can communicate only with other computers on the local network. It's the job of the NAT device (the host computer in an ICS system or a router) to connect to the Internet connection using a real Internet address, and it acts as an intermediary for the other computers. NAT is often used in conjunction with DHCP to make it easy for networks to share a single real Internet address.

Note that there is a difference between DHCP, which allows clients to use dynamic addresses, and NAT, which allows them to use internal, nonroutable addresses. It's possible for a network to have a pool of real, routable IP addresses and to serve them to clients with a DHCP server.

Basic Linksys Routers

The simplest Linksys router, the BEFSR11 EtherFast Cable/DSL Router, pictured in Figure 10-6, has just two ports on the back (not counting the power plug). Two other models, the BEFSR41 and BEFSR81, add 4-port and 8-port switches, respectively. Apart from the additional ports, all three models are essentially identical. (The BEFSR81 adds an advanced feature called Quality of Service (QoS), which is described later in the section "Quality of Service.")

The BEFSR11 is a good solution if you already have a network attached to a hub or a switch and you want to connect the network to the Internet through your DSL/cable modem. If, on the other hand, you haven't yet connected a network through a hub, you should consider the BEFSR41 or BEFSR81 (depending on the number of computers you need to connect), and use the ports in the router to create the network connection. If you need more wired Ethernet ports, you can buy a hub and connect it to the router through the Uplink port.

If you don't want to use wired Ethernet for your network, you still have router options. For instance, if you want to connect a wireless or HomePNA Phoneline network to a broadband Ethernet connection, Linksys makes routers

FIGURE 10-6   The Linksys BEFSR11 is the simplest device for routing a LAN to the Internet

that specifically perform such connections. (See Chapters 5 and 6 to learn about routers that work with other network topologies.)

If you're concerned about the security of your network, Linksys makes a special router with an advanced firewall that prevents many types of attacks against your network (discussed in Chapter 9).

If you need a Virtual Private Network (VPN), Linksys makes routers with integrated VPN features.

10

Router Ports

When looking at the back of your router, all the connections start (or end, depending on your point of view) on the back of your router. Using the Linksys BEFSR41 as an example (see Figure 10-7), I'll go over the ports, moving from left to right.

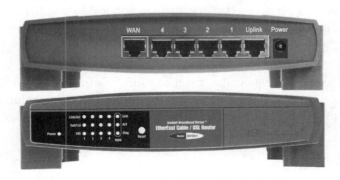

FIGURE 10-7   The Linksys BEFSR41 router has four Ethernet ports

WAN Port

Use the WAN port to connect the router to your DSL/cable modem. WAN means Wide Area Network, which is a term that's usually applied to a network that's spread across multiple locations. While the router doesn't really create a WAN, it does provide a separation point (and a barricade) between two networks: your LAN and the Internet (the Internet is a network too, remember).

LAN Port

You'll find a LAN port on the BEFSR11, but not on the BEFR41 or BEFSR81. Use this port to connect the router to the hub you're using for your network connections. Notice that the router also has Crossover Switch, which controls the wiring of the LAN port. The Crossover Switch sets the mode of the LAN port to either crossover (marked *X*) or straight-through (marked *II*). The choices relate to the way the cable pins meet at the connector. If you are connecting the LAN port directly to a computer, another stand-alone device, or to the Uplink port in a hub, select the crossover mode. For anything else, select straight-through. You can buy special crossover cables that do the same thing as the X mode in this switch, but the switch makes it easier to create a proper connection using normal straight-through cable.

> TIP   *If you're confused about which Crossover Switch selection to use, or what kind of cable you have, there's no need to worry. Just plug it in and try both positions until the connection works.*

Numbered Ports

The BEFR41 and BEFSR81 (see Figure 10-8) have a series of numbered ports: numbered 1 through 4 on the BEFR41; and 1 through 8 on the BEFSR81. These are regular Ethernet ports. You can use them to connect PCs to the network or to connect the router to a hub. (See Chapters 3 and 4 for more on cabling issues.)

Uplink

Use the Uplink port to connect the router to a hub. It's important to know that the Uplink port and Ethernet port 1 on the BEFSR41 are mutually exclusive—you can use only one at a time (if you use the Uplink port, port 1 is disabled).

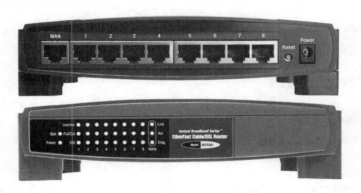

FIGURE 10-8   The BEFSR81 router has eight ports and (QoS)

Reset Button

Like the Reset button on your computer, the Reset button on the router clears data and restarts the device. To use it, hold the button for 2–3 seconds and then release it. Use the button only in case of an emergency—for example, if the links to the router are jammed and communication has frozen. Try following the tips in the troubleshooting section of your router's user guide before you press Reset.

NOTE   *If you hold the Reset button for longer than 5 seconds, it may cause the router to restore to factory defaults. If you do wish to restore the unit to factory defaults, Linksys suggests depressing the button for approximately 30 seconds to get a clean restore.*

It's possible, but unlikely, that the router could lock up to the degree that even the Reset button won't work. In that case, remove the power cable from the router for 3–5 seconds and then reinsert it. There's a good chance that this procedure will retain network connections through the router, but if you leave the unit powered down much longer, you may lose the connections.

NOTE   *On the BEFSR41, the Reset button is on the front of the unit.*

Power

This connector accepts the power adapter, the other end of which is plugged into a wall outlet (or, preferably, a surge protector). To turn off the unit, simply unplug it.

Front Panel LEDs

You'll notice several lights on the front panel of the router. At the far left, on its own, is the Power light, which is on when the router is powered up. To the right are some number of columns, the specific number depending on the router and how many ports it has. Each column has three indicators.

LAN Indicators

The LAN indicators show the status of the connection to the LAN port, as follows:

- The top indicator, Link/Act, is on continuously when there is a successful connection to a device on the LAN port. The LED flashes when data is being sent or received through the port.

- If the Full/Coll LED is on continuously, the LAN connection is *full-duplex*, meaning it is running at full speed both sending and receiving data. A flashing LED indicates that collisions on the connection are occurring, which means that the traffic load is heavy.

- The 100 LED turns orange when the router is connected to the LAN at 100 Mbps.

WAN Indicators

The WAN indicators show the status of the connection to the WAN port, as follows:

- The top WAN indicator, Link, is on continuously during a successful connection to a device, such as a cable or DSL modem, on the WAN port.

- The Act LED flashes when data is sent or received on the WAN port.

- The Diag LED turns on during the router's self-diagnostic stage while starting up. It turns off if the test is successful. If it is on for a long period of time, there is a problem with the unit. You need help. See Appendix C for information on obtaining support from Linksys.

In addition to these indicators, the BEFSR81 has a QoS LED, which flashes when the switch's Quality of Service function is being used. See "Quality of Service" later in this chapter.

Making the Connections

You must physically connect your router to your DSL/cable modem, and to the computers on your network. Depending on your current network topology, making the physical connections can be merely a matter of moving some cable, or you may need to install the cabling from scratch, or you may have to do a little of both.

> **NOTE** *Linksys advises that all nodes on the network be powered off while you make your connections.*

Attaching an Existing Hub/Switch to the Router

If you've already set up a wired Ethernet network before deciding to add a router, you don't have to abandon the hub or switch you're using (see Figure 10-9).

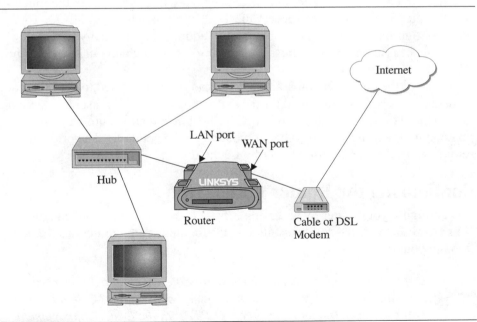

FIGURE 10-9 You can connect an existing hub to the router

To make this connection to the BEFSR11, connect a regular port on the hub to the LAN port on the router. Make sure to switch the Crossover Switch to the "X" position. You can use the Uplink port on your hub to connect to the LAN port on the router, but make sure to switch the Crossover Switch to the "*II*" position.

With the BEFSR41 or BEFSR81, you can connect from any of the regular data ports to the Uplink port on your hub, or from the Uplink port on the BEFSR41 to a regular port on the hub. Port 1 and the Uplink port on the BEFSR41 are mutually exclusive—you can use only one of them at a time.

If you had been connecting a DSL or cable modem through the hub, it should be connected through the WAN port on the router, which might open up a port on your hub.

 If you have an existing network, and you're using any form of Internet connection sharing, you must disable it. The router takes care of sharing the connection.

Configuring the Computers

You need to configure your computers to access the Internet through the router (see Chapter 8 to learn how to access the TCP/IP settings for your NICs). You must configure the computers to obtain an IP address automatically (the router takes care of issuing the IP addresses). Nothing else is enabled—no gateway, no DNS, no WINS, nothing.

If one of the computers on your network had been connected to the DSL/cable modem and its NIC is configured for the ISP settings, that NIC must be reconfigured as a client to obtain an address and other TCP/IP information automatically (matching the settings for the other computers on the network). The original settings from the ISP are used to configure the router.

Configuring the Router Connection

You configure your router by accessing it from one of the connected computers. No special software has to be installed on that computer; the router is accessed through your browser.

NOTE *Different router models may have small differences in features from those described here. For example, some routers may have a Login option for Point-to-Point Tunneling Protocol (PPTP). In the DHCP management section, some may have an option for changing the default lease time. Help is not available in most routers due to ROM restrictions.*

When you open the browser to begin configuration of the router, you may receive an error message. That's because the browser can't get to the home page you configured (because until you finish configuring the router, you don't have access to the Internet). But if your browser home page is set for *About: Blank*, you won't see an error message.

Follow these steps to begin configuring your router:

1. In the browser address bar, enter **http://192.168.1.1/** and press ENTER to open the Connect To dialog (it may take a few seconds for the dialog to appear).

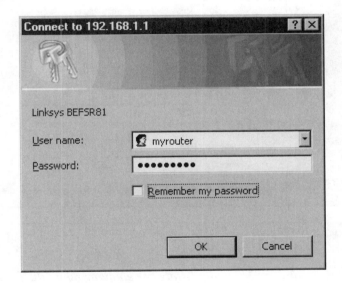

NOTE *This dialog may look slightly different if you're not doing this on a Windows 98 computer.*

TIP *Put the URL for the router on your Favorites list to make it easy to open the window later, in case you want to add or modify features.*

2. Leave the User field blank, and then go to the Password field and enter **admin** (in lowercase). Then click OK.

3. The Linksys Setup window appears, with the Setup tab selected, as seen in Figure 10-10.

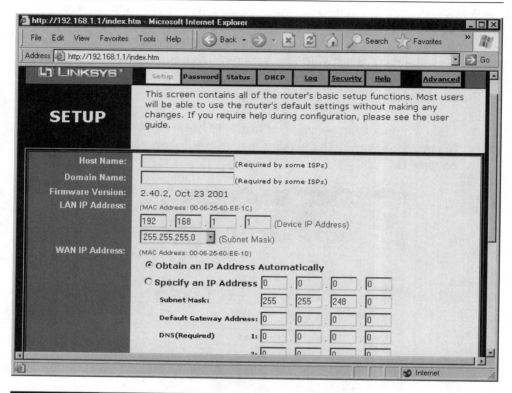

FIGURE 10-10   Configure your Internet connection through the router's Setup tab

> **NOTE**   *The Setup software has multiple tabs for configuring all the features offered by your Linksys router, and the tabs differ depending on the model.*

4. On the Setup tab, you specify the basic options for your Internet connection. You must configure this tab and restart your DSL/cable modem and the computers on the network before you set configuration options on the other tabs in the Setup window.

   ■ **Host Name and Domain Name**   These fields can usually remain blank, but if your ISP requires this information, fill in the data as instructed.

   ■ **Firmware Version**   This is the version number for the router's firmware, as well as the release date for the version. Firmware is programming code that is inserted into the read-only memory of a device. This technology provides a way to enhance the capabilities of hardware devices. When new firmware is available, you can download it from the Linksys Web site, along with instructions on how to insert the new code into the device's memory. (See Appendix C for more about obtaining new firmware from Linksys.)

■ **Device IP Address and Subnet Mask**   The default values for the router's IP address and subnet mask are preset and should not be altered.

■ **WAN Connection Type**   Click the arrow to the right of the text box and select a connection type.

The WAN connection specifications must match the instructions from your ISP. Linksys routers support five connection types, which are discussed next.

Obtain an IP Automatically

This is the default selection, because it's the most common. Your ISP instructs you to use this setting when DHCP services are provided by the ISP. If this is the correct setting for your ISP, you have nothing more to do in the Setup tab.

Click Apply, and then click Continue to save your settings. Close the browser. Power your DSL/cable modem off and on again. Restart all the computers on the network so they can establish the router's settings. You can return to this Setup utility at any time to configure any other features you want to use.

Static IP

Choose this option if the instructions from your ISP require a static IP address. The Setup window changes to display the fields you need for configuration (see Figure 10-11). Use the following guidelines to supply data in the fields:

■ **Specify WAN IP Address**   Enter the IP address for the router as seen from the WAN (Internet).

■ **Subnet Mask**   Enter the subnet mask as seen by the Internet and the ISP.

■ **Default Gateway Address**   Enter the IP address for the gateway.

■ **DNS (Required)**   Enter the IP address of the DNS server your ISP wants you to use. Your ISP provides at least one DNS IP address. Many ISPs provide a secondary DNS IP address. The Setup window also has a field for a third DNS IP address if your ISP provided one (which is unusual).

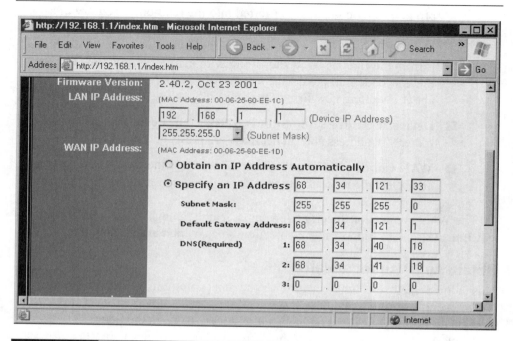

FIGURE 10-11   Use the information from your ISP to configure a static IP address

Click Apply, and then click Continue to save your settings. Close the browser. Power your DSL/cable modem off and on again. Restart all the computers on the network so they can access the router and its settings. You can return to this Setup utility at any time to configure any other features you want to use.

PPPoE

If your DSL provider uses Point-to-Point Protocol over Ethernet, select this option to enable the protocol (see Figure 10-12). Then configure your connection, using the following guidelines:

■ **User Name and Password**   Enter the data provided by your DSL ISP.

■ **Connect on Demand: Max Idle Time**   You can configure the router to disconnect from your DSL ISP after a specified amount of inactivity. Then, whenever you're disconnected as a result of inactivity, the connection is re-established as soon as a user attempts to access the Internet (by opening a browser or an e-mail application). Enter the number of minutes of

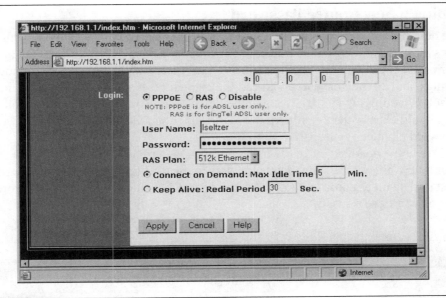

FIGURE 10-12   Enter your connection settings for PPPoE

inactivity that must elapse to cause the router to disconnect from your DSL ISP.

■ **Keep Alive: Redial Period**   Select this option to have the router periodically check the state of your Internet connection and reconnect to your ISP if the connection has been broken. Enter an amount of time that must elapse to cause the router to reconnect.

Click Apply, and then click Continue to save your settings. Close the browser. Power your DSL modem off and on again. Restart all the computers on the network so they can establish the router's settings. You can return to this Setup utility at any time to configure any other features you want to use.

RAS

RAS is used only in Singapore. Contact Singtel for information on the appropriate settings. After you've adjusted the settings, click Apply, and then click Continue to save your settings. Close the browser. Power your DSL/cable modem off and on again. Restart all the computers on the network so they can establish the router's settings. You can return to this Setup utility at any time to configure any other features you want to use.

Setting a New Router Password

The default router password is the same for all Linksys routers, so anyone who owns a Linksys router could gain entry to your router's configuration. In fact, any user on the local network could connect to the router and change the configuration settings, and all they have to do is read the manual or this book to know that the default IP address is 192.168.1.1 and the default password is admin. As a result, you should change the default password by using the fields available in the Password tab (see Figure 10-13).

Delete the dots that currently appear in the Router Password text box and enter a new password. Then, delete the dots in the next text box and enter the new password again to confirm it. You can use up to 63 characters for your password, but you can't use a space.

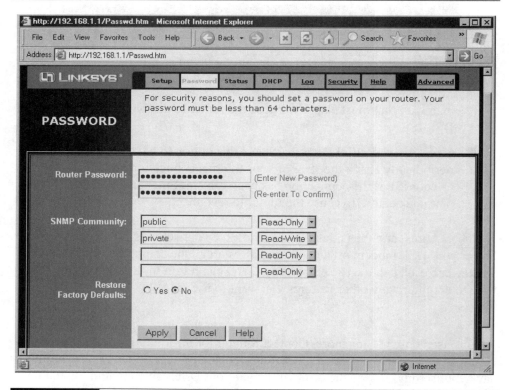

FIGURE 10-13   Change the default password so other users can't change the configuration

For added password security, don't enable the option to save the password and automatically log in when you open the router's configuration feature.

SNMP Community

Simple Network Management Protocol (SNMP) is a network protocol popular in large corporate networks for centralized monitoring and control of devices on the network. Such management requires separate management software. Linksys routers are compatible with all HP Openview-compliant software.

The SNMP Community section on the Password tab allows you to define up to four community names, which are used to manage SNMP access. Each community name can have either read-only or read-write access to the management information in the router. Each community name must be less than 31 characters.

SNMP makes sense only on very large networks with hundreds of users, and therefore it's beyond the scope of this book.

Restoring the Router to Factory Defaults

After setting all the configuration options, restoring the default settings is definitely a last-ditch solution. It's rare that an occasion would arise for such a drastic move, and don't even think about it unless you've exhausted all troubleshooting suggestions from Linksys technical support and they've told you that this is the only thing left to try.

Checking the Current Status of the Router

The Status tab displays the current status of the router and its configuration (see Figure 10-14). Most of the entries are self-explanatory, but the Login status may not be—it refers to whether or not Login is enabled for PPPoE or RAS connection types. If you're not using one of those connection methods, the Login status is marked Disabled. You cannot make changes to the values displayed on this page; it's only reporting your setup configuration. When you make changes to the Setup tab, those changes are reflected in the Status tab.

At the bottom of the Status page are three buttons related to DHCP management. The first two come into play if your router is a DHCP client on your ISP's network—in other words, if your router obtains an IP address automatically from the ISP's network. Clicking DHCP Release releases that address back to the ISP network. If you click this button, all the WAN settings on the Status page revert to zeros. Click DHCP Renew to tell the router to request a new address.

The third button, DHCP Clients Table, is the same as the button of the same name on the DHCP page (see the next section "Managing DHCP").

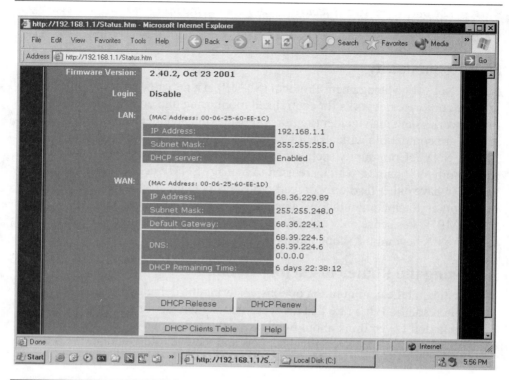

FIGURE 10-14   The Status tab displays configuration information

Managing DHCP

When you install a Linksys router, the router acts as the DHCP server. DHCP servers don't assign IP addresses permanently; they're leased to computers when the computers start up and request an IP address. When the lease expires, a new lease is assigned (computers don't have to reboot to request a new lease, as it's an automatic process). The settings for providing DHCP services are displayed on the DHCP tab (see Figure 10-15).

You can enable or disable the server by selecting the appropriate radio button. The Starting IP Address and Number Of DHCP Users fields tell you the range of addresses that will be assigned by the server. For example, if the starting address is 192.168.1.100 and the number of users is 50, which really means up to 50, DHCP

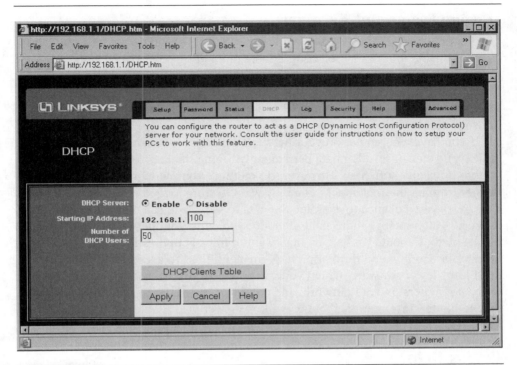

FIGURE 10-15   Configuration settings for your router-based DHCP server are displayed on the DHCP tab

addresses will be in the range 192.168.1.100 through 192.168.1.149. To see the current DHCP client data, click the DHCP Clients Table button.

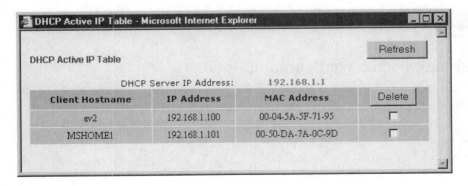

Logging Events and Warnings

Use the Log tab to enable logging and to view logs. By default, logging is disabled. You can enable logging by selecting Enable on the Log page. You can view the information being collected by opening the logs. The Incoming Access Log button displays information about incoming Internet Traffic, and the Outgoing Access Log button displays the URLs and IP addresses of Internet sites that users on the network accessed.

If you have a computer on your network with a fixed IP address (admittedly unlikely), you can save log data permanently. Using the logs to keep an eye on the system is usually sufficient. However, if you think your network is in some serious danger from an Internet attack, you may want to store logged information in files. This gives you a chance to examine the data to see if you can discern any patterns, especially attempts from the same IP address to enter your network. Even if you're not suspicious about attacks, you may want to track activities for some period of time by saving logged information in permanent files. To accomplish this, you need LogViewer software, which you can download from Linksys, install on one of the computers on your network, and configure the router to send the log data to that computer. Information about using LogViewer is available on the Linksys Web site.

Getting Help

Use the Help tab to travel to specific support pages on the Linksys Web site (see Figure 10-16). In addition to finding answers to questions, you can download a copy of the user guide, and you can even check to see whether there's a new firmware upgrade available for your router.

NOTE   *Appendix C has detailed information about the support options offered by Linksys.*

Advanced Setup Configuration Options

Clicking the Advanced tab opens a whole new set of tabs you can use to tweak your router's settings. (To return to the original window, and the original tabs, click the Setup tab.) Most of the options available in these tabs are unnecessary for home and small business networks, but you can read an overview of the functions in Chapter 9.

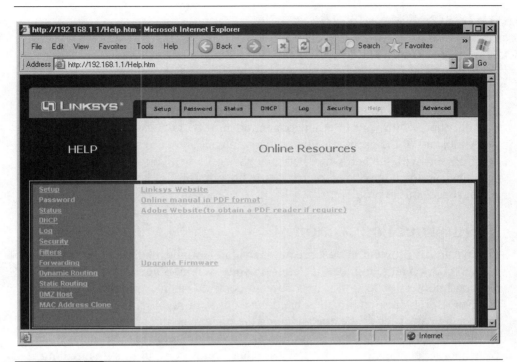

FIGURE 10-16   Click the appropriate link to get to the Linksys support page you need

Quality of Service

Quality of Service (QoS) is available only in the BEFSR81. QoS is a way to prioritize traffic to ports that require a certain level (or quality) of service. Streaming video is an example of traffic that should travel at a certain minimum rate. To turn QoS on, select the Enable radio button on the QoS tab.

There are two types of QoS functions: application-based and port-based (meaning the LAN port). With application-based QoS, you can specify that traffic utilizing a particular TCP port is to receive high or low priority, or no special treatment—that is, to disable QoS for that port. Five predefined TCP port applications appear in this screen: FTP, HTTP, Telnet, SMTP, and POP3. You can define three others and their prioritization by specifying their TCP ports.

You can also specify QoS based on the LAN port by specifying High Priority, Low Priority, or Disable for the appropriate port.

10

Troubleshooting and Tweaking Internet Connections

Networking is complicated. Hundreds of thick, complicated books have been written about networking, which is not to say that you need to know all that stuff. But things can go wrong, and this section describes some of the problems you may encounter with your Internet connection and what you can do about them.

Almost all of the problems you're likely to encounter are software problems, not problems with the hardware. Patience pays off when you attempt to solve these problems, and you may have to consider many possibilities before discovering the actual source of the problem.

No Internet Connection

This particular problem has a large number of potential explanations, so you may want to check a large number of things on your system. Sometimes, a faulty or missing Internet connection is beyond your control—such as problems with your ISP. Some problems, on the other hand, turn out to be stupid things you would never anticipate, such as the dog knocking the router's power outlet out of the wall.

Just because you can't get to your home page, don't jump to the conclusion that your Internet connection is down. Try another site. If you can't get to anything from your browser, check to see if your e-mail is also down. If you can't get to anything on the Internet, read on to learn about some other things to try.

If you're having problems connecting, try connecting from another computer on the local network. If only one computer has trouble connecting to the Internet, the problem is likely in that computer and not network-wide.

Check the Equipment Connections

Make sure that all the equipment involved in the Internet connection, from the computer to the modem to any routers you have installed, and any hubs or switches in the middle, are plugged into power outlets and turned on.

Similarly, check to see that all data cable connections are connected properly. Whether at a router, hub, or NIC, there's almost certainly a light that shines green when a connection is made. If you don't see lights where you expect them, manually check the plug.

Check the Internet Connection Device

Is your DSL/cable/telephone modem actually connected? Check the lights on this device carefully, as probably one or more lights indicate a connection to the Internet.

If there is no connection, try resetting the device. If it is a DSL device or cable modem, it should try to reconnect itself to the Internet. If you still get a nonconnection, the problem is at the ISP end. You may want to wait a while to give the ISP a chance to clear it up, or call them on the phone (if your phones are working).

If your broadband connection appears to be functional, but your computer connections still don't work, and this device is connected through a hub or router, you should try reconnecting it directly to a single PC. You may have to reconfigure that PC temporarily for the ISP settings—for example, if you have a static IP address from your ISP and have been using a router to provide NAT and DHCP, you will have to reconfigure the PC to use the static address.

Check TCP/IP Settings

If TCP/IP were not installed on the computer, you wouldn't ever have been able to get on the Internet. Nevertheless, it's possible that something happened that affected the TCP/IP configuration. If you are running Windows 95, 98, or Me, choose Start | Settings | Control Panel, and then double-click the Network applet to open it. The list of protocols and devices should contain both your network adapter and TCP/IP bindings to them. Scroll through the list to confirm this. Select TCP/IP and click Properties to see the TCP/IP properties. Confirm that the settings are correct.

In Windows XP, choose Start | Control Panel. Double-click the Network Connections applet to open it. You should see an entry for each network adapter in the system, and Windows XP is smart enough to tell you whether the connection is enabled or disabled. Right-click the connection object and select Status. If an obvious error message like "Network cable unplugged" appears—well, do something about it. Plug in the cable. If the connection is disabled, right-click its listing and select Enable. If you still don't have a functioning connection at this point, right click the connection again and select Repair. If this fails, check the TCP/IP properties to make sure they're set properly.

Check Network Communications

If you can communicate between two computers on the local network but not connect to the Internet, you've probably proved that the problem exists in the Internet connection hardware or the Internet connection itself.

10

To check whether you can communicate between two computers, you'll need to know either the computer name or IP address of one of them. To determine the IP address, choose Start | Run, and type **cmd**. At the command prompt, type **ipconfig**. You should see an IP address and some other information for each network adapter in the system. Write down the IP address for the local network adapter.

From another computer on the network, open a command prompt and type **ping x.x.x.x,** where x.x.x.x is the IP address of the computer on which you ran **ipconfig**. (You use the ping command to verify communications between two systems.)

If you get a series of error messages, such as "Request timed out" from the ping command, the computer on which ping is running cannot see the other computer. This could mean anything from a disconnected cable to a software crash. But you know that the problem is not necessarily on the Internet connection.

Check the Gateway

TCP/IP networking requires a computer or other device to function as a gateway, which is the device that sits between your network and the Internet. If you are using a router, it's probably acting as the gateway. Otherwise, the gateway is probably your ISP.

To determine your gateway, choose Start | Run and type **cmd**. At the command prompt, type **ipconfig**. The system should display the address of the gateway. Type **ping x.x.x.x** (where x.x.x.x is the IP address of the gateway system specified by ipconfig). If you get a series of error messages, such as "Request timed out," that means that your computer cannot communicate with the gateway system. This is what computer people call a "bad thing."

If your gateway is a router at your location, you should reset the router by pressing the Reset button and holding it for several seconds. The router will restart and attempt to reconnect to the local network and Internet. If it still fails, you need to contact Linksys technical support (see Appendix C). If your gateway is at your ISP's site, you need to contact your ISP.

Disable Windows XP Internet Connection Firewall

On Windows XP, if the Internet Connection Firewall (ICF) is enabled, you should disable it because it interferes with network communications. To disable ICF, follow these steps:

1. Choose Start | Control Panel | Network And Internet Connections.

2. Click Network Connections.

3. Right-click the listing for your Local Area Connection and choose Properties from the shortcut menu.

4. Select the Advanced tab.

5. Deselect the option to use ICF, and then click OK.

Invalid DHCP Lease

You may see a message about an invalid DHCP lease in Internet Explorer when you're trying to connect to a Web page. It's likely that your Internet access device tries to retrieve an Internet address automatically from the ISP, and sometimes the ISP's DHCP server is slow to respond to your system's request for an IP address. Before the ISP can supply an address, Windows times out (gets tired of waiting) and assigns the network adapter an APIPA number (see the sidebar "APIPA Addresses"). To fix the problem, follow these steps:

1. Choose Start | Run, type **cmd**, and then press ENTER.

2. Type **ipconfig** and press ENTER. The system displays the IP address assigned to each network adapter on this computer. The network adapter connected to the Internet should have an address of 169.254.*x.x*, where each *x* is between 0 and 255.

3. Type **ipconfig /release** to set the address to 0.0.0.0.

4. Type **ipconfig /renew** to request a new address for the adapter.

(For more information on the ipconfig command, see Appendix B.)

10

APIPA Addresses

Sometimes a network PC or some other network device, such as a print server, won't connect to the network. You determine, through the winipcfg program in Windows 98 or the ipconfig program in Windows XP, that the device has an IP address of 169.254.*x.x* (where each *x* value is between 0 and 255—the specific number is unimportant). These addresses are called APIPA addresses (Automatic Private IP Addressing), and their presence indicates that the device is set to obtain an IP address automatically from a DHCP server, but that no DHCP server could be found.

You can network multiple computers that have addresses in this range, but that's not the important point. These addresses are a signal that your DHCP server is unavailable. If you're running Windows ICS to share your Internet connection, the system running ICS is probably your DHCP server and there may be a problem with it. If you are using a router that is supplying addresses, check the router by using a Web browser from some other computer to run the administration program for it. You may need to reset the router or reboot the computer running the DHCP server.

Using Remote Control over the Network

One of my favorite power-user tips for networking is to use remote control. The key to this feature is that even though all your computers share an Internet connection and other resources, sometimes a specific computer is linked to certain software or tasks. The most common example is e-mail software, which usually is specific to the computer and the user who generally accesses that computer. Remote control lets you run programs on one computer from another computer on the network.

Let's take my case as a remote control example. I use one primary desktop computer for e-mail. As with most non-AOL e-mail users, my mailbox is stored on that computer, and if I run mail on another computer on my network I won't have access to my mail folders and stored messages.

So I use remote control. When I'm on my notebook computer on my deck, I open a remote session to my desktop computer (located upstairs) that has my mailbox, and then run my e-mail software.

Remote Control vs. Remote Access

The distinction between remote control and other types of remote network access can be a tricky one. All network usage involves some sort of remote access of files, printers, or something else attached to another computer somewhere. Remote control is different: You are sharing the entire computer. You are sitting at and using computer A, but in fact you are running programs on computer B.

With remote control, you run special programs on both computers, the one on which you want the programs to run (let's call it the *host*) and the one from which you want to control the host computer (the *guest*).

The remote control program on the guest lets you view and interact with programs on the host. You see the desktop, the Start menu, and so on for the host as you sit at the guest computer. When you press a key or move your mouse on the guest, that information is sent over the network connection to the host program, which executes the mouse movements or keystrokes. Any changes in the screen on the host are sent across the network to the guest, which displays them.

If you have an AOL dial-up account, you can use remote control to access the computer that has a modem and AOL installed on it. This doesn't allow multiple users to access the Internet simultaneously, but a single AOL account doesn't allow that anyway.

Remote Control Software Options

If you have Windows XP Pro (which is unlikely for small home and business networks, which usually run Windows XP Home Edition), you have built-in remote control software in the form of the Remote Desktop feature. With the Windows XP Remote Desktop feature, you can control the Windows XP Pro computer from any other Windows computer on the network. Only the host side of Remote Desktop requires Windows XP Pro. Any Windows system since Windows 95 can run the Remote Desktop Connection program, which comes on the Windows XP CD-ROM, or it can be downloaded from *http://www.microsoft.com/windowsxp/pro/downloads/rdclientdl.asp*.

If you're not using Windows XP Pro, numerous remote control programs are available from software companies. Remote control software has been around since the early 1980s and is very mature. You can find a rather good (and free) remote control program called Virtual Network Computing, or VNC, at *http://www.uk.research.att.com/vnc/*. It was written by AT&T Research in the United Kingdom and supports a wide variety of computers and operating systems. It's not quite as fancy as most of the commercial programs, but it is well regarded. So even if you just have two Windows 98 computers, you can control either from the other over your network using VNC.

Remote Control Performance Problems

Because all changes on the screen under remote control have to pass across the network (or over the Internet, if you're accessing the host computer from a remote location), applications that make a lot of changes in the screen in a short period of time perform badly when working in remote control.

The best examples of this are computer games, which also suffer from the fact that remote control software will often set the display on the remote system at a lower resolution and color depth than if you were working locally. Games aren't the only problem, though. Flash-based animations can be sluggish through remote control, even over a fast network connection.

Normal applications such as e-mail, word processing, and so on, work perfectly well. The slower the connection, the more the performance level is affected, but conventional applications can be tolerable for a while even over a dial-up connection. Across your home network, the performance level is just fine.

10

Tricks and Tips for Network Printing

When you go through the installation process for a printer (installing the drivers), an icon for that printer is placed in the computer's Printers folder (or Printers And Faxes Folder if you're using Windows XP). That icon represents a virtual printer, which means it's a collection of settings and configuration options that are used by the operating system when it sends a print job to the physical printer. Users actually send a print job to the virtual printer, and the operating system passes the job to the physical printer.

When users select the Print command in their software applications, they can set print options that are supported by the printer and the operating system. These options could include selections such as the tray from which to fetch the paper (if the printer has multiple trays), choosing between color or monochrome (if the printer is a color printer), and even whether to print the job to a file instead of to paper.

Once you understand the fact that you're printing to a virtual printer, and the operating system is the only user who can communicate with the physical printer, you can take advantage of this scenario.

Creating Preconfigured Printers

Because users print to a virtual printer, not the physical printer, you can create multiple virtual printers for the same physical printer. This makes it easier for all the users on the network to use specific features built into a physical printer.

If you have a printer with multiple trays (perhaps you have checks or letterhead in one tray and plain paper in the other tray), users must select the appropriate tray every time they use the Print command. Creating a separate virtual printer for each tray means you can make sure users don't accidentally use the wrong tray (isn't it annoying when you print a letter on checks?).

If you have a color printer, you can encourage users to print in monochrome unless they really need color for the print job; or at least you can make it easier for them to switch to monochrome. This means you won't have to replace the color cartridge as frequently, which means a substantial savings.

To create a separate virtual printer for each feature, you must install the same printer twice. The printer is probably already installed on your printer, so use the Add Printer Wizard to install another copy. Just go through all the steps, selecting the same printer, and the same port (probably LPT1). Windows doesn't complain if you add multiple printers to the same port. The wizard asks if you want to use the same driver you already installed (when you installed the first instance of the printer), and of course you do. The Windows XP If Wizard asks if you want to share this printer—click No, because it's easier to keep track if you change the configuration options before you create a sharename for the printer. (Don't bother sending a test document to the printer.) The wizard adds the printer to your system with a parenthetical number after the printer model name: Windows XP adds (Copy 1); Windows 98SE adds (Copy 2).

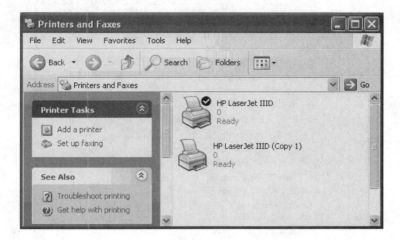

Right-click one copy of the printer and choose Properties from the shortcut menu. Find the Properties page that holds the configuration settings for the printer, which differs depending on the printer—there may be a Settings tab, or a Setup button. Configure the printer to reflect a single set of default options (see Figure 10-17).

Rename the printer icon to reflect its settings. Then share the printer and use a sharename that also reflects the settings (in fact, you can probably use the printer icon name as the sharename). For example, when you configure a two-tray printer that has letterhead in one tray and plain paper in the other tray, eliminate the letterhead tray in a printer named Plainpaper, and eliminate the plain paper tray in the printer named Letterhead.

The configuration options you select vary according to the printer's resources and features. In fact, you can create more than two copies of the same printer if you have more options than two virtual printers can handle. For example, you may want to preconfigure a printer for each of the following features:

- Plain paper, printing in Portrait mode

- Plain paper, printing in Landscape mode

- Letterhead

- Plain Paper, Landscape, 1200 dpi printing

- Plain Paper, Landscape, 600 dpi printing

- Envelope (even if it requires manually feeding the envelope)

10

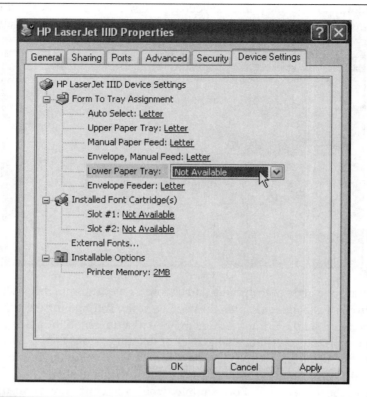

FIGURE 10-17 You can make a tray unavailable so that this virtual printer has only one type of paper

For color printers, you may want to create multiple printers, each with preconfigured settings for any of the choices the printer offers. For example, Figure 10-18 shows a variety of permutations and combinations for printing to a color printer. You can create enough virtual printers to handle the commonly used settings on your network.

Remember that in addition to renaming the printer to reflect its settings, you can use the Comment field on the General tab of the printer's Properties dialog to add information about the printer's settings. The text you add to the Comment field is visible to users on the network when they view the printer's listing in Network Neighborhood or My Network Places.

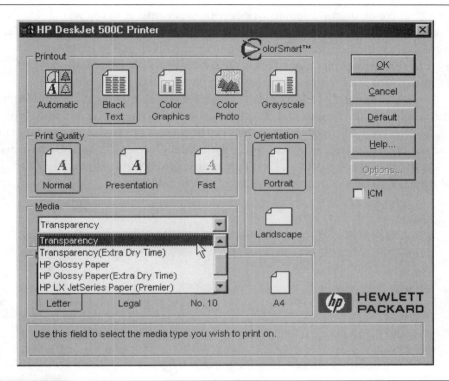

FIGURE 10-18   Preselect a combination of color choice, print quality option, and paper type to create each virtual printer

Creating a Printer for Text Files

Sometimes it's useful to print a document to a file instead of to a printer. For instance, you may have created a document at work (such as a report from a database or an accounting software application) that you want to take home and load in your word processor. If you use the Print command from the software window, and select the option to print to a file instead of to the printer, the resulting printer file can be sent only to the same printer model, which may not be the printer you have at home. That's because the printer driver controls the print file, which is filled with special codes that can be interpreted correctly by that printer only.

You can create a print file that works with every printer in the world. The file has no special codes, so anybody can print it to any printer. You can also load the file into any word processor, or into Notepad or Wordpad, and print it. Additionally, if you create a printer that's preconfigured to print to a file, you don't have to remember to choose the Print To File option on the Print dialog box.

To create a printer that automatically creates text disk files, start the Add Printer Wizard. Select Local Printer and deselect the option to have Plug and Play look for the printer (it wouldn't find it, since the printer doesn't physically exist). Select the manufacturer named Generic, and select the model Generic/Text only. Choose FILE as the port for this printer. Don't share this printer; instead, install it as a local printer (on LPT1) on every computer on the network.

Chapter 11

Networking Portable Computers

In one sense, networking portable computers is exactly the same as networking desktops. Windows fully supports networking on portable computers. You can set up a portable computer to support multiple network adapters and multiple networks, so you can, for example, move your notebook from the wired Ethernet network at the office to the wireless or home phoneline network at home.

Many modern notebooks have wired Ethernet and even wireless support built right in, but if yours doesn't, you can buy a PC Card that adds such support. You may also want to consider using USB network adapters, which can work in many desktops and notebooks.

Choosing and Installing a Network Adapter for a Notebook

Installing network adapters in portable computers is much like installing them in desktop systems. The hardware part is easy—for the most part, you will be using PC Cards, which you can just plug into and pull out of the notebook with ease. The software parts of the installation and configuration are identical to what you would find with a desktop PC.

Linksys Wired Ethernet PC Cards

Wired Ethernet is still the cheapest, fastest networking you can get, and it's the most common system used in business environments. Linksys makes a large number of wired Ethernet PC Cards for users with a variety of specific needs. The installation and configuration experience is largely the same for the Ethernet parts of all of them, so I won't describe them all in detail. See Appendix C for more information and contact information on Linksys products.

I will describe a representative product, the PCM100 EtherFast 10/100 Integrated PC Card. This card supports both 10 Mbps and 100 Mbps Ethernet and integrates the RJ-45 Ethernet outlet into the card (some other cards attach the outlet via a separate connector).

Installing the PCM100

Before you insert your PCM100 card into the PC Card slot in your portable computer, plug the Ethernet cable into the outlet on the card. Then insert the card into an available PC Card slot with the label facing up.

Windows XP   If you're running Windows 2000 or Windows XP, you may well be done at this point. With no device drivers to install, these versions of Windows support this card right out of the box. If you have functioning sound support, you should hear a faint bell noise; then your card is installed and software support loaded. If your network supports Dynamic Host Configuration Protocol (DHCP) for automatic TCP/IP addressing, you will also have an address, and you may be ready to go.

Your network may not support DHCP, or other Windows-related settings may need to be configured before you can access shared files on other computers or perform other tasks. Instructions for these functions are found in Chapter 8.

Windows 98SE   On Windows 98SE systems, you will need to load device drivers for the PCM100. After you insert the card or turn on the computer after inserting the card with the computer turned off, Windows detects the new card's presence and starts the Add New Hardware Wizard. Follow these steps:

11

1. A floppy disc should have been included with the card in the box. Insert the disk in the appropriate drive.

2. The opening screen of the wizard displays the card's name. Click Next to continue.

3. The next screen asks you whether it should search for the best device driver or let you choose one from a list. Select the first option (Search For The Best Driver For Your Device) and click Next.

4. The next screen asks you where Windows should search for the driver. Check the Specify A Location box and type **a:\win98** (*a:* is appropriate for a floppy disk; if your driver is on a different drive, substitute the appropriate drive letter). Click the Next button.

5. Windows looks for and finds the appropriate driver and tells you it has done so. Click Next to continue.

6. At this point, Windows actually copies the files from the disk to the computer. It's possible that Windows will ask you for your original Windows disc, so have it handy. If you do not, click OK, and when Windows can't locate the driver, try c:\windows\options\cabs. If that does not work, you

can also try respecifying the drivers on a:\win98 (sometimes Windows gets confused!).

7. Finally, the Add New Hardware Wizard tells you that it has finished installing the software for the new device. Click Finish to exit the wizard.

At this point, if your network supports DHCP for automatic TCP/IP addressing, you will also have an address and you may be ready to go. Your network may not support DHCP, or other Windows-related settings may need to be configured for you to access shared files on other computers or perform other tasks. Instructions for these functions are found in Chapter 8.

You may also want to check the Linksys Web site for updates to the device drivers and other software you've installed. See Appendix C for more information on how to contact Linksys. To configure Windows networking, see Chapter 8.

USB as a Wired Alternative for Portables

As I've already said, Linksys makes numerous wired Ethernet adapters for portable computers. All modern notebook computers have at least one USB port, so you should consider a USB-based network adapter as well. For example, the Linksys USB100M EtherFast 10/100 Compact USB Network Adapter and USB100TX EtherFast 10/100 USB Network Adapter are both reasonable solutions for a notebook user. See Appendix C for more on these products.

The Linksys WPC11 Wireless PC Card

The WPC11 Instant Wireless Network Adapter, Version 3.0, is your bread-and-butter wireless PC Card for notebook computers. (Wireless networking is described generally in Chapter 5.) Once you're ready, please try to remember that the installation procedures for Windows XP are different from those for all previous versions of Windows, so please read carefully.

> **NOTE** *Your portable computer will need a CD-ROM drive. If it doesn't have one, you'll need some way to get the files from the WPC11 CD-ROM onto some drive accessible to the notebook for the plug-and-play installation routine. If your laptop has an onboard Ethernet adapter, you can easily download the drivers from Linksys' Web site,* http://www.linksys.com/download.

Installing Under Windows XP

Like any PC Card, the WPC11 is a breeze to install. Plug it into the socket with the label side facing up. See Chapter 2 for more on PC Cards in general.

When the card is plugged in, or if you turn on the system after plugging it in while the system was off, the Windows Plug and Play feature will discover the wireless Network Interface Card (NIC). You will have to install the driver software for your wireless NIC. Put the CD-ROM that accompanies the WPC11 into the CD drive.

Windows XP automatically detects the new PC Card network adapter. First, a message appears above the notification area of the taskbar, telling you that Windows has found new hardware. At this point, Windows XP launches the Found New Hardware Wizard so you can perform a driver installation. Follow these steps:

1. Select the option Install The Software Automatically. Click Next.

2. If the wizard displays a window telling you that the driver is not tested for Windows, click Continue Anyway (don't worry, the driver is exactly what you need for Windows XP).

3. Click Finish in the next wizard window.

Windows XP may display a message above the notification area of the taskbar that a new network device is available, and that you should click the notice to run the Network Setup Wizard. See Chapter 8 for more on the Network Setup Wizard.

Installing Under Windows 98

With versions of Windows prior to Windows XP, you want to go about things differently. Put the CD-ROM that accompanies the WPC11 into the CD drive.

NOTE *You need to install the Linksys WPC11 software before you install the card itself. Do not install the PC Card until instructed to do so.*

After you insert the CD-ROM in the drive, Windows AutoPlay feature should load the Setup Wizard. If it does not, click Start, select Run, type **d:\setup.exe**, and press ENTER. Then, follow these steps:

1. Click the Install tab to begin the Setup Wizard.

2. Click Next at the welcome screen for the Install Shield Wizard.

3. Click Yes to accept the license agreement.

4. If you wish to choose a different location for the wireless software than the one indicated on the next screen, click Browse and select it. Click Next when you are finished.

5. In the next screen, the program asks you to choose between Infrastructure Mode and Ad-Hoc Mode. If you are using this card with an access point,

11

choose Infrastructure Mode. If you are setting up a peer-to-peer network, choose Ad-Hoc. Click Next when you are done.

6. If you chose Ad-Hoc Mode in the previous step, you will now be asked to select a channel for the wireless network. Much as cordless phones can use many channels within the same frequency, wireless networks can be switched between channels. Select one and make sure that all your other wireless adapters use the same channel.

7. The program will now ask you to enter the SSID of the network to which this card should connect. The default value, linksys, is also the default value for other Linksys cards and access points. Make sure to use the same value on all your equipment, and it's a good idea to change it from the default once you have your network set up. Click Next to continue.

8. Prior to copying the files to the hard disk, the wizard will restate your settings for you. Click Next if they are correct.

9. The wizard copies the files from the CD to the computer. Then you may see a screen indicating that the software does not have a digital signature, and that there is no guarantee that it will work with Windows. Don't worry, it will work. Click Yes to indicate that you want to continue.

10. At the end of the wizard, you are asked to reboot the computer. You don't have to do so at this point, but you must do so before continuing the setup of your wireless network.

After you have rebooted the computer, it's time to insert the card. Plug it into the socket with the label side facing up. See Chapter 2 for more on PC Cards in general. You may see some screens appear, but you should not need to provide any more input. The card installation should be finished.

You may want to check the Linksys Web site for updates to the device drivers and other software you've installed. See Appendix C for more information on how to contact Linksys. To configure Windows networking, see Chapter 8.

Configuring the WPC11

For versions of Windows prior to Windows XP, the WPC11 uses the Linksys Instant Wireless Configuration Utility that you installed, along with the device driver software, prior to installing the card itself. For Windows XP, you will use Windows' integrated configuration support for Wi-Fi networking.

Both these configuration utilities are described in detail in Chapter 5.

Other Wireless Alternatives for Portables

You may also want to consider the WPC54A Instant Wireless PC Card, which supports the 802.11a standard instead of the much more popular 802.11b standard of the WPC11. The WPC54A, covered in detail in Chapter 5, operates at much higher speeds than 802.11b equipment but is more expensive and has much less peripheral hardware support. For example, where Linksys makes several routers with integrated access points for 802.11b, the company makes one wireless access point for 802.11a. Just something to keep in mind.

Likewise, all modern notebook computers have at least one USB port, so a USB network adapter is also an alternative to consider. For example, the WUSB11 Instant Wireless USB Network Adapter, Version 2.6, supports 802.11b and, being a USB device, can be easily moved to a desktop computer as well. The WUSB11 is also covered in detail in Chapter 5.

Linksys Home Phone Networking PC Cards

One of the simplest methods of home networking is to use your home telephone lines. This type of network doesn't interfere with voice or fax communications, and you already have all the cables going through the walls. Home phone networking is described more generally in Chapter 6.

I'll describe two phoneline networking PC Cards here: the PCM200HA HomeLink Phoneline 10M Integrated PC Card and the PCM100H1 HomeLink Phoneline + 10/100 Network PC Card.

The PCM200HA has two phoneline ports integrated onto the card so that you can connect to the network and to a phone or, alternatively, so that you can connect between other computers on the network.

The PCM100H1 has no ports integrated, but it uses a separate attachment, called a coupler, that plugs into a small outlet on the card. This coupler has the same two phone plugs as the PCM200HA, but it also has a single 10/100 wired

Ethernet connector. You cannot use both wired Ethernet and phoneline networking at the same time. Shown here is the card without the coupler:

The PCM100H1 can be a great solution for you if you use wired Ethernet at the office and PhoneLine networking at home.

Installing the PCM200HA

Insert the PCM200HA card into an available PC Card slot with the side with the red HomeLink logo facing up. Attach the appropriate phone cable or cables to the plugs in the card. Even though one is labeled Phone and the other HomeLink, they're equivalent. It doesn't matter which plug you choose for what.

Windows XP   After you plug it into the PC Card socket, Windows XP automatically detects the new PC Card network adapter. First, a message appears above the notification area of the taskbar telling you that Windows has found new hardware. At this point, Windows XP launches the Found New Hardware Wizard so you can perform a driver installation. Follow these steps:

1. Insert the CD-ROM that came with the card into your CD-ROM drive.

2. Select the option Install The Software Automatically. Click Next.

3. If the wizard displays a window telling you that the driver is not tested for Windows, click Continue Anyway (don't worry, the driver is exactly what you need for Windows XP).

4. Click Finish in the next wizard window.

5. Windows XP may display a message above the notification area of the taskbar that a new network device is available and that you should click the notice to run the Network Setup Wizard. See Chapter 8 for more on the Network Setup Wizard.

Windows 98SE   On Windows 98SE, you will need to load device drivers for the PCM200HA. After you insert the card or turn on the computer after inserting the card with the computer turned off, Windows detects the new card's presence and starts the Add New Hardware Wizard. Follow these steps:

1. Insert the CD-ROM that came with the card into your CD-ROM drive.

2. The opening screen of the wizard displays the card's name. Click Next to continue.

3. The next screen asks you whether it should search for the best device driver or let you pick one from a list. Select the first option (Search For The Best Driver For Your Device) and click Next.

4. The next screen asks you where Windows should search for the driver. Check the box labeled CD-ROM and click the Next button.

5. Windows looks for and finds the appropriate driver and tells you it has done so. Click Next to continue.

6. At this point, Windows actually copies the files from the disk to the computer. It's possible at this point that Windows will ask you for your original Windows disc, so have it handy. If you do not, click OK, and when Windows can't locate the driver, try c:\windows\options\cabs. If that does not work, you can also try respecifying the drivers on a:\win98 (sometimes Windows gets confused!).

7. Finally, the Add New Hardware Wizard tells you that it has finished installing the software for the new device. Click Finish to exit the wizard.

At this point, if your network supports DHCP for automatic TCP/IP addressing, you will also have an address and you may be ready to go. Your network may not support DHCP, or other Windows-related settings may need to be configured, for example, for you to access shared files on other computers. Instructions for these functions can be found in Chapter 8.

You may also want to check the Linksys Web site for updates to the device drivers and other software you've installed. See Appendix C for more information on how to contact Linksys. To configure Windows networking, see Chapter 8.

Installing the PCM100H1

Insert the PCM100H1 card into an available PC Card slot with the side with the green arrow facing up. Be careful when plugging the coupler into the card, as you can break the part if you force it in the wrong way. The plug is "keyed" so that it can plug in only one way with the "Press Here to release" label facing up. Attach the appropriate cable or cables to the coupler.

Windows XP The PCM100H1 does not ship with Windows XP drivers. You will have to go to the Linksys support Web site to download current drivers, copy them to the portable computer on which you will be installing the card, and then begin the driver installation process.

On a computer with Internet access, use your Web browser to surf to *http://www.linksys.com/download*. Follow these steps:

1. Click the large list box and scroll through it to find PCM100H1 – HomeLink Phoneline + 10/100 Network PC Card.

2. In the smaller list box below it, select Windows XP.

3. Click the Downloads For This Product button.

4. Click the Driver link.

5. Right-click the linked word "here" in the line "Click here to download the Driver" and select Save Target As.

6. Select a location to which the file should be downloaded (you may want to use the floppy disk, since you'll probably need to copy it there).

7. Copy the file to the computer on which you will be installing the card. The file is small enough to store on a floppy disk.

8. The file is a Zip file, which is a compressed archive containing other files. You will need to extract the files from the Zip; you may have your own favorite tool, but Windows XP has built-in support for it, as shown in Figure 11-1. Locate the file in Windows Explorer, right-click it, and select Explore. Copy the contents of the file to a directory you can create on the hard disk, such as c:\linksys.

Now you're ready to begin the actual installation process. After you plug it into the PC Card socket, Windows XP automatically detects the new PC Card network adapter. First, a message appears above the notification area of the taskbar telling you that Windows has found new hardware. At this point, Windows XP launches the Found New Hardware Wizard so you can perform a driver installation. Follow these steps:

1. Select the option Install From A List Or Specific Location (Advanced) and click Next.

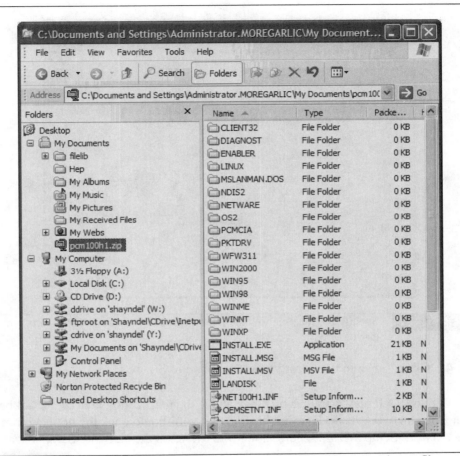

FIGURE 11-1   Windows XP has built-in Zip file support so you can explore a file

2. In the next wizard window, select the option Search For The Best Driver In These Locations, and clear the check box labeled Search Removable Media. In the field labeled Include This Location In The Search, type **c:\linksys** (substitute the location you used in the steps above when you extracted the files from the Zip), as shown in Figure 11-2.

3. If the wizard displays a window telling you that the driver is not tested for Windows, click Continue Anyway (don't worry, the driver is exactly what you need for Windows XP).

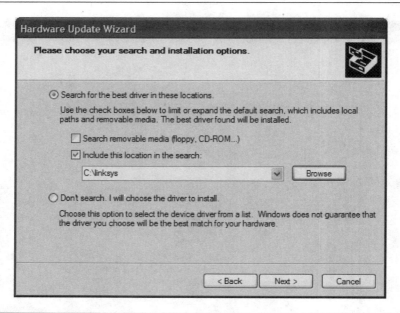

FIGURE 11-2   Specify the location to which you copied the Windows XP drivers you downloaded

4. Click Finish in the wizard window shown in Figure 11-3.

Windows XP may display a message above the notification area of the taskbar that a new network device is available and that you should click the notice to run the Network Setup Wizard. See Chapter 8 for more on the Network Setup Wizard.

Windows 98SE   On Windows 98SE, you will need to load device drivers for the PCM100H1. After you insert the card or turn on the computer after inserting the card with the computer turned off, Windows detects the new card's presence and starts the Add New Hardware Wizard. Follow these steps:

1. A disk, either a floppy or CD-ROM, was included with the card in the box. Make sure the disk is in an appropriate drive.

2. The opening screen of the wizard displays the card's name. Click Next to continue.

3. The next screen asks you whether it should search for the best device driver or let you pick one from a list. Select the first option (Search For The Best Driver For Your Device) and click Next.

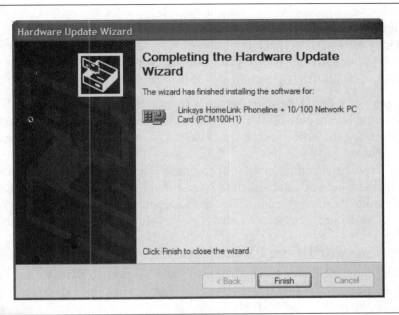

FIGURE 11-3   Finally, you're done installing the PCM100H1

4. The next screen asks you where Windows should search for the driver. Check the box labeled Specify A Location and type **a:\win98** (*a:* is appropriate for a floppy disk; if your driver is on a different drive, substitute the appropriate drive letter). Click the Next button.

5. Windows looks for and finds the appropriate driver and tells you it has done so. Click Next to continue.

6. At this point, Windows actually copies the files from the disk to the computer. It's possible that Windows will ask you for your original Windows disc, so have it handy. If you do not, click OK, and when Windows can't locate the driver, try c:\windows\options\cabs. If that does not work, you can also try respecifying the drivers on a:\win98 (sometimes Windows gets confused!).

7. Finally, the Add New Hardware Wizard tells you that it has finished installing the software for the new device. Click Finish to exit the wizard.

At this point, if your network supports DHCP for automatic TCP/IP addressing, you will also have an address and you may be ready to go. Your network may not support DHCP, or other Windows-related settings may need to be configured, for example, for you to access shared files on other computers. Instructions for these functions are found in Chapter 8.

You may also want to check the Linksys Web site for updates to the device drivers and other software you've installed. See Appendix C for more information on how to contact Linksys. To configure Windows networking, see Chapter 8.

Switching the PCM100H1 Between Network Types   Switching the PCM100H1 between home phone networking and wired Ethernet, as you might do when moving between the office and home, is easy. Just unplug it from one wire and plug in the other.

If you reboot the computer after changing the network cables, Windows should just see the new network and attach to it (assuming you have configured access to network resources, as defined in Chapter 8). Depending on the version of Windows and the network configuration, Windows may switch you over without a reboot.

USB Options For Home Phone Networking

All modern notebook computers have at least one USB port, so a USB home phone network adapter is also an alternative to consider. For example, the USB200HA HomeLink Phoneline 10M USB Network Adapter has two integrated phoneline network ports and, being a USB device, can be easily moved to a desktop computer as well. The USB100H1 HomeLink Phoneline + 10/100 USB Network Adapter has the usual two ports plus a 10/100 wired Ethernet port, much like the PCM100H1 described above. See Appendix C for more product and contact information from Linksys.

Moving Between Networks (Home/Office)

Many companies don't like to think about it, but a lot of employees take their notebooks home and work on them there. If you've set up a home network, you might want to connect your notebook to it at home. This means you'd have two sets of network settings, one for the office and one for home. Or, you might travel between multiple offices and have multiple network settings. In any event, this scenario presents a special challenge for Windows.

If you've got hardware that isn't ancient, all versions of Windows since Windows 95 are good at handling multiple network adapters in the computer. But Windows networking is more complicated than that, and the real problem comes with the software network settings.

At work, if you're not working at a small company, your computer probably logs onto a Windows domain or a Netware network, something very different from your network at home, which is probably what Windows calls a *workgroup*. If you shut down your computer at work, take it home, and connect to your network, when you boot up you won't be connected to your home network. You'll have to make several changes, potentially complicated ones, and then when you take your computer back to the office you'll have to switch them back.

Windows XP is much better at this sort of switch than previous versions of Windows, but it still doesn't do everything you'd want it to. Windows 98 is just plain bad at it.

But there is a solution that's easy and cheap. A $14 shareware program makes it easy to switch between as many network configurations as you'll ever need, and it handles everything.

Switching a Windows 98 System by Yourself

Windows 98 is so bad at this that it's almost sad. How bad your situation is depends on what your networking configurations are at home and work. It's probably best for you to make these changes just before you shut down your computer at one location to bring it to another. The switches may force you to reboot anyway, so when you turn your computer on at the new location it will just work.

Changing Your TCP/IP Settings

I won't go into great detail here because the subject is covered extensively in Chapter 8. However, if you are using the same network adapter for two different networks on Windows 98, and if they are not both using DHCP (the Obtain An IP Address Automatically option), you will have to use the TCP/IP properties settings to switch the addresses when you move between networks. Simple enough?

Luckily, if you have multiple network adapters, one for each network you use, Windows maintains separate TCP/IP settings for each and will automatically switch between them. For this reason, if you have two networks of the same type, for example wired Ethernet at home and the office, it may be easier just to use two different network adapters and physically switch them.

If you use one adapter and both networks use DHCP for all settings that the servers provide, you may be able to get away without any reconfiguration of TCP/IP settings when switching networks (although you still have to change Windows network settings, as described in the next section).

But if even one network uses static settings, you'll have to change them before booting onto the other network. What's worse, you'll have to write them down somewhere, because Windows has no way to save them and restore them for you (NetSwitcher does this; see the "Using NetSwitcher" section). You'll need to go to the Network applet, either from Control Panel itself or by right-clicking and selecting Properties on the Network Neighborhood. In the list of network components, find and select the TCP/IP binding to the network adapter you have to switch, and then click Properties. Note everything in this dialog. You'll have to save it and enter it everytime you switch the adapter between networks.

Switching Windows Networks in Windows 98

Like the infomercial says, "But wait, there's more!"

You also have to switch the setting that tells Windows what network you are on. This is a global setting for all network adapters, so even if you are using one adapter for each network to which you connect, you will have to change this setting when you switch networks, and it will force a reboot.

Two basic ways are used to organize Windows networks: domains and workgroups. Your computer may be a member of a domain at work, and when you log into the computer, you are actually logging into the domain. Your login dialog will have an extra field in such cases, displaying the domain name. Domains are great for large networks, but they're too complicated and too much work for home networks. A workgroup, which you probably have at home, is simply a collection of stand-alone computers, but when they all say they are in the same workgroup, they can see each other for purposes of sharing files and printers and other things.

To switch your computer from a domain setting to a workgroup setting, follow these steps:

1. Go to the Network Control Panel applet, either from Control Panel or by right-clicking and selecting Properties on the Network Neighborhood.

2. On the Identification tab, if you've put it in previously, you'll see your workgroup name. If it's not there, type it into the Workgroup field.

3. Back to the Configuration tab, find and double-click the Client for Microsoft Networks line in the list of networking components. The Log On To Windows NT Domain check box (see Figure 11-4) will be checked; uncheck it.

4. Click OK, and you'll have to reboot.

To switch back to the domain from the workgroup, reverse that last step. On the Configuration tab of the Client for Microsoft Network Properties dialog, the Log On To Windows NT Domain check box will be unchecked; check it.

Switching a Windows XP System by Yourself

Windows XP saves you from the manual part of switching TCP/IP addresses, but not the part about switching between domains and workgroups.

Each network adapter—more specifically, each network connection—can have a TCP/IP configuration and an alternative configuration. Here's how to configure this:

1. Select Network Connections in Control Panel.

2. Right-click the connection you want to configure and select Properties.

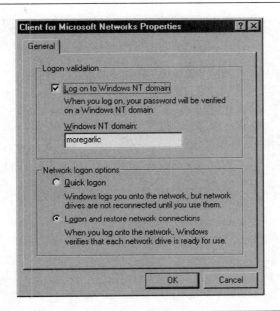

Switch between a workgroup and a domain and you'll have to change the Log On To Windows NT Domain setting

3. In the list in the middle of the dialog, locate and double-click Internet Protocol TCP/IP. The Internet Protocol (TCP/IP) Properties dialog (see Figure 11-5) appears.

The properties in Figure 11-5 are set, as most home network users will be, to obtain addresses automatically from the network. As with Windows 98, if both networks are configured this way, which is a possibility, that's all you have to do, although there is still the matter of telling Windows what domain or workgroup you're logging into. But on either network, the adapter will request configuration information from the DHCP server and get the appropriate address.

On the other hand, if one or both of the networks uses a static address, you can configure the other on the Alternate Configuration tab (see Figure 11-6).

On the Alternate Configuration tab, you can specify the basic TCP/IP information, including address, subnet mask, gateway, DNS servers, and WINS servers (WINS servers aren't really basic information except in some all-Microsoft IT departments).

Alternatively, you can specify Automatic Private IP Address (APIPA), which is a Microsoft TCP/IP-specific feature. It's the address range 169.254.x.x, which is owned by Microsoft. In Windows, when an adapter requests a DHCP address and fails to see the DHCP server, it gets one of these APIPA numbers. If all the

11

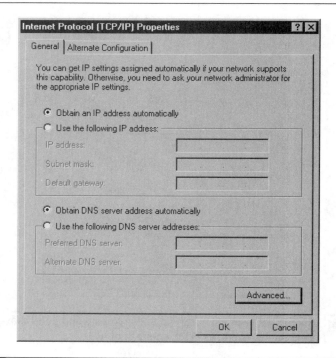

Windows XP lets you define a second TCP/IP configuration for an adapter in case the first one fails

computers in your local network are in the APIPA range they should communicate, but there will be no gateway or DNS servers, so you won't get out to the Internet.

Switching Windows Networks in Windows XP

As with Windows 98, if you switch between a domain and a workgroup, or between different domains or different workgroups, you have to change the setting in Windows that names the domain or workgroup to which you are logging in.

NOTE   *Windows XP Home Edition cannot join a Windows domain. Only Windows XP Pro has this feature.*

In Windows XP, launch the System applet in Control Panel. If you're in the Categories view of Control Panel, click Performance And Maintenance and then System.

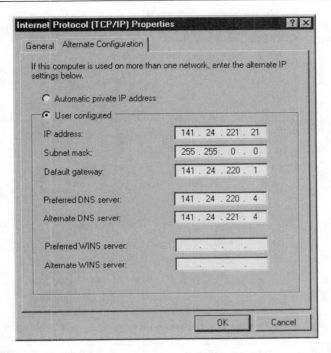

FIGURE 11-6   The Alternate Configuration only contains basic TCP/IP information

On the Computer Name tab of the dialog, click the Change button. At the bottom of the dialog (see Figure 11-7), you can select either Workgroup or Domain and fill in the appropriate name in the appropriate field. Click OK to close and save the changes.

Using NetSwitcher

A shareware utility program called NetSwitcher can be downloaded for free from *http://www.netswitcher.com*. This utility consolidates this whole process into a single-user interface. If NetSwitcher works for you, the author requests a $14 payment that will also entitle you to support.

NetSwitcher saves not just these networking options for your Windows system, but also numerous other options that might change from one location to another. It saves your Windows telephone dialing rules (such as your area code); your wireless network SSID; mapped drives and file and printer shares on network servers; Internet

In Windows XP, you still have to select between workgroup and domain membership

proxy server settings; e-mail client configuration, including default e-mail client assignment; AOL Instant Messenger login information; and even lists of programs that start up with Windows from your Startup folder and registry.

You can save a complete set of all of these options, called a *location*, for each network on which you might run your program, and in one operation restore that location at the next reboot. In fact, NetSwitcher eliminates numerous reboots that Windows would have you perform; in many cases, all you need to do is log in.

Instructions for the program can be found on the Web site, and a large number of options can be configured in the program. But the basics of the program aren't hard to figure out. When you install it, the program immediately asks if you want to save the current configuration so that you can restore it later on.

You don't need to change your configuration in Windows to define new configurations to boot your system. You can load the main NetSwitcher program (see Figure 11-8), make the changes in that program, and save the changed location as a new location.

For example, you could load your NT Domain login location from your network at the office, uncheck the NT Domain Logon check box, enter your home

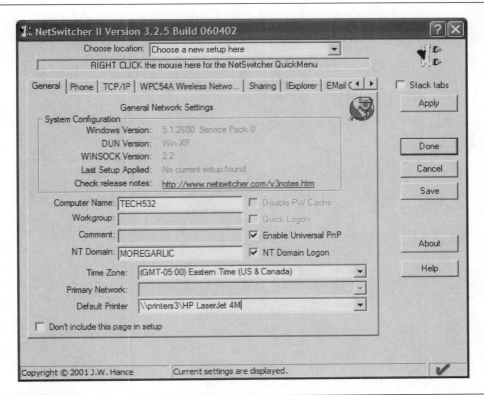

FIGURE 11-8   NetSwitcher has a large number of options you can save and restore for different networks on which you would run your computer

Workgroup name, and save the results as "Home Network On Workgroup" or some such name. Then, you click the Apply button to save the settings to Windows itself. Then you could just log in to the workgroup—or you could shut the computer down and go home, and when you got home, Windows would log you on to the workgroup.

A word of warning: In many cases, all involving Windows 2000 or Windows XP clients, where configuring your computer to connect to or disconnect from Windows domains is an issue, you will need help from your network administrator to configure the software. Specifically, someone with sufficient network rights will have to enter their username and password into the program to give it permission to disconnect you from the domain before you take it home and reconnect you when you bring it back. This will have to be done only once, but it means you'll have to explain to an admin what you are doing—which you really should anyway since this person is in charge of the network.

Chapter 12

Sharing Network Resources

In a network environment, you can share certain components on one computer with the other computers on the network. These components are called shared resources, and they include drives, folders, modems, and printers. In this chapter, I'll cover sharing files and printers.

When you create a shared resource, the commonly used jargon for that resource is a *share*. Other standard terminology you'll encounter for shared resources includes the following:

- *Sharename* is the name of a share (all shares are named).

- *Local computer* is the computer at which you're currently working.

- *Local user* is the user who is working at a specific computer.

- *Remote computer* is another computer on the network.

- *Remote user* is the user who is accessing a share from a remote computer.

> NOTE *Appendix A is a glossary of networking terms, and you should check it whenever you come across a phrase you don't understand.*

Sharing Files

To share files across the network, you share their containers, which are drives and folders. Sharing does more than provide access to files for other users on the network; it's also handy when you want to work on your own files, but the computer you usually use isn't available at the moment. In most home networks, there are more users in the household than computers, so it's common to share computers. If Dad usually sits at the computer in the den and saves his documents on that computer, when his daughter is using the den computer Dad can go to any computer in the house and access the documents on the den computer. In fact, he can work on those documents as if he were sitting in front of the computer in the den.

File Sharing Is Hierarchical

When you share a file container, every part of the container is shared. This means if you share a drive, you share every folder, subfolder, and file on that drive. If you share a folder, you share every subfolder and file contained in that folder.

To keep your system safe, it's not a good idea to share a drive. In addition, limit your shares to the folders that contain document files, because sharing software and system files can be very dangerous—remote users could inadvertently change or remove those files. Share your document folder, or share only specific subfolders within your document folder.

The exception to this safety rule is an external drive—CD, Zip, Jaz, and so on. When you share an external drive you cannot share a folder on that drive, because the folder structure changes depending on the media that's inserted in the drive. Instead, you share the drive, making its current contents available to remote users.

Shares and the Network Browse Window

Once you understand that sharing is hierarchical, your logical brain tells you that the best way to share a large number of files is to share the highest container in the hierarchy. For example, if your My Documents folder has many subfolders (each dedicated to a particular type of document), you should share My Documents. Then, when anyone on the network (including yourself, if you're working on a different computer) needs to get to any file in any subfolder, it takes only a couple of double-clicks to open the hierarchical set of folders to get to the target file.

It's actually safer and more efficient to share the subfolders, especially since you can skip any subfolders that hold files you deem "private" and don't want to share with other users on the network. In fact, for your "private" subfolder, you can create a hidden share that only you can access when you're working on a different computer (see the section "Using Hidden Shares" later in this chapter).

Shares automatically appear in the network browser window (Network Neighborhood in Windows 98SE, and My Network Places in Windows XP/Me/2000), so any user can quickly access them from a remote computer. Additionally, a share can be mapped to a drive letter, which means a remote user can access the files in a share without opening the network browser window. This is extremely useful when data files for applications that everybody on the network uses (for example, QuickBooks) are kept on one computer on the network. See the section "Mapping Shares to Drive Letters" later in this chapter.

Sharing Files in Windows XP

When you run the Windows XP Network Setup Wizard, file sharing is enabled as part of the process. Windows XP uses a feature called Simple File Sharing, in which a share is either available or it's not. You cannot limit access to certain users by forcing the use of passwords, as you can with Windows 98SE shares. If you're using Windows XP Home Edition, you cannot turn off Simple File Sharing.

12

Sharing the My Documents Folder

The icon for the My Documents folder you see in Windows Explorer is almost certainly not a folder—it's a shortcut to a folder. When you right-click the My Documents icon, you don't see a Sharing command; the Sharing command appears only when you access the real My Documents folder. The shortcut is pointing to the My Documents folder that belongs to the currently logged on user. The real My Documents folder is found in one of the following locations (substitute the logon name of the user for <UserName>):

- In Windows 98/Me, the shortcut for the "My Documents" folder is pointing to a folder that's located at C:\Windows\Profiles\ <UserName>\My Documents.

- In Windows XP/2000, the shortcut for the "My Documents" folder is pointing to a folder that's located at C:\Documents and Settings\ <UserName>\My Documents.

If you're using Windows XP Professional with the NTFS file system, you can turn off Simple File Sharing and use NTFS security to restrict the activity of remote users (for example, permitting remote users to read files, but not change or delete them). For more information about NTFS and configuring permissions on shares, see the list of books on administering networks and computers in Appendix C.

NOTE   *The Windows XP Network Setup Wizard even creates a special folder named Shared Documents, which is automatically shared using the sharename "SharedDocs." Although this share is designed to make its contents available to all the users who log on to the computer, you can also make it a network share.*

Sharing Folders in Windows XP

Most of the time, you'll want to share your My Documents folder, or one of the subfolders you created to hold documents of specific types (for example, budgets, letters, contracts, and so on). To share a folder in Windows XP, follow these steps:

1. In My Computer or Windows Explorer, right-click the folder and choose Sharing and Security from the shortcut menu to open the folder Properties dialog with the Sharing tab in the foreground (see Figure 12-1).

Hicksville
Fire Dept.
Volunteers
Wanted

Call
516-933-6444
For Information

Protect Your
Dreams...
Volunteer

Protection Hook & Ladder Co. No. 1
Independent Engine & Hose Co. No. 2
Citizens Engine Co. No. 3
Volunteer Hose Co. No. 4
Emergency Co. No. 5
Hook & Ladder Co. No. 6
Engine Co. No. 7
Floodlight Heavy Rescue Co. No. 8

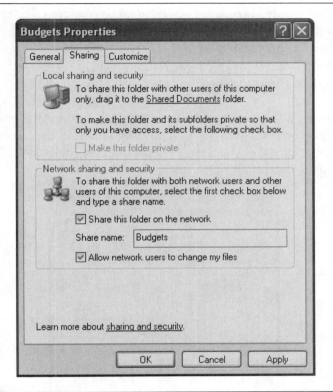

FIGURE 12-1	Enable sharing and name the share

2. In the Network Sharing and Security section, select Share This Folder on the Network.

3. Enter a sharename for this folder, which is the name remote users see when they view the folder in Network Neighborhood or My Network Places. By default, Windows uses the folder name, but you can change it.

NOTE *Changing a sharename doesn't change the folder name.*

4. If you don't want remote users to be able to create, change, or delete files in this folder, clear the check box labeled Allow Network Users to Change My Files.

 *If you prevent remote users from creating or changing files in a shared folder, that restriction also affects you when you're working with the files from a remote computer.*

5. Click OK to create the share.

To stop sharing a folder, just deselect the sharing option. After you create a share, the folder icon you see in My Computer or Windows Explorer changes to include another graphical element—a hand cradling the folder icon. This gives you a quick way to determine which folders are shared.

Sharing Drives in Windows XP

When you attempt to share a drive in Windows XP, the system issues an admonition, citing the dangers of exposing all the folders and files contained on the drive to remote users.

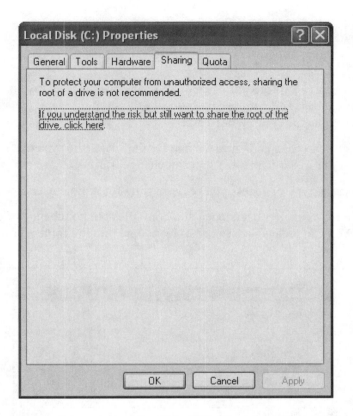

The warning is valid, and you should heed it. However, if you have some reason to share all the contents of your hard drive, you can display the Sharing tab by clicking the link that says you understand but you want to share the drive anyway. Incidentally, the same warning appears for any drive, even removable drives such as the CD drive. Sharing removable drives doesn't present the same danger to your system, because the disks you insert in those drives don't contain important system files that remote users could change or remove.

Sharing Files in Windows 98SE

In Windows 98SE (and Windows Me), you can share a drive or a folder using identical steps, because those operating systems don't issue a warning about the dangers of sharing a drive (but you should still avoid sharing a drive). Follow these steps to create a share:

1. In Windows Explorer, or My Computer, right-click the drive or folder you want to share and choose Sharing from the shortcut menu, which will open the Sharing tab (see Figure 12-2.)

2. Select Shared As and enter a name for the share (the system automatically enters the folder name, but you can change it).

3. Select the type of access you're permitting for remote users:

   ■ *Read-Only* lets users open and copy files but not change or delete files. You can create a password to let people into the folder for read-only

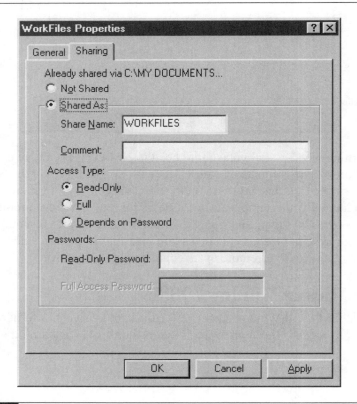

FIGURE 12-2   Windows 98SE provides password protection to enhance security

access, or skip the password requirement to let all users access the share with read-only permissions.

■ *Full* lets users do whatever they wish in the folder. You can create a password to let people into the folder for full access, or skip the password requirement to let all users access the share with full permissions.

■ *Depends On Password* allows different access levels, depending on the password the user enters.

4. Click OK to create the share.

Notice that Windows 98 tells you when the folder you're working on is a subfolder of a folder that's already shared (see the text on the top of the Sharing tab in Figure 12-2). You can create the new share anyway, in order to make it appear in the network browse window. That way, a remote user (including yourself, if you're working on a different computer) can open the folder quickly, or can map a drive to the share.

Windows 98SE Passwords for Shares

The password feature for shares in Windows 98 is very handy. You can share the folder and then give the password only to certain people. In fact, you can keep the password to yourself, so you can get into the folder when you're working at a different computer. When a remote user (which could be you) attempts to open the folder, a dialog appears for entering the password.

If the user doesn't enter the correct password, she can't open the share. However, if the share is a subfolder and the parent folder is shared, a remote user can open the parent folder and then enter the password-protected folder without entering a password. This is another example of why it's important to share only specific subfolders.

Using Hidden Shares

A hidden share doesn't show up in the network browse window, so remote users won't open the share and see its files. However, anyone who knows the share exists (which would usually be only the person who created the hidden share) can get to it. Hidden shares are handy for keeping private documents away from remote users, while maintaining the option to get to the private files when you're working at a different computer.

> **NOTE** *Only the share is hidden, not the folder itself, which means its hidden attribute only works on remote users. The folder is a normal accessible folder to anyone working on the computer.*

A hidden share isn't hidden if any of the containers above it are shared. If you create a hidden share for a subfolder in My Documents, you cannot share My Documents, nor the drive on which My Documents exists (because both containers are parents of the hidden share). If you do share the My Documents folder, when remote users open the folder, they'll see the folder you thought you'd hidden. If you want to share the My Documents folder, and you also want a private, hidden folder, create a separate folder outside of the My Documents folder on the hard drive and use it to save your personal stuff (and don't share the hard drive).

Creating a Hidden Share

To hide a share, all you have to do is make the last character in the sharename a dollar sign ($).

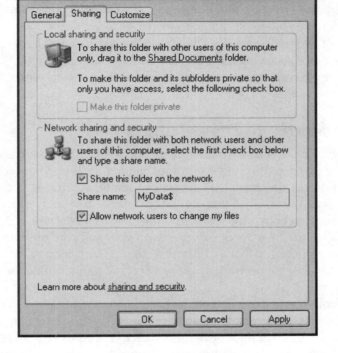

Because you're probably the only person who will access this share from a remote computer, be sure the option Allow Network Users to Change My Files is enabled in Windows XP. Also, be sure you provide full access in Windows 98SE (you don't need a password for a hidden share—that would be overkill).

Accessing a Hidden Share from a Remote Computer

To access a hidden share from a remote computer, choose Start | Run and enter the path to the share, using the format **ComputerName\ShareName**, and click OK. For example, enter **kitchen\mynovel$** to get to the hidden share named

12

mynovel$ on the computer named kitchen (uppercase or lowercase characters are irrelevant, and don't forget that dollar sign!). A window opens, displaying the contents of the share, and you can go to work.

This format (a double-backslash before a computer name and a single backslash before a sharename) is called the Universal Naming Convention (UNC), and it's designed to let network users access resources on the network without opening the network browse window.

Mapping Shares to Drive Letters

Mapping is the technical term for assigning a drive letter to a share on a remote computer. The mapped drive letter becomes another drive on your local computer. This is a useful trick for shares you access constantly, because all the drives on your computer appear in My Computer and Windows Explorer, which means you don't have to open a network browse window to get to this share.

You can also use the mapped drive letter in your software programs when you want to open or save a file that's in a remote share. Using a drive letter is much easier than browsing the network to get to a specific remote folder in order to open or save a document.

You can only map a drive letter to a share, not to a subfolder of a share. For example, if Drive C on a remote computer is shared, you cannot map a drive to a folder on that drive if that folder isn't also shared. If you share a folder, you cannot map a drive to one of its subfolders unless that subfolder is also explicitly shared.

> NOTE *The fact that you can only map a drive to a resource that's been explicitly shared is a Windows rule. If you've worked in a corporate setting and your company used Novell NetWare, you know it's possible to map a drive to any subfolder. This feature is called Map Root, and it's not available in Windows.*

Creating a Mapped Drive

To map a drive letter to a share, open the network browse window (My Network Places in Windows XP/Me/2000, or Network Neighborhood in Windows 98SE). Double-click the icon for the computer that has the share you want to map, which displays all the computer's shares.

Right-click the icon for the share you need, and select Map Network Drive from the shortcut menu. The Map Network Drive dialog opens so you can assign a drive letter to the share, and also decide whether you want to make the mapping permanent. Click OK or Finish (depending on the version of Windows you're using) to map the drive. A window opens to show you the contents of the mapped share. You can work on files, or close the window if you're merely creating the mapped drive and you aren't ready to work on the files.

Selecting a Drive Letter   In all versions of Windows except Windows XP, the system automatically selects the next available drive letter on your computer. The next available drive letter changes depending on whether you have multiple drives on the computer or you've previously mapped a drive letter to a share.

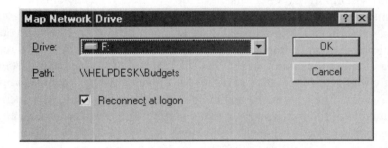

In Windows XP, mapped drives start with *Z*, and then work backwards through the alphabet. For example, if this is the second mapped drive you're creating, its default drive letter is *Y*.

12

Regardless of the version of Windows you're using, you don't have to accept the default drive letter. Click the arrow to the right of the Drive field and select another drive letter if you wish.

Permanent Mapping vs. Temporary Mapping   You can also decide whether you want this mapped drive to be permanent, which means when you shut down Windows, the next time you start up the share is remapped and once again becomes a drive letter on your computer. By default, Windows assumes you want to map this drive permanently, and the Reconnect at Logon option is selected. If you only want to map the drive temporarily, click the check box to clear the check mark.

Automatic reconnections of mapped shares can be tricky, however. If you select the option to reconnect your mapped drive at logon, the order in which you start your computers becomes important. The computer that holds the shared resource should boot before the computer that has the mapped drive. That way, when the computer with the mapped drive searches for the resource in order to complete the mapping process, the resource is available. This, of course, presents a seemingly insurmountable problem if you have two computers on the network and each of them is mapping drives to shares on the other.

Don't worry, this is all workable. When a computer that has drives mapped to remote shares boots and cannot find the computer that holds the drives, an error message appears at the end of the startup process. The error message tells you that the permanent connection is not available, and it will ask if you want to reconnect the next time you start the computer. Click Yes.

After both (or all) computers have booted, open My Computer or Windows Explorer. You can see the mapped drive, but there's a red X mark under the icon, which indicates the connection is "broken." Click the icon to access the mapped share—because the remote computer is now available, the red X goes away and you can access the files you need.

Windows 98SE has a better idea—an option that stalls the attempt to connect to a mapped drive until you actually access it. You can configure this option with the following steps:

1. Put the Windows 98SE CD in the CD drive (exit the setup program if it starts automatically).

2. Choose Start | Settings | Control Panel.

3. Open the Network applet in Control Panel.

4. Select Client For Microsoft Networks and click Properties.

5. Select Quick Logon.

6. Click OK twice to close the Network Properties dialog, and to transfer files from the Windows 98SE CD to your hard drive.

Network Browse Window Shortcuts Are Confusing

If the Map Network Drive command is not available on the shortcut menu, the resource is not explicitly shared and you cannot map it. However, that statement isn't as straightforward as it seems. Windows XP automatically browses the network on a frequent basis, and puts a shortcut for each share it finds in the My Network Places window. Shortcuts are not really icons for shares, so you won't see the command for mapping a drive on the menu that appears when you right-click the icon. The shortcuts are handy when you want to access a share, but the only way to map a share is to get to the icon for the share instead of the icon for its shortcut. To do this, you must open the Entire Network icon or the Workgroup icon, and open the appropriate computer to see its shares.

Sharing Printers

The ability to share printers in a network is almost as big a motivation for installing a network as the desire to share an Internet connection. Without a network, households and small businesses with multiple computers have two choices for printing:

- Buy a new printer every time you buy a new computer.

- Teach users how to copy documents to a floppy disk, walk to the computer that has the printer, insert the floppy disk, open the appropriate software, load the document in the software, and print the document—whew!

Of course, when you have a network you *can* buy a printer for each computer—perhaps a high-speed laser printer for one computer, and a color inkjet printer for the other computer—and then everyone can use either printer, depending on the type of document they're printing.

You have two choices for setting up printer sharing in your network:

- Use a hardware device called a print server.

- Use the Windows software features to share a printer that's attached to a computer.

12

Using Linksys Print Servers to Share Printers

You gain two enormous advantages when you use a hardware print server to share printers on a network instead of the standard printer sharing features offered by Windows:

■ Speed, because the Linksys print servers soup up the speed at which data is delivered to the printer

■ Location, because you can put your printers in a place that's convenient for all users on the network, instead of attaching individual printers to individual computers (especially important if the computers aren't near each other)

Linksys offers several types of print servers (see Appendix C for more information). I happen to use the three-printer-port EPSX3 because it fits my own network setup best, so I'll use that model as the basis of this discussion. However, setting up a Linksys hardware print server is very much the same regardless of the model. Installing the Linksys print server requires several steps, all of which are quite easy. You start by physically installing the device to both your printer and your network. Then you must install and configure drivers for the print server and for the printers attached to the print server.

Physical Installation of the Print Server

You must make all the physical connections for your print server before you can start setting up printers on the computers on your network. Attach your printer to the printer port at the back of the print server. If your printer is attached to a computer, remove the connector from the back of the computer and connect it to the print server. If you're attaching multiple printers to a print server that handles multiple printers (mine does), repeat this step for each printer.

Use the RJ-45 port (the LAN port) on the back of the print server to attach the print server to your network hub/switch or the computers on your network (depending on your network setup and the print server model you're using). Use a standard Ethernet cable. For example, the print server I use has one RJ-45 port that connects to the hub into which I connect my network computers. If you're using a print server that has multiple RJ-45 ports, you can use those ports to connect multiple computers, such as a Linksys EFSP42, which acts as a hub as well as a print server.

Connect the power supply to the print server and plug it into an outlet. The print server has no On/Off switch—you power it by plugging it in. As soon as you power up the print server, the LED lights on the front of the device should glow to indicate the presence of power, printer connections, and computer connections.

Installing the Print Server Driver

All the computers on the network use the print server to access printers, so you must install the print server's driver on those computers. On each computer, insert the Linksys CD that came with your print server. Then, launch the print server setup process by using either of the following methods:

- Choose Start | Run, enter **d:\driver\win9xnt\setup.exe**, and click OK (substitute the drive letter for your CD drive if it isn't D).

- Open Windows Explorer or My Computer and navigate to the driver\win9xnt folder on the CD, and then double-click setup.exe.

The Linksys PrintServer Drive Wizard opens with a welcoming message. Click Next to begin installing the drivers. The next window displays the location on your hard drive where the drivers will be installed (C:\Program Files\Linksys\ PrintDriver). If you have some compelling reason to change that location, click Browse and select a different folder. Otherwise, click Next. The wizard displays the new entries that will be installed on your Programs menu.

Click Next to have the setup program copy the files from the CD to your hard drive. When the wizard displays the Setup Complete window, the option Configure Print Driver Now is preselected.

12

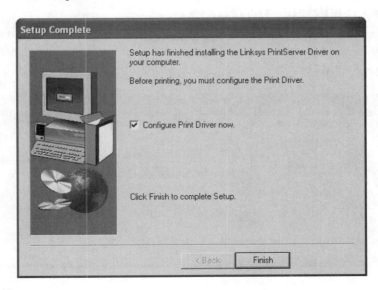

Setup Complete

Setup has finished installing the Linksys PrintServer Driver on your computer.

Before printing, you must configure the Print Driver.

☑ Configure Print Driver now.

Click Finish to complete Setup.

< Back   Finish

Click Finish to complete the installation process and begin the process of configuring the port(s) and the printer(s) attached to the port.

How to Handle Static IP Addresses with the Print Server

At this point in the installation and configuration process, the Linksys software is able to find the print server on your network and display its ports only if the print server received an IP address from the DHCP server on your network. That DHCP server is either the host computer for your Internet Connection Sharing, or a router you installed to share an Internet connection among all the computers on your network.

If your network is using static IP addresses (addresses that were supplied by your ISP, and assigned to each computer on the network), you won't see the print server in this window until you give the device an IP address. You do that with the Linksys Bi-Admin program, which is covered in the next section, "Installing the Bi-Admin Print Server Manager Tool." Before you can use the Bi-Admin utility, you must know the name assigned to your print server. The name of the print server is printed on the bottom of the unit. You should write it down so you don't have to look for it when you need it (the print server has to be connected to the printer and the network, which can make it difficult to turn it upside down to read the name). The name of my print server is SC991156, and the name you find on your print server has a similar naming pattern. After you read the sections on using the Bi-Admin software to assign a static IP address to the print server, you can perform the printer driver installation tasks that are discussed in this section.

Installing the Printer Driver(s)

To begin the next phase, which is installing the drivers for the printers attached to the print server, the wizard opens a window that displays the Program menu items for the Linksys print server.

NOTE *You can also reach the Linksys setup program at any time by selecting it from the Programs menu.*

Double-click the shortcut labeled Print Driver Setup. The system displays a message that reminds you to make sure all the physical connections are ready to go.

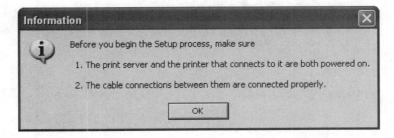

Click OK to see the Printer Port Setup window, which displays the name of your print server and lists its port(s). Figure 12-3 shows my Linksys three-port print server, which automatically tried to identify each printer connected to its ports. You'll notice it failed to identify the printer on port 3, which is a very old dot-matrix printer that holds checks (so I don't have to change paper when I want to print checks). However, I have printer drivers from the manufacturer for this printer so I'll be able to install and use it.

To install the actual printer drivers to the local computer, select a port (your print server model may only have one port to select) and click Next. The system adds the port to your computer (and informs you of that fact with a message dialog). The Configure Printer port dialog opens automatically so you can either select an existing printer (a printer driver that's already installed on the local computer) or add a printer, as follows.

If the printer you're configuring had previously been installed on this computer, you'll see an existing driver. Select its listing and click Connect. Windows links the printer to its already-installed driver and returns you to the Printer Port Setup dialog. Click the Refresh button to update the display—the port listing has an asterisk to indicate that both the port and the printer are installed.

If the printer you're configuring doesn't have an existing driver on this computer (no listing appears in the Existing Printers box), click Add New Printer. The Windows Add Printer Wizard opens, and you need to go through the wizard to add the printer, using the same steps you'd use if you were adding a printer that's attached to this computer. Windows has drivers for a lot of printers, but if you have drivers from the printer's manufacturer, use the Have Disk option and follow the wizard's prompts to install the printer. When you're returned to the Print Port

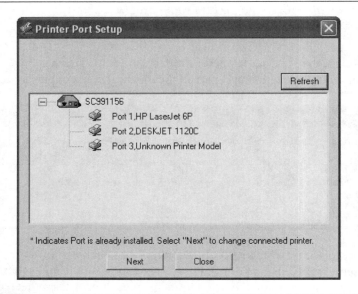

FIGURE 12-3   The print server displays its port(s)

Setup dialog, click the Refresh button to update the display—the port listing has an asterisk to indicate that both the port and the printer are installed on this computer.

If you open your Printers folder in Control Panel, you'll see the printer (or multiple printers) you installed. This means the printer shows up when you use the Print dialog in software, so you're all set for printing no matter which computer on the network you're using.

Installing the Bi-Admin Print Server Manager Tool

Linksys supplies a utility program to manage your print server, called the Bi-Admin Management utility. You can use this software to check the status of, troubleshoot, and generally manage the print server.

You also need this software to configure a static IP address for your print server if you're using static IP addresses on your network. Your ISP provided a range of static IP addresses for you to use on your network, and you must have an "extra" static IP address for the print server.

The Bi-Admin utility should not be installed on every computer that's accessing the print server; instead, you should install it on the computer used by the person with the most knowledge of networking features (the program is powerful, and choosing incorrect options could cause problems with your print server). To install the utility, put the Linksys CD in the CD drive and take one of the following actions:

- Choose Start | Run and enter **d:\utility\biadmin\setup.exe** (substitute the appropriate drive letter if your CD drive isn't D).

- Open the CD drive in Windows Explorer or My Computer and navigate to the \utility\biadmin subfolder, and then double-click setup.exe.

Either way, the Bi-Admin Setup Wizard launches so you can install the software. Follow the wizard's prompts, clicking Next to move through all the wizard windows. After all the files are copied, the wizard opens the folder for the Programs listing for the utility. You can start the program now by clicking the Bi-Admin shortcut, or you can close the window and access the program from the Programs menu when you're disposed to use it.

Using the Bi-Admin Print Server Manager Tool

When you launch Bi-Admin, the program opens a window that asks you to confirm the protocol you're using for network communication (which is TCP/IP). Click OK to start the program, which first scans your network to find the Linksys print server you've installed.

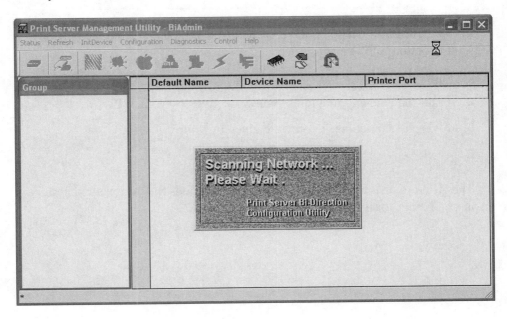

Assigning a Static IP Address to the Print Server

If you're using static IP addresses on your network, the Bi-Admin program won't find the print server when it scans your network. Here are the steps you must take to attach your print server to your network by assigning it a static IP address:

1. In the Bi-Admin software window, choose InitDevice | Set IP Address to open the Set IP Address dialog.

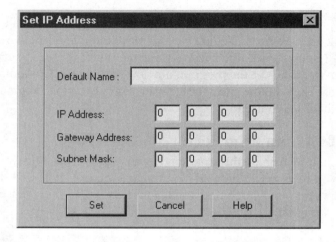

2. In the Default Name field, enter the name you copied from the label at the bottom of the print server.

3. Enter the IP address you're assigning to the print server.

4. Enter the gateway IP address you were given by your ISP.

5. Enter the subnet mask you were given by your ISP.

6. Click Set.

The Bi-Admin software rescans your network, finds the print server, and displays a listing for it in the software window.

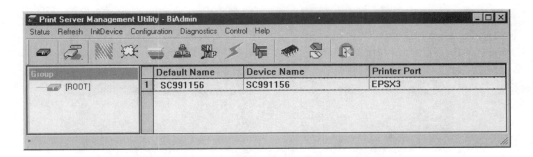

Using the Bi-Admin Management Tools

The Bi-Admin software offers plenty of tools to help you manage your print server, the printer(s) attached to the print server, and printing services for your network. I'll go over a few of the useful utilities here (see the Help files to learn about all the things you can do with this software).

Status Menu   The Status menu offers the following useful commands: Backup/Restore Device Information and Print Status.

Backup/Restore Device Information (which you can open quickly by using its toolbar icon, which is the first icon on the left) opens a window that contains all the technical information about your print server and the printers attached to it. You can save this information to a file, and then use that file to restore the settings if some disaster occurs.

12

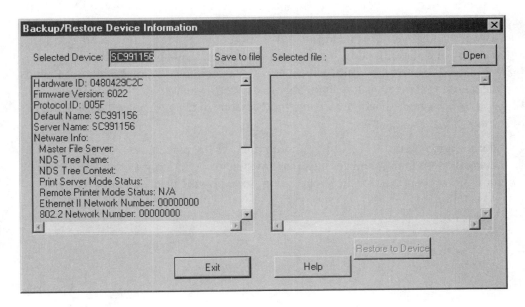

Printer Status (which is accessible quickly via the second icon on the toolbar) provides a way to check the current status of the printer(s). If you have more than one printer, select a port to see the status of its attached printer.

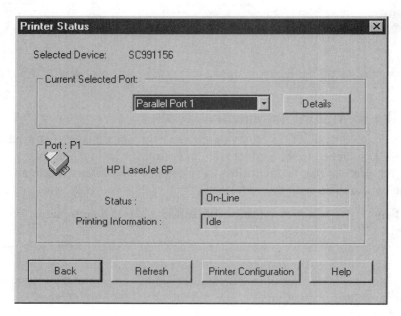

InitDevice Menu   If you're not comfortable with network protocols and technical settings, using the commands in the InitDevice menu can be dangerous to the health of your print server. Tread carefully! If you used the Set IP Address command to establish a static IP address for your print server, that's probably the last time you'll need to access the InitDevice menu. It's a good idea to think of the commands that are on this menu as tools you should only use when you're talking to Linksys support personnel. There aren't any good reasons to change the name, IP address, or any other device setting.

Configuration Menu   The Configuration menu is the place to make changes to the network operating system settings (for any network operating system) and other configuration options for the group being served by the print server.

Diagnostics Menu   If users are having trouble printing, use the Print Test Page command on this menu to send a test document to the printer port. If the test document prints, the problem is with the user's setup. If the test document doesn't print, check the connections between the print server and the printers.

Control Menu   Use the Abort Mail Print Job command on this menu to stop printing over the Internet Printing Protocol (IPP), if you've enabled that feature to service remote locations. Usually, IPP isn't used in small networks.

Using Windows Printer Sharing Features

If you don't have a print server hardware device, you can use the built-in Windows printer sharing features to give everyone on the network a way to use any printer on the network. This makes any computer that is attached to a printer a print server for that printer—if you have three computers with printers, you have three print servers on your network.

In this section, I'll go over the steps involved for sharing a printer and for installing and using a printer that's attached to another computer. I'm assuming you've already taken the steps to install printers and their drivers on your computers. I'll use a lot of the standard terminology that's applied to discussions of shared printers, so here are some guidelines to make this section easy to understand:

- The printer that's attached to the computer you're working on is a *local printer*.

- A printer that's attached to another computer on the network is a *network printer* (sometimes called a *remote printer*).

Sharing a Printer in Windows XP

To share a printer that's connected to a computer running Windows XP, follow these steps:

1. Choose Start | Control Panel to open the Control Panel window.

2. Select Printers and Other Hardware, and then select View Installed Printers or Fax Printers to open the Printers and Faxes window.

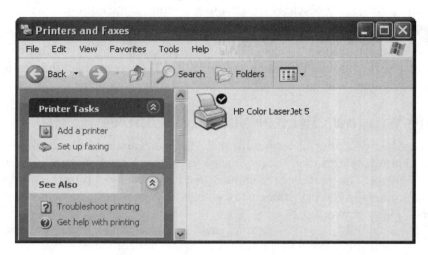

3. Right-click the icon of the printer you want to share, and choose Sharing to open the Sharing tab of the printer's Properties dialog.

4. Select Share This Printer and name the share. Windows usually suggests a name based on the printer's model, but you can change the sharename to suit yourself. As you can see in Figure 12-4, I find it helpful to add text that indicates information about the printer. In this case, the printer sharename indicates the printer type, and the name of the computer to which the printer is attached (so people don't wander around looking for their print jobs).

5. Click OK.

6. The icon for the printer now sports a hand cradling the printer graphic, indicating that this is a shared printer.

NOTE *When you install a printer on a Windows XP computer that's attached to a network, during the installation process you're asked whether you want to share the printer with other users. In this section, I'm assuming you either installed your printer before you installed your network, or you didn't share the printer if you installed it after you created your network (and you're ready to share it now).*

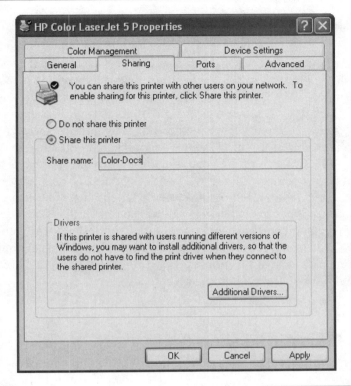

FIGURE 12-4   Select the option to share the printer, and also provide a sharename

If you create a printer sharename that has more than eight characters, Windows displays a message warning you that computers running only MS-DOS won't be able to access the shared printer. I suspect this isn't a problem for your network, so when Windows asks if you're sure you want to use the sharename you invented, just click Yes.

More important, however (and not referred to in the message you see), is the fact that if you create a printer sharename that has more than 12 characters, Windows 98SE users won't see the printer share when they open Network Neighborhood. As a result, be sure to count the characters as you create a sharename for the printer.

NOTE   *You can provide printer drivers for this printer for remote users who are running earlier versions of Windows. See the sidebar "Installing Additional Drivers" for more information.*

Installing Additional Drivers

Windows XP has a button labeled Additional Drivers on the Sharing tab. If you click the button, you see a list of Windows versions for which you can preinstall drivers for this printer. This means that users working on a computer running Windows 98SE, for example, can install the printer drivers using the files on the Windows XP computer, instead of accessing driver files from the Windows 98SE CD or a printer manufacturer's driver disk. However, in order to preinstall the drivers on the Windows XP computer, you must insert the Windows 98SE CD or a printer manufacturer's driver disk. Since you're unlikely to have a Windows 98SE CD handy on a desk or table that's holding a Windows XP computer, I think it's easier to let each user on the network install his or her own drivers when installing the printer that's connected to the Windows XP computer. However, if you want to preinstall the drivers, click Additional Drivers and follow the prompts to complete the installation. Then, when remote users install this printer, they can indicate that the drivers are available on the Windows XP print server.

Sharing a Printer in Windows 98SE

To share a printer that's attached to a Windows 98SE computer, follow these steps:

1. Choose Start | Settings | Printers to open the Printers folder.

2. Right-click the icon for the printer and choose Sharing from the shortcut menu.

3. Select Shared As and either accept the default sharename or change it (see Figure 12-5).

4. Click OK.

NOTE   *In Windows 98SE, you can password-protect the printer in the same way you can password-protect folder shares. However, it's unusual to have a reason to do that.*

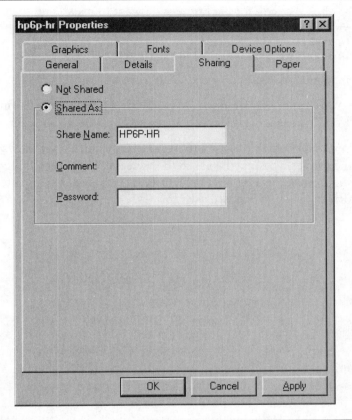

FIGURE 12-5   Share the printer by selecting the Shared As option and creating a sharename

Installing a Remote Printer

In order to use a printer that's on a remote computer, you must install it on your local computer (which means installing the printer drivers on the local computer). To locate and install a remote printer, follow these steps:

1. Open Network Neighborhood or My Network Places.

2. Double-click the computer that has the printer you want to install, to display all the shares for that computer (including printer shares).

3. Right-click the icon for the printer you want to install and then choose the appropriate command:

   ■ In Windows XP, choose Connect from the shortcut menu.

   ■ In Windows 98SE, choose Install from the shortcut menu.

4. The Add Printer Wizard opens to begin installing the printer (in Windows XP, you first see a message telling you to click OK to look for a driver).

5. Follow the wizard's prompts to install the printer. If Windows has drivers for the printer, you may be asked to insert the Windows CD. If you're using drivers from the printer's manufacturer, click Have Disk or enter the path to the drivers when the wizard asks for it.

Windows XP Remote Printer Installation

The manner in which Windows XP handles any hardware installation could be described as "magical." If the operating system recognizes a Plug and Play device and has built-in drivers for the device, it automatically installs it. You don't see a dialog, you don't have to walk through a wizard—you don't have to do anything.

Windows XP manages remote printers in the same magical way. If you share a printer on another computer and Windows XP has the drivers for the printer already installed on the local hard drive, you don't have to install that remote printer. Wait a few minutes and then open the Printers and Faxes window in Control Panel. Voilà! You'll see the remote printer listed as an installed printer. You see, Windows XP browses the network every few minutes, behind the scenes, looking for anything new. When it finds a new shared printer for which it has installed drivers, it automatically adds it. If it doesn't have an installed driver, it ignores it until you manually install the printer. This phenomenon is common when the same or similar printers (printers that use the same driver files) are installed on both the Windows XP and other computers (which is the case in many small networks).

Part IV

Appendixes

Appendix A

Glossary of
Network Terminology

10BaseT   Also called twisted pair cable, 10BaseT is the current standard in Ethernet cable. 10BaseT looks like telephone cable, but it is manufactured differently, and it's designed to transmit data rather than voice. The cable's wires are twisted along the length of cable; hence the name twisted pair cable. Two types of 10BaseT are available: unshielded twisted pair (UTP) and shielded twisted pair (STP). In STP, the cable wires are encased in metal, which lessens the possibility of interference from other electrical devices, radar, or radio waves. Using 10BaseT requires the purchase of a hub. Each network computer's NIC is connected to a length of 10BaseT cable, which is then connected to the hub. The hub disseminates data to the computers' NICs.

100BaseTX   A networking standard that supports data transfer rates up to 100 Mbps, ten times faster than the original Ethernet standard. Often referred to as *Fast Ethernet,* the official standard is IEEE 802.3u.

1000BaseT   Provides 1000 Mbps (gigabit) Ethernet service.

10Base2   Commonly known as coaxial cable or thinnet cable. This network cable looks like a thin version of the cable that your cable television company uses. 10Base2 used to be the standard cable for Ethernet, but most companies have abandoned their 10Base2 systems in favor of 10BaseT. (See 10BaseT.)

Active Application   The software application in which you are currently working. Its window is in the foreground of your screen. Other applications that may be open are in the background of your screen and are called inactive applications.

Adapter   A circuit board installed in a PC that provides connectivity to a network.

ADSL   Asymmetric Digital Subscriber Line. This technology uses standard telephone lines to produce high-speed connections to the Internet. ADSL supports data rates of 1.5 to 9 Mbps when receiving data (*downstream rate*) and from 16 to 640 Kbps when sending data (*upstream rate*).You need a special ADSL modem, telephone lines that support the technology, and an Internet host server that maintains ADSL modems that can connect to your modem. (See SDSL.)

ASCII   American Standard Code for Information Interchange. This standard assigns a number to each key on your keyboard. Internally, your computer uses the number to read and write keyboard characters.

ASCII Text File   A file that contains nothing but ASCII characters without special formatting.

Auto-negotiate   The process of automatically determining the correct settings, such as determining the speed of Ethernet transmissions.

Bandwidth   The transmission capacity of a device, including how much data the device can transmit in a fixed amount of time. Usually expressed in bits per second (bps).

Banner   The NetWare term for a separator page, which is a form that accompanies each print job. (See Separator Page.)

Barrel Connector   A tube-shaped device that enables you to join two lengths of 10Base2 cable in a network. (See 10Base2.)

Baud Rate   The speed at which information is transferred. Also referred to as bits per second (bps).

BIOS   Basic In/Out System. Part of a PC that controls and manages the hardware in the computer.

Bit   The smallest unit of digital information. A bit is either on or off (to the computer, on is 1 and off is 0).

Bit Error Rate (BER)   In a digital transmission, the percentage of bits with errors, divided by the total number of bits that have been transmitted, received, or processed over a given time period. The rate is typically expressed as 10 to the negative power. BER is the digital equivalent to signal-to-noise ratio in an analog system.

Bit Error Rate Test (BERT)   A procedure or device that measures the bit error rate of a transmission. (See Bit Error Rate.)

Bitmap   A graphic image stored as a pattern of dots (called pixels).

Bits Per Second (Bps)   Measurement of the speed at which data is transferred.

BNC Connector   A round device shaped like a fat ring, a BNC connector looks like a smaller version of the connector at each end of your cable television cable. Installed at each end of a length of coaxial cable (also called 10Base2 or thinnet), the BNC features a center pin (connected to the center conductor inside the cable) and a metal tube (connected to the outer cable shielding). A rotating ring on the metal tube turns to lock the male connector ends to any female connectors. (See 10Base2.)

Boot   The process of starting the computer and loading the operating system. Some people think the term originates from the adage "pulling oneself up by one's bootstraps."

A

Bottleneck   A delay in the transmission of data through the circuits of a computer's microprocessor or over a TCP/IP network. The delay typically occurs when a system's bandwidth cannot support the amount of information being relayed at the speed it is being processed.

Bridge   A device that connects different networks.

Broadband   A data transmission technology in which multiple signals share the bandwidth of a device.

Brownout   A drop in electrical voltage that can destroy a variety of computer components (hard drive, chips, and so on). You can prevent brownout damage by purchasing a voltage regulator. (See Voltage Regulator.)

Buffer Underrun   A problem that occurs when burning data to a CD. It indicates that the computer is not supplying data quickly enough to the CD writer. Recording to a CD-R (for compact disc, recordable) is a real-time process that must run nonstop without any interruption, and the CD-R drive stores incoming data in a buffer so that slowdowns in the data flow will not interrupt the writing process. A buffer underrun error occurs when the flow of data was interrupted long enough for the recorder's buffer to empty.

Bus   A slot on your computer's motherboard into which you insert cards, such as network interface cards. (Technically, the name of the slot is *expansion* slot, and the bus is the data path along which information flows to the card. However, the common computer jargon is bus.)

Byte   The amount of memory needed to specify a single ASCII character (eight bits). Kilobytes (1000 bytes) and megabytes (1,000,000 bytes) are usually used to describe the amount of memory a computer uses.

Cable Modem   A modem that connects to your cable television company's cable lines (but doesn't interfere with TV transmissions). Cable modems are significantly faster than standard telephone modems but aren't yet available everywhere. Their speeds are measured in millions of bytes per second rather than in thousands of bytes per second like standard modem speeds. (See Modem.)

Cache   Random-access memory (RAM) that is set aside and used as a buffer between the CPU and either a hard disk or slower RAM. The items stored in a cache can be accessed quickly, speeding up the flow of data.

Cascading Menu   A menu that is opened from another menu item. Also called a hierarchical menu or submenu. In Windows, a menu item displays a right arrow if it opens a cascading menu.

CAT 5 (Category 5)   The American National Standards Institute/Electronic Industries Association (ANSI/EIA) standard for twisted pair cable that is the standard for Ethernet networks.

CD-ROM   Compact Disc-Read Only Memory. Discs that contain programs or data. CD-ROMs can hold more than 600MB of data. You can only read data on a CD-ROM; you cannot write (save) data.

Centronics Interface   The connector on a parallel (printer) cable that attaches to the printer.

Check Box   A small square box in a dialog box that can be selected or cleared to turn an option on or off. When the check box is selected, an X or a check mark appears in the box.

Client   A computer that uses hardware and services on another computer (called the host or server). Also called a workstation.

Client/Server Network   A network scheme in which a main computer (called the host or server) supplies authentication services and sometimes supplies files and peripherals shared by all the other computers (called clients or workstations). Each user who works at a client computer can use the files and peripherals that are on his individual computer (called the local computer) or on the server.

Clipboard   An area of memory devoted to holding data you cut or copy, usually used to transfer data between applications or between parts of a data file. Typically, you transfer data to the clipboard by using an application's Copy or Cut command, and you insert data from the clipboard by using the application's Paste command.

Cluster   A unit of data storage on a hard or floppy disk.

Coaxial Cable   Cable used in 10Base2 networks. (See 10Base2.)

COM Port   Also called a serial port. A connector where you can plug in a serial device cable, usually attached to a modem. Most PCs have two COM ports, COM1 and COM2.

A

Computer Name   A unique name assigned to a computer on a network to differentiate that computer from other computers on the network.

Concentrator   (See Hub.)

CPU (Central Processing Unit)   The computing component of a computer. Also called the processor.

CSMA/CD   Carrier Sense Multiple Access/Collision Detection. The LAN access method that Ethernet uses. When a device wants access to the network, it checks to determine whether the network is quiet (senses the carrier). If the network is not quiet, the device waits a random amount of time before retrying. If the network is quiet and two devices access the cable at exactly the same time, their signals collide, and both devices retreat to wait another random amount of time before trying again.

Daisy Chain   Connected in a series, one after another. Transmissions go to the first device, then the second device, and so on.

Database   A collection of data that is organized in a way that makes it easy to access.

Data Packet   A frame in a packet-switched message. Most data communication processes divide messages into packets. For instance, Ethernet packets can be from 64 to 1518 bytes long.

Default Button   In some dialog boxes, a command button that is selected automatically if you press ENTER. In most dialog boxes, the default button has a bold border to make it discernible.

Default Gateway   The routing device that is used to forward all traffic that is not addressed to a device within the local LAN.

Defrag   To take fragments of files and put them together so that every file on a hard drive has all of its contents in one place. Defragging makes opening files a much faster process because the operating system doesn't have to look all over your hard drive for all the pieces of a file that you want to open.

Device Driver   Software files that allow your operating system to communicate with hardware, such as network interface cards, or peripherals, such as printers. For example, a printer driver translates information from the computer into information the printer can understand and manage. (Also called drivers.)

DHCP   Dynamic Host Configuration Protocol. A protocol that lets network administrators manage the assignment of IP addresses. Each computer using TCP/IP gets an IP address automatically.

Dial-Up Networking   A feature in Windows that enables your modem to dial out and connect to a server, either on the Internet through an Internet service provider (ISP), or to a server in a company network.

Directory   Part of the structure for organizing your files on a disk. A directory can contain files and other directories (called subdirectories). In Windows, directories are usually called folders.

DMZ   Demilitarized Zone. Allows one IP address to be exposed to the Internet, creating a host for the other computers that access the Internet.

DNS   Domain Name System. The way that domain names are located and translated into IP addresses.

Document   A data file that you create in a software program.

Document Window   The window within a software program's window that holds the document. More than one document window can be open at a time.

Domain   A group of computers under the control of one security database.

Download   To receive a file transmitted over the network (including the Internet). The opposite of *upload*, which means transmitting a file over the network.

Driver   Software that provides the operating system with information about a device, enabling the operating system to control the device.

Dynamic IP Address   An IP address that is assigned automatically, usually by a DHCP server.

Dynamic Routing   Forwarding data via different routes, based on the current condition of network circuits.

Embedded Network Card   A network interface card that is built into a computer's systemboard.

Ethernet   The most widely used of the several technologies available for cabling Local Area Networks. (See LAN.)

Expansion Slot   A slot on your computer's systemboard into which you insert cards, such as network interface cards. Also called a *bus*.

Extension   The period (.) and characters at the end of a filename that usually identifies the kind of information a file contains. For example, text files usually have the extension ".*txt*", and Microsoft Word files usually have the extension ".*doc*".

A

Failover   A backup operation that automatically switches to a standby database, server, or network if the primary system fails or is shut down.

Fast Ethernet   Ethernet that communicates at 100Mbps.

Fault Tolerance   The ability of a system to react automatically to an unexpected software or hardware failure. There are many levels of fault tolerance, from being able to continue operations in the event of a power failure (back up battery systems) to mirroring all operations (every operation is performed on one or more duplicate systems).

Firewall   Software or hardware that protects a computer on the Internet from unauthorized, outside intrusion. Companies that have one or more servers exposed to the Internet use firewalls to allow only authorized employees access to the servers.

Firmware   Programming code that is written into read-only memory, so it is retained even when the device is not on.

FTP   File Transfer Protocol. A protocol used to transfer files over TCP/IP.

Full Duplex   The ability of a device to transmit data in both directions simultaneously.

Gateway   A device that interconnects networks.

Gigabit   When used to describe data storage, it equals 1024 megabits. When used to describe data transfer rates, it equals 10^9 (1,000,000,000) bits.

Gigabits Per Second (Gps)   A measurement of data transfer speed. A gigabit equals 1,000,000,000 bits.

Gigabyte (GB)   1000 megabytes.

GPF   General Protection Fault. In Windows, this means the memory protection feature detected an illegal instruction from a program, causing the program to crash.

Graphical User Interface (GUI)   A way of interacting with a computer using graphics instead of text. GUIs use icons, pictures, and menus to display information and accept input through a mouse and a keyboard.

Half Duplex   Data transmissions that can travel in only one direction at a time.

Home Phoneline Networking Alliance   An association working to ensure adoption of a single, unified home telephone line networking standard and to bring home telephone line networking technology to the market.

Host   The main computer on a client/server network that supplies the files and peripherals shared by all the other computers. Also called a *server*.

HTML   Hypertext Markup Language. The language used to create Web pages, it define the location and characteristics of each element on the Web page.

HTTP   Hypertext Transfer Protocol. The protocol used for transferring files to and from World Wide Web (WWW) sites.

Hub   The home base of a 10BaseT network to which all lengths of cable from the network computers are attached. (One end of each cable length attaches to the concentrator; the other end of each length attaches to a computer's network interface card.) Also called a concentrator.

IDE   Integrated Drive Electronics. A type of hard drive controller.

IEEE   Institute of Electrical and Electronics Engineers, which oversees standards.

Interrupt   A signal that a device sends to the computer when the device is ready to accept or send information. (See IRQ.)

I/O   Short for Input/Output. The process of transferring data to or from a computer. Some I/O devices handle only input (keyboards and mice), some handle only output (printers), and some handle both (disks).

IP   Internet Protocol. The method by which data is sent from one computer to another computer on the Internet, or on a network using TCP/IP.

IP Address   A number that identifies a computer's location on the Internet or on a network using TCP/IP.

IPSec   Internet Protocol Security. A series of protocols used to implement security during the exchange of data over a network.

IRQ   Interrupt Request. An assigned location in memory used by a computer device to send information about its operation. Because the location is unique, the computer knows which device is interrupting the ongoing process to send a message.

ISA Bus   ISA (Industry Standard Architecture) is a standard bus that has been used for a number of years. It's a 16-bit card, which means that it sends 16 bits of data at a time between the systemboard and the card (and any device attached to the card). (See Bus, EISA Bus, Systemboard, and PCI Bus.)

A

ISDN Modem   A modem that offers faster transmission speeds than a standard modem. (ISDN stands for Integrated Services Digital Network, in case you were wondering.) The drawback is that an ISDN modem is generally more expensive than a standard modem and requires a special ISDN phone line (which is more expensive than a standard phone line).

ISP   Internet service provider. A company that provides Internet access to individuals and businesses.

Java   A programming language produced by Sun Microsystems. Java is used to provide services over the Web. A Web site can provide a Java application (called an *applet*) which you download and run on your own computer.

JPEG   A format for graphic image files. JPEG images are usually smaller than other types of image files, due to compression features. However, the compression features are sometimes rather primitive, so it may be difficult to reproduce the image properly.

Jumper   A small piece of plastic in a network interface card that "jumps" across pins. Whether or not pins are "jumpered" determines settings components in a computer.

Kbps   Kilobits per second. A measure of data transfer speed. One Kbps is 1000 bits per second.

Keyboard Buffer   An area in memory that keeps track of the keys you typed, even if the computer did not immediately respond when you typed them. If you hear a beep when you press a key, you've exceeded the size of the buffer.

Kilobyte   1024 bytes. Usually abbreviated K, as in 1024K. Used to describe the size of memory and hard drive storage.

LAN   Local Area Network. Two or more computers connected to one another so that they can share information and peripherals.

Latency   The delay between the time a communication or process request is made, and when it begins.

LCD   Liquid Crystal Display. Technology used for laptop computer displays as well as many other electronic devices.

LMHOSTS File   In Windows, a plain text file that tells your computer where to find another computer on a network. The file resides in the Windows directory, and it lists the IP addresses and computer names of computers on the network.

Local Computer   The computer you sit in front of when you access a remote computer. (See Remote Computer.)

Local Printer   A printer attached to the computer you're using.

LPT1   The name used to refer to the first parallel port on a computer. The second parallel port, if there is one, is LPT2.

LVDS   Low Voltage Differential Signaling. A low noise, low power, low amplitude method for high-speed data transmission over copper wire. LVDS differs from normal input/output. Normal digital I/O uses 5 volts as a high (binary 1) and no volts as a low (binary 0). The differential adds –5 volts as a third option, which provides another level for encoding, therefore providing a higher maximum data transfer rate, using fewer wires.

MAC Address   Media Access Control address. A unique number assigned by the manufacture to an Ethernet networking device (such as a network adapter), which lets the network identify the device at the hardware level.

Mapping   To assign a drive letter to a shared resource on another computer to access that shared resource more easily. You can map another computer's drive, folder, or subfolder. The drive letter that you use becomes part of the local computer's set of drive letters. The drives you create are called *network drives*.

Mbps   Megabits per second. A data transmission measurement of 1 million bits per second.

Megabit   When used to describe data storage, 1024 kilobits. When used to describe data transfer rates, 1 million bits.

Megabyte   1024 kilobytes (approximately 1 million bytes). Usually abbreviated MB.

Megahertz   The speed at which a computer runs, set by the processor. Usually abbreviated MHz.

MIDI   Musical Instrument Digital Interface. The protocol for communication between electronic musical instruments and computers.

MIME   Multipurpose Internet Mail Extension. The standard for transferring binary information (files other than plain text files) via e-mail.

Modem   A communications device that enables a computer to transmit information over a telephone line.

A

Modular Duplex Jack   A device that plugs into a telephone wall jack to convert that single telephone jack into two jacks so that you can plug in two phones; a phone and a modem; or, in the case of a telephone line network, a telephone and a telephone line network cable. Also called a *splitter*.

Monochrome Printer   A printer that prints in black and shades of gray (rather than a color printer, which prints in colors). Some people call this a black-and-white printer, despite the fact that no white ink is involved.

Motherboard   For a PC, a plane surface that holds all the basic circuitry, and the CPU. Also called a *systemboard*.

Multimedia PC   A PC that contains a CD-ROM drive, sound card, and speakers.

Multiprocessor   A computer system that uses more than one CPU running simultaneously for faster performance.

NAT   Network Address Translation. The translation of an IP address used within a network to a different IP address that is known within another network.

NDIS   Network Driver Interface Specification. A Windows device driver feature that enables a single NIC to support multiple network protocols (for example, both TCP/IP and NetBEUI).

NetBEUI   NetBIOS Extended User Interface. The transport layer for NetBIOS communication.

NetBIOS   Network Basic Input/Output System. A software program that permits applications to communicate with other computers that are on the same cabled network.

Network Drive   A drive that is located on another computer on the network.

Network Interface Card (NIC)   The primary hardware device for a network, a NIC attaches a computer to the network cable. Technically, NIC refers only to internal cards, because network controllers are available for USB and other ports. However, the term is often used generically to describe any network controller.

Network Printer   A printer attached to a remote computer on the network. (A printer attached to a local computer on the network is called a *local* printer.)

Network Resource   A device located in a computer other than the local computer.

Node   A connection point for distributing computer transmissions. Usually applied to computers on a network.

Object Linking and Embedding (OLE)   A software system that allows programs to transfer and share information. When a change is made to a shared object in the first program, any document in any program that contains that object is automatically updated.

Packet   A chunk of information sent over a network (including the Internet).

Parallel Port   A connection on a PC, usually named LPT1 or LPT2, where you plug in a cable for a parallel device (usually a printer).

Pathname   In DOS, a statement that indicates a filename on a local computer. When you use a pathname, you tell your computer that the target folder is on the local computer. Anyone working at another computer on the network must use a UNC statement to access that folder.

PC Card   A device for a laptop computer that is designed to use PCMCIA slots on the computer.

PCI bus   Peripheral Component Interconnect bus. The PCI bus is built for speed and is found in most new computers. It comes in two configurations: 32-bit and 64-bit. (32-bit means that the bus sends 32 bits of data at a time between the systemboard and the card; 64-bit means that the bus sends 64 bits of data at a time.) Its technology is far more advanced—and complicated—than that of the ISA bus. (See Bus, EISA Bus, ISA Bus.)

PCMCIA   A device for a laptop computer, such as a NIC or a modem, that works like an expansion slot (bus) in a desktop computer. A PCMCIA card is about the size of a credit card. Also called a PC card.

Peer-To-Peer Network   A network in which all the computers are connected without any network-wide authentication procedures (which is the case in a client/server network).

Peripheral   Any device connected to a computer: a monitor, keyboard, removable drive, CD-ROM drive, scanner, speakers, and so on.

Permission Level   A setting that controls users' access to shared resources on a network. The person who creates a shared resource decides which type of permission level to grant, such as Read-Only, Full, or Depends on Password.

Persistent Connections   Mapped drives linked to a user (a logon name) rather than a computer. If multiple users share a computer, the mapped drives that appear are those created by the user who is currently logged on. (See Mapping.)

A

Plug and Play   A software feature that reviews all the hardware in your computer during startup. When a new Plug and Play hardware component is detected, the software installation procedure begins automatically.

POP   Post Office Protocol. A protocol for downloading e-mail from an e-mail server.

Port   A connector located on the back of your computer into which you can plug a peripheral device, such as a keyboard, mouse, printer, and so on. Computers also have virtual ports. (See Virtual Port.)

POST   Power-On Self-Test. The internal circuitry, memory, and installed hardware that a computer performs on itself when you turn it on.

PPP   Point to Point Protocol. A protocol for communication between two computers using a serial interface (usually a telephone line). Usually used to describe the way an ISP provides a connection so the provider's server can respond to your output, pass it on to the Internet, and bring Internet responses back to you.

PPPoE   Point to Point Protocol over Ethernet. A method of encapsulating PPP in a way that provides authentication processes in addition to transporting data.

PPTP   Point to Point Tunneling Protocol. A protocol that allows PPP to be tunneled through an IP network. Usually used for secure access from one location to another over a Virtual Private Network (VPN).

Print Queue   The lineup of documents waiting to be printed.

Print Server   On a network, a computer to which a shared printer is attached.

Print Spooler   The place on your hard drive where printer jobs are lined up, waiting to be sent to the printer. (See Print Queue.)

Profile   The computer environment that belongs to a particular user.

Protocol   Standardized rules for transmitting information among computers.

Proxy Server   A server that acts in place of a client computer. For example, a proxy server performs all the functions of a Web browser for all the individual computers accessing the Internet.

RAM   Random-Access Memory. The memory used by the operating system and software to perform tasks. The phrase "random-access" refers to the ability of the processor to access any part of the memory.

Registry   A database that keeps track of the configuration options for software, hardware, and other important elements of your Windows operating system.

Remote Computer   On a network, a computer other than the one you're working on.

Remote User   A user who's accessing one computer but sitting in front of another computer.

Resolution   The number of dots (pixels) that make up an image on a screen or printed document. The higher the resolution, the finer and smoother the images appear.

RG-58 cable   The specific type of coaxial (10Base2) cable used in networks. (See 10Base2.)

RIP   Routing Information Protocol. A routing protocol (part of TCP/IP) that determines the route to a destination based on the smallest number of hops.

RJ-11   Registered Jack-11. The connector at each end of a length of telephone cable for telephones and telephone line networking schemes.

RJ-45   Registered Jack-45. The connector at the end of Ethernet twisted pair cable.

Root Directory   A section of your hard drive that is not part of a directory (folder). It holds files needed for booting.

Router   A device that connects subnetworks together.

SDSL   Symmetric Digital Subscriber Line. A technology that allows a high-speed connection to the Internet over standard telephone lines. SDSL supports data rates up to 3Mbps. It differs from ADSL in the fact that it supports the same data rates for both upstream and downstream traffic. (See ADSL.)

Separator Page   A form that accompanies each print job and prints before the first page of the job. The form displays the name of the user and prints ahead of the first page of each document so that multiple users of a printer can easily identify their documents. Also called a *banner* (in NetWare).

Server   A computer on a network that functions as a supplier of services to users. Also called a *host*.

Shared Resources   Files, folders, printers, and other peripherals attached to one computer on a network that have been configured for access by remote users on other computers on the network. (See Remote User.)

A

Slot   (See Expansion Slot.)

SMTP   Simple Mail Transfer Protocol. The protocol used to transfer e-mail between computers on the Internet. It is a server-to-server protocol, so other protocols (such as POP) are needed to transfer e-mail to a user's computer.

Sneakernet   The inconvenience you have when you don't have a network. With sneakernet, information is exchanged between computers by copying files to a disk from one computer, walking to another computer (not necessarily wearing sneakers), and then loading the files from the disk into the second computer.

SOHO   Small Office/Home Office. A description of computer (usually network) environments.

Splitter   (See Modular Duplex Jack.)

Static IP Address   A permanent IP address assigned to a node in a TCP/IP network.

Static Routing   A permanent routing system for forwarding data in a network, which cannot adjust to changing conditions. (See Dynamic Routing.)

STP Cable   Shielded Twisted Pair cable. A type of 10BaseT cable in which metal encases the cable's wires, lessening the possibility of interference from other electrical devices, radar, radio waves, and so on.

Subnet Mask   A method of splitting IP networks into a series of subgroups (subnets). Usually LANs are computers that have the same subnet mask.

Switch   A device that connects network devices, allowing a large number of network devices to share a limited number of ports.

System Files   The files that Windows installs to make the operating system run.

T-connector   A T-shaped connector used to connect 10Base2 to a NIC on a network without interrupting the cable run. (See Network Interface Card, 10Base2.)

TCP/IP   Transmission Control Protocol/Internet Protocol. A set of standardized rules for transmitting information. TCP/IP enables Macintosh, IBM-compatible, UNIX, and other dissimilar computers to jump on the Internet and communicate with one another, as long as each computer uses TCP/IP.

Terminator   A device with BNC connectors that lets you "cap off" the empty cross-bars of T-connectors at the beginning and end of a 10Base2 cable run. (See 10Base2, BNC Connector, T-Connector.)

TFTP   Trivial File Transfer Protocol. A version of FTP that has no security (password) capabilities.

Thinnet   (See 10Base2.)

Topology   The way a network is laid out.

Twisted Pair Cable   (See 10BaseT.)

UNC   Universal Naming Convention. A formatted style used to identify a particular shared resource on a particular remote computer. The format is \\Computername\sharename.

Uninterruptible Power Supply (UPS)   A mega-battery that plugs into the wall outlet. You plug your computer and monitor into the UPS outlets. If power fails, your computer draws power from the battery to give you enough time to shut down your computer properly.

Upload   To send data over a network (including the Internet). Opposite of download (receive data).

URL   Uniform Resource Locator. Used on the World Wide Web (WWW) to identify the address of a resource on the Internet. For example, www.microsoft.com.

UTP   Unshielded Twisted Pair. 10BaseT cable that does not have a metal shield. (See STP.)

Virtual Drive   A drive that doesn't really exist; you add a new drive letter, but you don't add any new physical drives to a computer. (See Mapping.)

Virtual Port   A nonphysical port through which a computer accepts data from remote computers (including over the Internet). For example, HTTP (the protocol you use when interacting with a Web page), uses port 80. Ports work by "listening" for data and will usually automatically accept data if it's the right type of data for that port.

Voltage Regulator   A device connected on one side to an outlet and on the other side to a computer. The device measures voltage coming from the outlet and then adjusts the voltage to make sure the voltage delivered to the computer is within a safe range.

VPN   Virtual Private Network. A technique for creating private communication channels (called *tunnels*) between LANS.

A

Wake-on-LAN   A technology (built into network adapters) that allows a computer to be powered on remotely over a network.

WAN   Wide Area Network. A network connected by public networks (usually telephone lines), covering remote geographical areas, consisting of two or more LANs.

Wizard   An interactive program that walks you through a software installation process.

Workgroup   The group to which the computers on a peer-to-peer network belong.

Workstation   (See Client.)

Y-Connector   An adapter shaped like the letter *Y* that connects two devices to one input device. For example, you can use a Y-connector to connect both a modem and a telephone line NIC to a length of cable that's inserted in a wall jack for a telephone line network. The two ends at the top of the Y connect to the back of the computer (one end connects to the modem; the other connects to the NIC). The single end at the bottom of the Y connects the cable between the computer and the wall jack. (See NIC.)

Appendix B

Advanced Network Tools

If all goes well (and it usually does), after you connect all the hardware and finish all the software configuration chores, the computers on your network will see each other and will find the Internet, and you can just start using your network. Every once in a while, however, you may have a small problem with the way your network is functioning, and you may have to dig around the operating system to find and solve the problem. Luckily, lots of tools exist to help you dig. In addition to diagnosing and solving problems, you can use network tools to learn about the way networks work.

Windows Graphical Network Tools

Windows works in a GUI (pronounced *gooey*), which stands for graphical user interface, so it's not surprising that many of its built-in tools are GUI tools. However, few of Microsoft's network tools are GUI tools. Most of the network tools and utilities are text-based programs that you run from the command line, and they're discussed later in this chapter, in the section "Command Line Tools." However, the few GUI network tools that come with Windows, or are available from Microsoft's Web sites, are important and useful.

WINIPCFG

Winipcfg is available in Windows 95/98/98SE/Me and presents a graphical view of a computer's TCP/IP configuration. It provides a way to renew the computer's DHCP lease of the IP address. To run winipcfg, choose Start | Run, type **winipcfg,** and click OK. The program opens with a display of the basic TCP/IP information for the network adapter(s) installed in the computer.

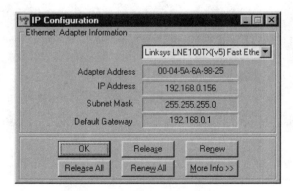

If you have multiple network adapters (perhaps one adapter for a DSL/cable modem, and another adapter for the LAN), select an adapter from the list in the drop-down box at the top of the window to see its configuration settings.

The Release, Renew, Release All, and Renew All buttons are only available for adapters that have DHCP addresses (IP addresses assigned by a DHCP server). If you run the program on the computer that's acting as the DHCP server (your ICS host), the buttons are grayed out.

- Click Release to remove the DHCP lease for the selected adapter, which removes the adapter's IP address.

- Click Renew to retrieve a new address for the selected adapter from the DHCP server.

- Click Release All to remove the DHCP leases from all the adapters in the computer.

- Click Renew All to retrieve new addresses for all the adapters in the computer.

- Click More Info to expand the window so it reveals more information about the computer's TCP/IP configuration (see Figure B-1).

While it's unusual to have a need to release and renew IP addresses, under some circumstances you may have to perform this task.

If a computer fails to find the DHCP server during startup, Windows assigns an automatic private IP address (APIPA) to the LAN adapter. APIPA addresses are assigned in the range 169.254.x.x, and they permit computers to communicate over a LAN, but won't work for Internet connection sharing. If the failure to find the DHCP server resulted from the order in which computers started up (you should always start the DHCP server first), after the DHCP server is up and running, the client computers usually find the DHCP server and get a leased IP address. You can force the computer to obtain an IP address from the DHCP server by using the Release and Renew buttons in the winipcfg window.

If you move a computer from one LAN to another (usually a scenario that involves a laptop), you can use the Release and Renew buttons to assign the computer an IP address that is guaranteed to be unique on the network.

B

WNTIPCFG

Wntipcfg is the Windows NT/2000/XP version of Winipcfg. Unfortunately, it isn't built in to the operating system, but you can download it from *http:// www.microsoft.com/windows2000/techinfo/reskit/tools/existing/wntipcfg-o.asp*. Click the link labeled WntIpcfg_setup.exe and save the file on your hard drive. To install the program, double-click the downloaded file and follow the prompts to complete installation.

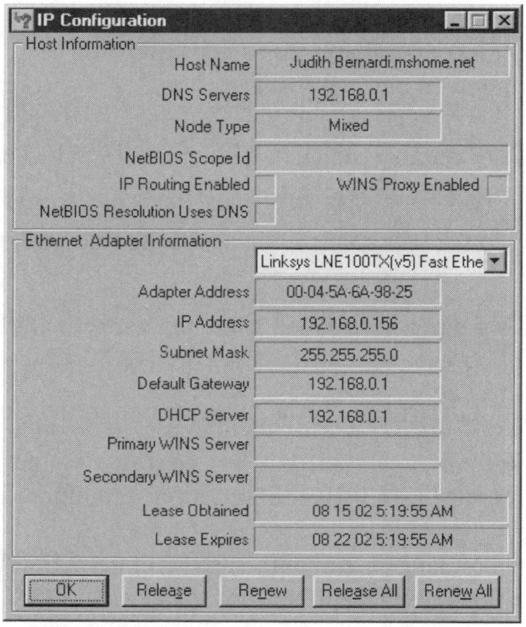

FIGURE B-1 The detailed view of winipcfg provides plenty of information about the TCP/IP settings for this computer

To run Wntipcfg, open Windows Explorer or My Computer and navigate to the folder in which you installed the program (the default installation folder is C:\Program Files\Resource Kit). Double-click the program's listing to open a window that offers the same information and tools as Winipcfg.

> **NOTE** *For Windows NT/2000/XP, a command line tool, Ipconfig, is available. This tool is a more powerful version of Wntipcfg. Ipconfig is discussed later in this chapter, in the section on command line tools.*

Network Connection Properties

You can use the Properties dialog of the network adapter to check settings and repair errors. A great deal of information about configuring adapter settings is found throughout this book, in the chapters specific to the network topology you're using (Ethernet, wireless, and so on). However, you can also do some troubleshooting from the Properties dialog. The following sections cover some of the settings you should check if you're having problems with network communications.

Workgroup Name

Be sure every computer on the network is logging on to the same workgroup. By default, Microsoft names the workgroup MSHOME, but if you chose a different name, you may have forgotten to make the change on one computer.

In Windows 98SE, follow these steps to ascertain the name of the workgroup:

1. Choose Start | Settings | Control Panel to open the Control Panel window.

2. Double-click the Network applet to open the Properties for your network adapter(s).

3. Click the Identification tab to see the workgroup name.

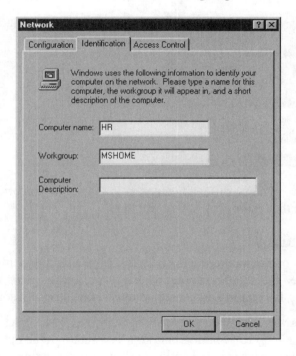

In Windows XP, follow these steps to see the name of the workgroup:

1. Choose Start | Control Panel.

2. Click Network and Internet Connections.

3. In the left pane (the Network Tasks list), click My Network Places.

B

4. In the left pane, click View Workgroup Computers and look for the workgroup name at the bottom of the left pane.

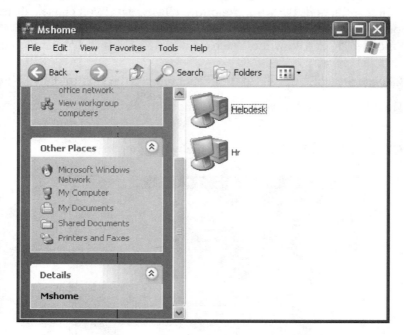

If the workgroup name differs on any computer, you must correct the errant entry and reboot that computer.

Shared Resources

You can't access one computer on the network from a remote computer unless you've configured the target computer to share its resources. This is a two-option process: enabling file sharing and creating at least one shared resource.

Enabling File Sharing　In Windows 98SE, open the Network applet in Control Panel, and click the File and Print Sharing button. Make sure that the option to share files is selected (and also make sure the option to share printers is selected if the computer has a printer).

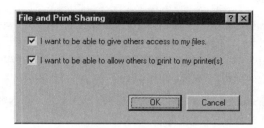

In Windows XP, right-click the icon for the LAN connection and make sure the option File and Printer Sharing for Microsoft Networks has a check mark in the check box.

Checking Shared Resources

Make sure at least one folder (or drive) is shared on each computer. The quick way to check is to open Windows Explorer or My Computer and look for drive and

B

folder icons that include a picture of a hand. However, if your shared folders are subfolders, or subfolders of subfolders, it's more difficult to check for shared folders (you have to navigate too far down into the drive and folder structure). Fortunately, you have some tools to help you find the folders you've shared.

Windows 98SE Net Watcher   In Windows 98SE, you can use Net Watcher to display information about your shares. Open Netwatcher by choosing Start | Programs | Accessories | System Tools | Net Watcher. To see a list of the shared resources on the computer, click the Show Shared Folders icon on the toolbar (see Figure B-2).

When you select a share, the right pane displays the name of any remote computer that's connected to that share. In Figure B-2, you can see that a user from the computer named Helpdesk is accessing the share named Linksys. To ascertain the name of the user, click the Show User icon on the toolbar. To disconnect a user, click the Disconnect User icon on the toolbar. (The user gets no warning message before being disconnected, so if you use this tool be prepared to hear some screaming.)

You can also use the tools in Net Watcher to remove a share (the icon is named Stop Sharing), and to add a share. Read the Net Watcher Help files for more information about using this versatile and powerful networking tool.

If Net Watcher isn't listed on your System Tools menu, you need to install it using the following steps:

1. Put the Windows 98SE CD in the CD drive.

2. Choose Start | Settings | Control Panel to open the Control Panel window.

3. Open the Add/Remove Programs applet.

4. Click the Windows Setup tab.

5. Select the System Tools listing and click Details.

6. Click the check box next to the Net Watcher listing, to place a check mark in the check box.

7. Click OK twice and follow the prompts to install Net Watcher.

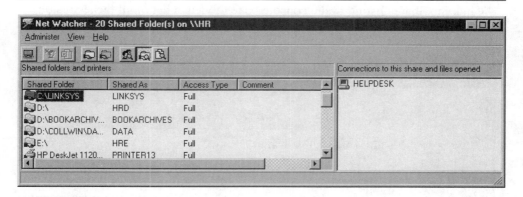

FIGURE B-2   Net Watcher displays information about all the shared resources on a computer

Windows XP Shared Folders Management Console   In Windows XP, you can use a Microsoft Management Console (MMC) to view information about the shares on the computer. To open the Computer Management MMC, choose Start, right-click the My Computer listing, and choose Manage from the shortcut menu. In the Computer Management MMC window that opens, expand the Shared Folders listing in the console pane (the left pane) by clicking the plus sign. This reveals listings for the three categories of information you can view with the MMC: Shares, Sessions, and Open Files.

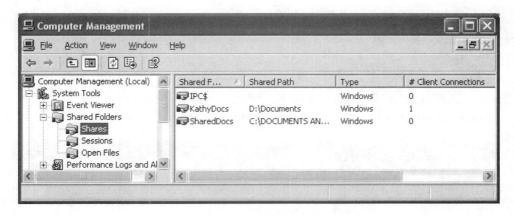

B

Click the Shares listing in the console pane to view a list of all the shares on the computer. Notice that you can also see whether any users are connected to any shares.

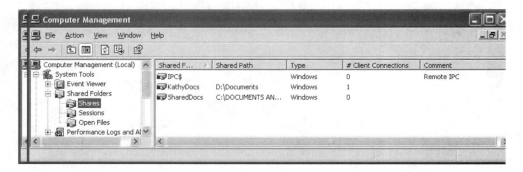

Click the Sessions listing in the console pane to see which users are connected to this computer's shares. The Action menu offers a command to disconnect all the sessions if you have some reason to do so.

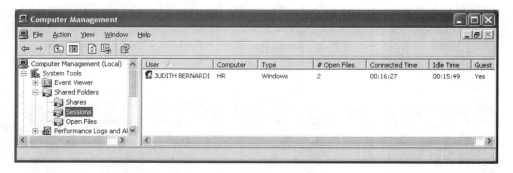

Click the Open Files listing to see the files being used by remote users. The Action menu offers a command to disconnect (close) all open files.

Disable Windows XP Internet Connection Firewall

Make sure that on a Windows XP computer, the LAN connection isn't running Internet Connection Firewall (ICF). ICF doesn't provide any configuration options to permit access from the computers on your network (you can easily configure third-party firewalls such as ZoneAlarm to allow network computers to access a Windows XP computer). To disable ICF, right-click the LAN connection, choose Properties from the shortcut menu, and click the Advanced tab. If a check mark appears in the check box for ICF, click the check box to remove the check mark (it's a toggle).

 Only remove ICF from the LAN connection, not from the connection to your modem.

Windows XP Network Diagnostics Tools

If you're running Windows XP, you have some additional graphical tools built in to the operating system for diagnosing and solving network connectivity problems. You can access these tools with the following steps:

1. Choose Start | Help and Support to open the Help and Support Center.

2. Under Pick a Task, click the link labeled Use Tools to View Your Computer Information and Diagnose Problems.

3. In the Tools list (the left pane), click Network Diagnostics.

You can click Scan Your System to have Windows XP look at all the settings involved in your network and Internet connections. Or, you can customize the scanning process by clicking Set Scanning Options. This tool is most useful if you're working with Microsoft support personnel, because it checks settings in the registry (the database that controls Windows). However, the tool performs a couple of tests on network hardware and indicates the results with a Passed/Failed indicator.

After scanning your system, the Network Diagnostics tool displays a report on the screen, as seen in Figure B-3. The report displays the categories the tool uses to analyze your network settings.

You can expand any category by clicking the plus sign, and you'll see the details for that category. Most of the details won't make sense to you, unless you have a good understanding of the registry. To maintain a permanent copy of the

B

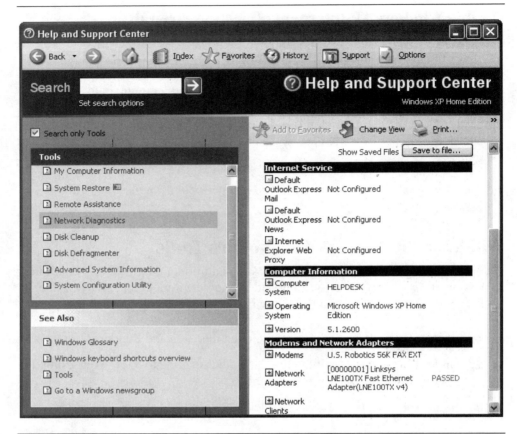

FIGURE B-3   The Network Diagnostics tool reports its findings sorted by category

report, click Save to File. The system saves the file in two places on your hard drive.

The filename is Netdiag XY, where X is the date (in the format DDMMYYYY) and Y is the time (in the format HHMMSS). You can retrieve the file later by clicking Show Saved Files.

If you find the test results overwhelming, you can focus on specific network settings by selecting the option Set Scanning Options. A window opens to display the actions the tool performs, and the categories for which the tool checks settings (see Figure B-4). You can enable or disable any of these settings by inserting or removing a check mark. To make your selections permanent, click Save Options.

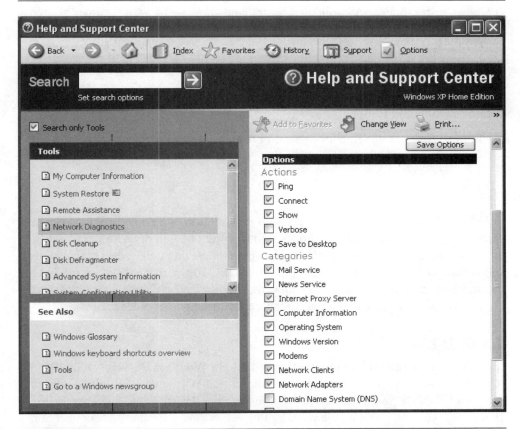

FIGURE B-4   Select the actions and categories you want Network Diagnostics to cover when it scans your system

Command Line Tools

Some of us are very comfortable working at the command line (called *text mode*), because we started working with computers before graphical interfaces such as Windows existed. Text mode was the only mode available. People who were introduced to computers after graphical interfaces became the norm often have a tough time with command line tools.

Even though the interface that Windows sports has introduced new and fancier graphics, command line tools continue to be part of the operating system. There's a good reason for this—text-based tools are very powerful. Working in text mode is always faster than working in a GUI tool, and some text-based commands aren't even available in a graphical format.

Command line tools operate in a command prompt window, which you reach in either of the following ways:

- In Windows XP, choose Start | All Programs | Accessories | Command Prompt.

- In Windows 98SE, choose Start | Programs | MS-DOS Prompt.

NOTE   *Type **exit** to close a command window.*

Most of the command line tools return information, which is displayed on your screen. If you want to save the information to a file you can open and examine at any time, you can invoke a feature called *redirection*. Saving output data permanently can be useful for working with support personnel. To redirect the data provided by a command line tool, use the following syntax: command > filename.txt (substitute the real command name and a real filename for these placeholder names).

Ipconfig

Ipconfig is a command line tool that's available in Windows 98/ME/NT/2000/XP. It's a particularly useful tool on systems running DHCP, because it allows you to see which TCP/IP values have been configured by DHCP. (If you have an assigned IP address, you can see it by viewing the Properties dialog for the LAN connection.)

To see the current IP address, open a command prompt, type **ipconfig**, and press ENTER. The system returns information about the current IP address.

```
Command Prompt                                                    _ □ ×

C:\>ipconfig

Windows IP Configuration

Ethernet adapter Local Area Connection:

        Connection-specific DNS Suffix  . :
        IP Address. . . . . . . . . . . : 192.168.0.1
        Subnet Mask . . . . . . . . . . : 255.255.255.0
        Default Gateway . . . . . . . . :

PPP adapter Mindspring:

        Connection-specific DNS Suffix  . :
        IP Address. . . . . . . . . . . : 63.14.144.236
        Subnet Mask . . . . . . . . . . : 255.255.255.255
        Default Gateway . . . . . . . . : 63.14.144.236

C:\>_
```

To gain more information, and perform additional tasks, you can use
parameters with ipconfig, as follows:

ipconfig [/all | /renew [*adapter*] **| /release** [*adapter*]] **(WinNT/2000/XP)**
ipconfig [/all | /renew_all | /release_all] (Win98/ME)

where

- ■ **all** displays all information about all connections. As you can see in
  Figure B-5, both the LAN connection and the dial-up Internet connection
  settings are shown. Note that the computer in Figure B-5 is the ICS host,
  and therefore doesn't need DHCP services to gain an IP address for the
  LAN connection.

- ■ **/renew** [*adapter*] - **/renew_all** renews the DHCP configuration parameters
  (IP address lease). This option is only available if the computer is running
  the DHCP Client service. If you have multiple adapters and want to renew
  the lease for only one adapter, type the adapter name that appears when
  you use ipconfig without parameters.

- ■ **/release** [*adapter*] - **/release_all** releases the current DHCP lease. This
  option is only available if the computer is running the DHCP Client service.
  The option disables TCP/IP on the local system, or on a specific adapter.

Ping

Ping is a command line tool that lets you verify the connection to a remote computer.
It's available in all versions of Windows and requires the TCP/IP protocol. Ping

B

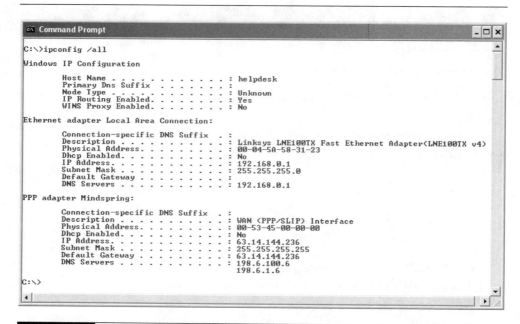

FIGURE B-5   Everything you need to know about a computer's TCP/IP configuration is available when you use the /all parameter with ipconfig

works by sending an Internet Control Message Protocol (ICMP) Echo Request message to a remote computer. ICMP is a message control and error-reporting protocol that uses IP datagrams, where the messages are processed by the IP software and are not seen by the user. The messages all request a reply, and the user can see whether a reply is received and the length of time it takes to receive that reply. You can use ping for a variety of tasks, depending on the function you need to check:

- To make sure that the TCP/IP protocol is installed and running on your computer

- To see if your computer is correctly connected to the network and receiving an IP address from a DHCP server

- To see if your computer can connect to the Internet host computer on the LAN, or on the Internet

- To see if your computer is getting DNS resolution services, which translates IP addresses to computer names (on the LAN) or domain names (on the Internet)

Check TCP/IP

One quick way to see whether TCP/IP services are running properly on your
computer is to perform a test, called a *loopback test*, with the ping command. In
the command window, type **ping 127.0.0.1** and press ENTER. TCP/IP sends four
message packets and waits for replies, displaying the progress in the command
window.

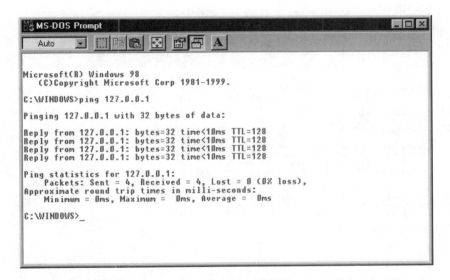

```
Microsoft(R) Windows 98
    (C)Copyright Microsoft Corp 1981-1999.

C:\WINDOWS>ping 127.0.0.1

Pinging 127.0.0.1 with 32 bytes of data:

Reply from 127.0.0.1: bytes=32 time<10ms TTL=128
Reply from 127.0.0.1: bytes=32 time<10ms TTL=128
Reply from 127.0.0.1: bytes=32 time<10ms TTL=128
Reply from 127.0.0.1: bytes=32 time<10ms TTL=128

Ping statistics for 127.0.0.1:
    Packets: Sent = 4, Received = 4, Lost = 0 (0% loss),
Approximate round trip times in milli-seconds:
    Minimum = 0ms, Maximum =  0ms, Average =  0ms

C:\WINDOWS>_
```

If the loopback test fails, it means the IP stack on the local computer isn't
working properly. This could mean the TCP drivers are corrupted, or the network
adapter has failed. Remove and reinstall TCP/IP protocol, and if the loopback test
still fails, replace the adapter.

Check Network Services

You can use ping to make sure your computer is getting IP address and gateway
services from a host computer on your network. First, use winipcfg (Windows 98SE)
or ipconfig (Windows XP) to determine the IP address of the computer. Then, enter
ping *x.x.x.x* (replace "x" with the IP address) and press ENTER. If the network routing
system is correct, this command merely forwards the packet to the loopback address of
127.0.0.1. The resulting display should look similar to the results from pinging the
loopback address. If the loopback test succeeds, but pinging the local IP address fails,
you probably have a problem with the driver for your network adapter, or with the
routing taking place on the ICS host computer.

B

Check Connection to the Gateway

To make sure your computer can reach the Internet gateway on your LAN, ping the IP address of the gateway computer. Usually, the gateway is the computer acting as the Internet connection host on your LAN, but if you have static IP addresses, the gateway is at your ISP. In a command window, enter **ping** *x.x.x.x* (substitute the IP address of the gateway for "x") and press ENTER. The system returns the information about the replies.

```
Microsoft(R) Windows 98
    (C)Copyright Microsoft Corp 1981-1999.

C:\WINDOWS>ping 192.168.0.1

Pinging 192.168.0.1 with 32 bytes of data:

Reply from 192.168.0.1: bytes=32 time=1ms TTL=128
Reply from 192.168.0.1: bytes=32 time<10ms TTL=128
Reply from 192.168.0.1: bytes=32 time<10ms TTL=128
Reply from 192.168.0.1: bytes=32 time<10ms TTL=128

Ping statistics for 192.168.0.1:
    Packets: Sent = 4, Received = 4, Lost = 0 (0% loss),
Approximate round trip times in milli-seconds:
    Minimum = 0ms, Maximum =  1ms, Average =  0ms

C:\WINDOWS>
```

If ping fails, it's likely you have a problem with the router/gateway device, or the cabling.

Check DNS

To make sure the DNS functions are operating properly, you should check both the local network and the Internet. To check the local network, enter **ping** *ComputerName* (substitute the name of a computer on your network for ComputerName) and press ENTER. The system displays the information about received replies, along with the IP address to which the name resolved.

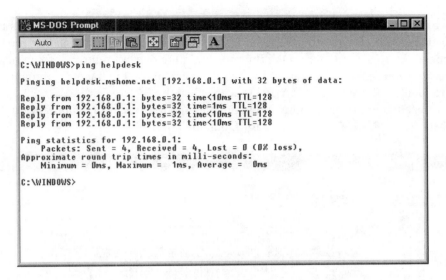

```
MS-DOS Prompt                                          _ □ ✕
Auto      ▼   [□] 🗐 🗈  ⊞  🖻 🖨  A

C:\WINDOWS>ping helpdesk

Pinging helpdesk.mshome.net [192.168.0.1] with 32 bytes of data:

Reply from 192.168.0.1: bytes=32 time<10ms TTL=128
Reply from 192.168.0.1: bytes=32 time=1ms TTL=128
Reply from 192.168.0.1: bytes=32 time<10ms TTL=128
Reply from 192.168.0.1: bytes=32 time<10ms TTL=128

Ping statistics for 192.168.0.1:
    Packets: Sent = 4, Received = 4, Lost = 0 (0% loss),
Approximate round trip times in milli-seconds:
    Minimum = 0ms, Maximum =  1ms, Average =  0ms

C:\WINDOWS>
```

To check DNS services on the Internet, enter **ping *DomainName*** (substitute
the URL for an Internet site for DomainName) and press ENTER. The system
displays the information about received replies.

Ping uses name resolution to resolve a computer name into an IP address. If
pinging by IP address succeeds but pinging by name fails, the problem is name
resolution, not network connectivity. Make sure that DNS server addresses are
configured properly for the computer (either by naming a DNS server or by indicating
DNS services are assigned automatically).

Ping is a powerful and useful command line tool, and has numerous parameters
you can use to perform a variety of tasks. Many of those tasks are outside the
scope of this discussion, but if you're interested in learning more about ping, see
the Windows Help files.

Tracert

When you connect to an Internet server, your computer doesn't establish a direct
connection to that computer—instead, you move through a number of Internet servers
to get there. You start at your ISP, then move through the Internet backbone, then

B

move through other servers. Each move is called a *hop*. Tracert (which stands for trace route) traces and reports the hops. If you use the ping command to verify connectivity to a computer on the Internet, and ping doesn't return all four packets properly (you see a result that says timeout), you can use the tracert command to try to identify the source of the problem.

To use tracert, open a command window and enter **tracert *DomainName*** (substitute the URL for a Web site for DomainName).

```
C:\>tracert ivens.com

Tracing route to ivens.com [64.226.173.212]
over a maximum of 30 hops:

  1    <1 ms    <1 ms    <1 ms  dsl092-230-065.phl1.dsl.speakeasy.net [66.92.230.65]
  2    16 ms    15 ms    16 ms  gw-081-239.dsl.speakeasy.net [66.92.239.1]
  3    10 ms     9 ms    10 ms  border1.fe5-14.speakeasy-27.ext1.phi.pnap.net [216.52.67.91]
  4    11 ms    11 ms    11 ms  core1.fe0-1-bbnet2.phi.pnap.net [216.52.64.65]
  5    11 ms    12 ms    12 ms  sl-gw26-pen-5-1-0.sprintlink.net [144.232.190.201]
  6    11 ms    12 ms    12 ms  sl-bb25-pen-0-7.sprintlink.net [144.232.5.185]
  7    11 ms    12 ms    12 ms  sl-bb21-pen-8-0.sprintlink.net [144.232.5.237]
  8    13 ms    13 ms    13 ms  sl-bb23-rly-0-0.sprintlink.net [144.232.20.32]
  9    15 ms    14 ms    13 ms  sl-bb21-rly-9-0.sprintlink.net [144.232.14.133]
 10    28 ms    26 ms    26 ms  sl-bb20-atl-10-1.sprintlink.net [144.232.9.198]
 11    27 ms    26 ms    26 ms  sl-gw21-atl-9-0.sprintlink.net [144.232.12.110]
 12    29 ms    30 ms    29 ms  sl-il-3-0.sprintlink.net [160.81.204.10]
 13    30 ms    30 ms    30 ms  64.224.0.99
 14    31 ms    30 ms    30 ms  ivens.com [64.226.173.212]

Trace complete.
```

If any hop produces a timeout, or takes an excessive length of time (50 milliseconds or more) to return a packet to tracert, you've probably discovered the source of your Internet connectivity problem. If the errant server is at your ISP, you can call the support number to see what's going on. Frequently, when an ISP is performing maintenance tasks on servers, connectivity is slow or temporarily unavailable. If the errant server is out on the Internet, you can't do anything except wait for the problem to be resolved. At least you know the problem is on the Internet, and not in your configuration settings.

NOTE   *If you see asterisks instead of an IP address at any hop, it means that server is configured for extra security, to avoid displaying its IP address to the world. Doing a tracert to microsoft.com produces such a result.*

Pathping

Pathping, which is available only in Windows XP and Windows 2000, is a useful utility that combines the power of ping with the power of tracert. You can use pathping to show each hop across the Internet as you travel to a target site, and see statistics about the way the data packets were handled by each server. The statistics are computed by continuous pinging of servers, which is time-consuming (so you don't want to try this with the slow speed of a telephone modem).

To accomplish its mission, pathping sends data packets to each server (actually, to the routers on each server), and then computes results based on the packets returned from each hop. The returned data shows the degree of packet loss at any given hop, so you can determine which server might be causing connectivity problems.

Nbtstat

Nbtstat is a powerful diagnostic tool that displays information about current TCP/IP connections that are using NBT (NetBIOS over TCP/IP). You're most likely to use this tool at the direction of a technical support person, but if you're having connectivity issues, this program is a good way to determine if the problem stems from duplication of a computer name or IP address.

Windows computers communicate with each other using the Server Message Block (SMB) network command protocol. (SMB is now called Common Internet File System, or CIFS, for no apparent reason, because I think the word "Internet" is confusing—SMB is used on LANs—maybe Microsoft just likes having the word "Internet" in all the cute names it gives its technology features.) SMB hosts use the computer name (called the *friendly* name) to identify computers, and the friendly name used to be called the NetBIOS name. SMB doesn't use the NetBIOS interface, but the phrase "NetBIOS name" dates back to earlier days in networking, when NetBIOS was the communication protocol—today we use TCP/IP. TCP/IP doesn't know (or care about) friendly names, so Windows uses an application called NetBIOS-Over-TCPIP Helper (NBT) to translate friendly names to IP addresses.

NBT registers the friendly name of each computer on the network, as each computer boots into Windows. It uses a Windows Internet Naming Service (WINS) database to store the information. If you're using WINS for name-to-IP address resolution (and you're probably not—instead, you're probably using DHCP), you can access the information that NBT has stored with the nbtstat command line tool. If you're not using WINS, NBT gathers the information it needs by periodically browsing the network.

Ntbstat has many parameters, and you can see all of them, along with explanations, by entering **nbtstat** at the command line. It's important to note the following two syntax rules for ntbstat:

- You enter parameters with a minus sign instead of a forward slash.

- Capitalization counts—entering the parameter -R is not the same as entering the parameter –r.

B

For this discussion, I'll go over some of the commonly used parameters when investigating network connectivity problems.

- **nbtstat -a** *RemoteComputerName* lists the remote computer's name table, indicating whether or not the computer name is registered on the network. For instance, to see information about a computer named helpdesk, entering **nbtstat -a helpdesk** produces a display that shows the computer named Helpdesk is registered (several times, due to periodic browsing) as a unique name. The display also indicates the name of the workgroup (MSHOME), and the MAC address of the adapter on the computer named helpdesk. Unique names are imperative, because any computer name that isn't unique to the network has serious connectivity problems.

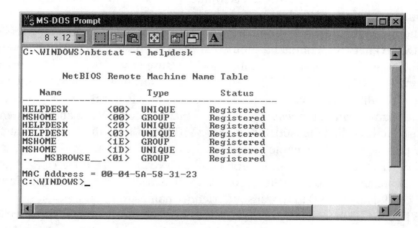

- **nbtstat -A** *RemoteIPaddress* is the same as using -a except instead of using the computer's friendly name, you enter its IP address.

- **nbtstat -n** displays the NetBIOS name for the local computer, also indicating whether the name is unique to the network. A status of Registered indicates that the name is registered by broadcast or WINS.

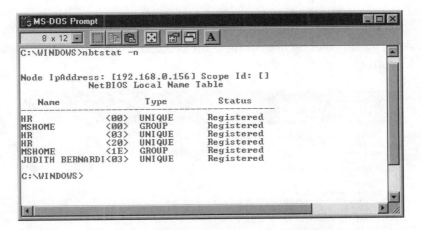

■ **nbtstat -r** lists the names of remote computers that have been resolved and registered via broadcast or via WINS.

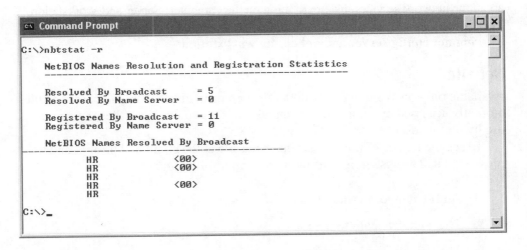

Net Commands

Windows has a slew of commands you can use to view network settings, perform network tasks, and troubleshoot network problems. All the commands start with the word "net" and have a second word that calls the specific net command. In this section, I'll discuss several of the useful net commands that run in a peer-to-peer (workgroup) environment.

Net Config

In Windows 98SE, entering **net config** at the command line returns information about the current computer and network software.

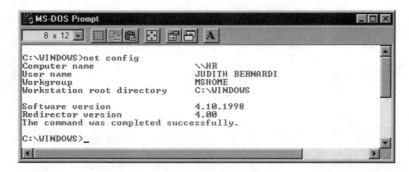

In Windows XP, entering **net config** at the command line returns information about the network services that are running on the computer: Server and Workstation. You can obtain additional information about the services (see Figure B-6) by entering **net config server** and **net config workstation**.

Net File

Available only on Windows XP/2000, this command displays the filenames of files currently accessed by remote users, and also allows you to close files that are in use by remote users.

To see the names of files in use, enter **net file** at the command prompt and press ENTER. The system returns the following information:

- An ID number for the file

- The complete path to the file

- The name of the remote user who is using the file

- The number of locks on the file (indicates that the file is locked and cannot be accessed by anyone else, including you)

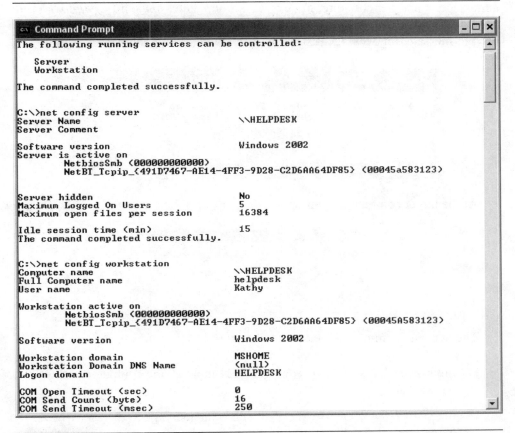

FIGURE B-6   You can view detailed information about the Server and Workstation services on a Windows XP computer

To close a file that's in use (and release the lock if it's locked), enter **net file ID# /close** (substitute the ID number you saw when you entered the command net file for ID#).

Net Send

Available only in Windows XP/2000/NT, this command lets you send messages to other computers on the network. The messages are displayed on the screen. To send

B

a message to another computer in your workgroup, enter **net send** *ComputerName* *MessageText* (substitute the name of a computer for ComputerName, and the text of your message for MessageText) at the command prompt and press ENTER.

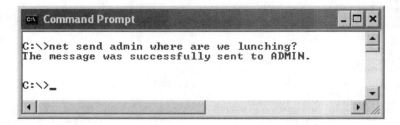

At the target computer, a pop-up window displays the message.

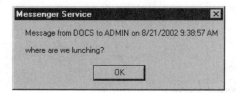

The net send command supports additional useful syntax values, as follows:

■ **net send** *** *MessageText* sends the message to all the computers in the workgroup.

■ **net send** *UserName MessageText* sends the message to the user who is logged on as *UserName* (useful if you don't know which computer that user is working on). If the user isn't logged on, no message is sent.

■ **net send** **/users** *MessageText* sends the message to all logged on users.

You need to be aware of the following rules for using net send:

■ If a UserName or ComputerName contains a space, enclose the name in quotation marks.

■ The message text cannot exceed 128 characters, including spaces.

Net Share

Available only in Windows XP/2000, you can use net share to manage the shared resources on a computer. The available parameters and syntax rules for net share are quite robust, and I'll discuss some of the commonly used (and useful) methods for using this command. (You can get more information about net share in the Windows XP/2000 help system.)

■ Entering **net share** (with no parameters) lists all the shared drives and folders on the computer.

■ Entering **net share** *ShareName* displays information about that share, including the name of any user who is currently accessing the share.

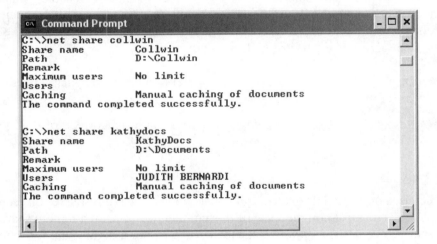

■ Entering **net share** *ShareName* **/users:***number* sets the maximum number of users (the number you enter for *number*) who can simultaneously access the share.

■ Entering **net share** *ShareName* **/unlimited** specifies that an unlimited number of users can simultaneously access the share.

■ Entering **net share** *ShareName* **/delete** stops sharing the resource named in *ShareName* (the folder isn't deleted, it's just no longer shared).

B

Net Time

Use the net time command to synchronize your computer's clock with the clock of another computer on the network that you know has the correct time. For computers logging on to a Windows 2000 domain, time synchronization is automatic, and Windows 2000 domain controllers are set to synchronize the time with an external reliable clock, over the Internet. When you're working in a peer-to-peer network (a workgroup), you can use a Windows XP computer as the computer that synchronizes its clock over the Internet, and then use the net time command to synchronize all the other computers on the network to that computer. See the section "Synchronizing Time Over the Internet" later in this chapter to learn how to use a Windows XP computer as a network timekeeper.

To synchronize a computer's clock with the clock of another (reliable) computer on the network, enter **net time *ComputerName* /set /yes** (substitute the name of the reliable computer for ComputerName) at a command prompt and press ENTER. The system performs the following tasks automatically:

- Displays the current time of the computer to which you synchronized your computer

- Resets the time (and the date, if the current date is incorrect) of your computer

Net Use

The net use command lets you control connections to shared resources on remote computers. The most common use of this command is to map a remote shared folder to a drive letter. *Mapping* is the technical term for assigning a drive letter to a share on a remote computer. The mapped drive letter becomes another drive on your local computer. This is a useful trick for shares you access constantly, because all the drives on your computer appear in My Computer and Windows Explorer, which means you don't have to open a network browse window to get to this share. Using a drive letter is much easier than browsing the network to get to a specific remote folder in order to open or save a document.

> NOTE *You can also map drives from the network browser (My Network Places or Network Neighborhood), which is discussed in Chapter 12.*

To map a remote share to a local drive letter, enter the following command at the command prompt and then press ENTER:

net use *x*: *ComputerName**ShareName*

where

- *x:* is the drive letter you want to use for this share.

- *\\ComputerName* is the name of the computer that has the share.

- *\ShareName* is the name of the share.

If you're unsure about which drive letter is available, enter an asterisk (*) instead of a drive letter, followed by a colon, Windows will assign the share the next available drive letter on your computer, using the following rules:

- Windows XP starts at z: and works backwards.

- All other versions of Windows start at the first unused drive letter on the computer and work forwards.

To see the mapped drives on your computer, enter **net use** at the command prompt and press ENTER. The system returns information about mapped drives; the status, the local drive letter that's been assigned to a share, and the name of the share on the remote machine.

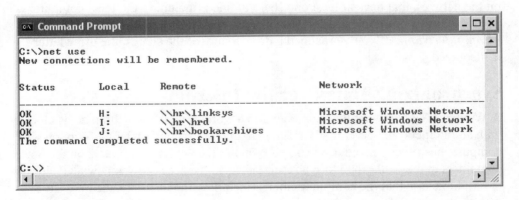

```
C:\>net use
New connections will be remembered.


Status       Local      Remote                    Network

-------------------------------------------------------------------
OK           H:         \\hr\linksys              Microsoft Windows Network
OK           I:         \\hr\hrd                  Microsoft Windows Network
OK           J:         \\hr\bookarchives         Microsoft Windows Network
The command completed successfully.

C:\>
```

- To disconnect a mapped drive, enter **net use** *x:* **/delete** (substitute the drive letter you want to disconnect for "x") and press ENTER.

- To disconnect all mapped drives, enter **net use * /delete** and press ENTER.

The real beauty of the net use command is the ability to use it in batch files, to automate transfer of files between computers. I use the command in a batch file that backs up files from one computer on my network to another. Following is a copy of one of my batch files for backing up important files. You can see I create a mapped drive (the share is drive C of the computer named admin), and then I use Xcopy (and its powerful parameters) to back up my files to a parent folder named adminbu (which stands for admin backup) that I created on the local computer.

```
REM SET UP A MAPPED DRIVE FOR THE \\SERVERNAME\SHARENAME FOR THE DRIVE
OF THE SOURCE COMPUTER
net use i: \\admin\admin-c
REM BEGIN COPYING
xcopy i:\figures\*.* c:\adminbu\figures /s/e/h/i/r/c/v/y
xcopy i:\"documents and settings"\administrator.WESTERN\"my
documents"\*.* c:\adminbu\"my documents" /s/e/h/i/r/c/v/y
xcopy i:\cuteftppro\*.* c:\adminbu\cuteftpro /s/e/h/i/r/c/v/y
xcopy i:\eudora\*.* c:\adminbu\eudora /s/e/h/i/r/c/v/y
xcopy i:\quickbooks\*.qbw c:\adminbu\quickbooks /s/e/h/i/r/c/v/y
REM REMOVE THE MAPPED DRIVE (TO AVOID AN ERROR THE NEXT TIME THE BATCH
FILE RUNS)
net use i: /delete
```

Net View

Net view displays information about the computers on your network that share resources. Entering **net view** at the command prompt returns a list of all the computers on the network that have at least one share defined (including the local computer).

To see a list of all the shares available on a specific computer, enter **net view** *ComputerName*. If you've mapped a drive to any of the shares, the drive letter is displayed.

Synchronizing Time Over the Internet

A Windows XP computer that's operating in a workgroup can synchronize its clock with an Internet time server that's accurate to the millisecond. After the Windows XP computer has synchronized its clock, you can use the net time command on the other computers in the workgroup to sync their clocks to the accurate Windows XP clock.

Making sure that the computer clocks (including the date) are accurate isn't just an exercise for the terminally fussy—it's important for time-stamped data. For example, if users on your network are accessing a network-wide database (including accounting software), the time stamp for each addition or modification of a record is important. Additionally, your e-mail software Inbox is probably sorted by date/time, and the date/time stamp on your outgoing messages may be important to recipients.

Understanding Time Synchronization

To use the time sync feature, you designate one Windows XP computer on your network as the time source. That computer's clock is synchronized with an Internet time server once a week. This is, obviously, much easier to accomplish if you have an always-on Internet connection through a DSL/modem cable. If, however, you're using a telephone modem, or a DSL connection that isn't always on, you can elect to sync the computer's clock manually.

The time sync works automatically—the Windows XP computer reads the time from the Internet time clock and resets its own clock (unless the clocks already match, of course). However, before attempting the synchronization, the Windows XP computer must have the correct date (some Internet clocks won't provide information to a computer that has the wrong date). You can check the computer's date setting by hovering your mouse over the time display at the right edge of your taskbar. If the date is wrong, double-click the time display to open the Date and Time Properties dialog, and specify the correct date. Click OK to close the dialog and reset the computer's date.

To establish the settings for synchronizing time on your Windows XP computer, double-click the time display at the right edge of the taskbar to open the Date and Time Properties dialog. Click the Internet Time tab, seen in Figure B-7.

Changing the Time Server

You can change the Internet time server if you wish (the default time server is run by Microsoft). If you click the arrow to the right of the Server field, you'll see an entry for a time server run by the United States government (time.nist.gov), which you can select.

You can also enter the name of a time server you prefer if you want to use one that is not in the drop-down list (useful if you live outside the United States).

CAUTION   *Only time servers that use the Simple Network Time Protocol will work. You can't use an Internet address that uses the Hypertext Transfer Protocol (HTTP).*

Time servers, which are available around the world, are maintained in a hierarchy. Primary (stratum 1) servers are the most accurate, but secondary (stratum 2) servers are generally either synchronized perfectly with stratum 1 servers or are

B

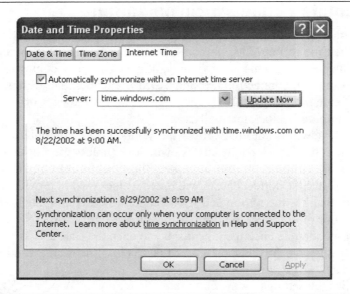

FIGURE B-7   Be sure synchronization is enabled, and choose an Internet time server

only slightly off the clock ticks of the stratum 1 servers. The difference, a matter of a few nanoseconds, certainly won't create a problem for you. Big deal!

- For a list of stratum 1 servers, visit *http://www.eecis.udel.edu/~mills/ntp/clock1.htm.*

- For a list of stratum 2 servers, visit *http://www.eecis.udel.edu/~mills/ntp/clock2.htm.*

TIP   *Because stratum 1 time servers are very busy and can time out, you should select stratum 2 servers as your external NTP servers.*

Each list contains the NTP time servers available for public access, including any restrictions on their use. The lists are sorted by country code.

Synchronizing the Time Manually

If you don't have an always-on Internet connection, or if your Windows XP computer was not running during the last scheduled sync, you'll see a failure message when you open the Internet Time tab of the Date and Time Properties dialog. You can, however, update the Windows XP clock manually. Start your Internet connection and then click Update Now.

You may want to use the manual update method even if you have an always-on Internet connection. For instance, if your Windows XP clock doesn't maintain its accuracy over the course of a week, you can sync time daily, or semiweekly.

Updating Clocks on the Network Computers

Once you have a reliable clock on the network, you should update the time on all the other computers on your network by using the net time command, and pointing the computers to the reliable Windows XP computer. See the discussion on the net time command earlier in this chapter.

B

Appendix C

Getting Help and Support

This book is focused on helping you understand, install, and configure the hardware for your home or business network. A lot of additional information that can help you manage, tweak, and secure your network is available in other books, most of which contain a great amount of detail about specific features and functions. Some of these books are about basic features and functions, others cover advanced troubleshooting techniques. Information about specific books is in this appendix.

Linksys maintains a robust support system, providing information online and through trained support personnel. Information about Linksys support, and about Linksys products for networks, is in this appendix.

Books

Linksys Networks: The Official Guide is about installing, configuring, and maintaining networks, and we assume you've already set up basic operating system configuration settings. We even assume you know how to install a printer, a DSL/cable/telephone modem, and other peripherals. However, if you're working with a new computer or a new version of Windows at the same time you're setting up a network, you can get information about basic operating system chores from other books published by McGraw-Hill/Osborne.

Windows XP Books

Windows XP: The Complete Reference by Levine & Levine-Young, McGraw-Hill/Osborne (0-07-219297-6)
Windows XP Headaches: How to Fix Common (and Not So Common) Problems in a Hurry by Simmons, McGraw-Hill/Osborne (0-07-222461-4)

Windows 2000 Books

Windows 2000: The Complete Reference by Ivens, McGraw-Hill/Osborne (0-07-211920-9)
Windows 2000: A Beginner's Guide by Matthews, McGraw-Hill/Osborne (0-07-212324-9)

Windows 98 Books

Windows 98: The Complete Reference by Levine, McGraw-Hill/Osborne
(0-07-882343-9)

Security Books

Hacking Exposed by McClure, Scambray, Kurtz, McGraw-Hill/Osborne
(0-07-219381-6)
Hacking Exposed Windows 2000 by McClure & Scambray, McGraw-Hill/Osborne
(0-07-219262-3)

Network Protocols Books

Networking: A Beginner's Guide, Second Edition by Hallberg,
McGraw-Hill/Osborne (0-07-213231-0)

Hardware Books

Troubleshooting, Maintaining & Repairing PCs, 5th Edition,
McGraw-Hill/Osborne (0-07-213272-8)
PC Hardware by Ron Gilster, McGraw-Hill/Osborne (0-07-212990-5)
Bigelow's PC Technician's Troubleshooting Pocket Reference by Bigelow,
McGraw-Hill/Osborne (0-07-212945-X)

Internet Books

Internet: The Complete Reference, Second Edition by Levine-Young,
McGraw-Hill/Osborne (0-07-219415-4)

Linksys Support

Linksys offers fast and free 24-hour technical support 7 days a week to assist
customers with setup, troubleshooting, and other product-related questions.

C

Online Support

Visit *www.linksys.com* for online support, which includes a variety of educational and technical information sites.

Education

Click Educate Me on the Linksys home page to learn more about small networks and the topologies (Ethernet cable, wireless, phoneline, and powerline) you can use to connect those networks.

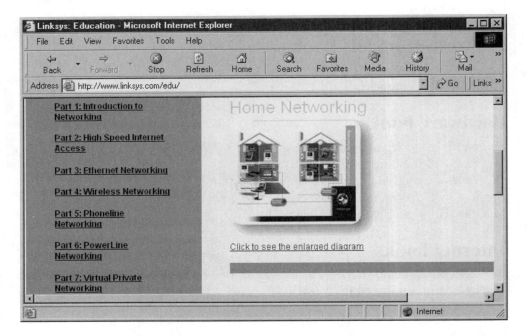

You can head right for information about a particular topology or go through all the available topics to help your decision-making process. Each information-filled page has a button to change the display to a printer-friendly version, so you can print the information you need and use it as you plan your network.

Knowledge Base

Click Support on the Linksys home page, and then click Knowledge Base to access a Linksys support database that contains a wide range of information. All you have to do is enter a phrase or a question.

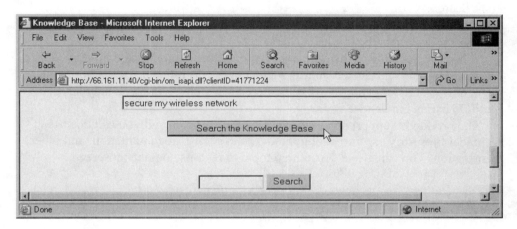

Then, click on the articles that seem most appropriate. Linksys ranks the articles according to their relevancy to your query, so you can usually find what you need quickly.

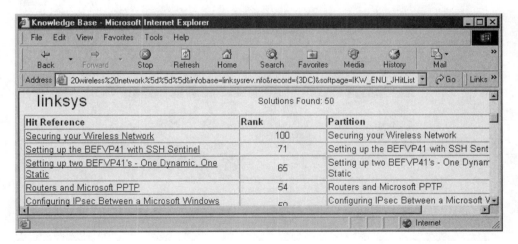

Product Support Pages

Click Support on the Linksys home page, and then click the icon for Support Pages to locate helpful information and tools for your Linksys products. Start by selecting a product from the drop-down list, as seen in Figure C-1. Then click Search.

You can also select the option Search By Keywords, and enter a word or phrase that describes the product. Then click Search.

When the Search Results page appears, click the listing for the product you're investigating. If you selected your model from the drop-down list on the search page, only one listing appears. If you entered a search phrase, you may have multiple listings to choose from.

The product's support page appears (see Figure C-2), and you can download technical files (drivers, firmware upgrades, and so on), documentation, and other information. You can also select a help topic to read its contents onscreen.

NOTE   *The type and amount of support files differ by product.*

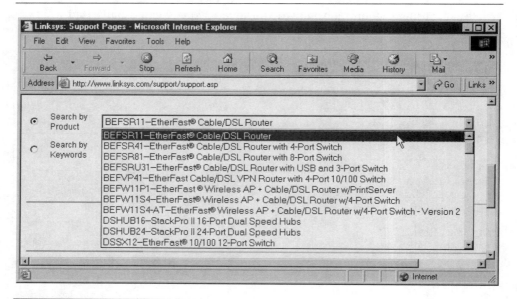

FIGURE C-1   Select the Linksys product you want to learn about

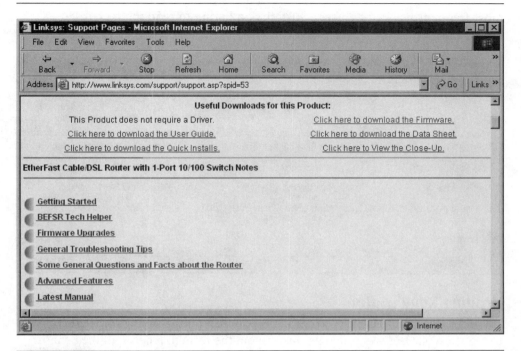

FIGURE C-2   Plenty of information is available for this product

Linksys User Guides (and other documentation) are PDF files, which require Acrobat Reader. If you don't have a copy of Acrobat Reader, you can download the software (it's free) from either of the following Web sites:

- *http://www.adobe.com* (follow the links to Acrobat Reader)

- *http://www.admin911.com/downloads/ar500enu.exe* (*www.admin911 .com* is also a support site for this book—it will contain corrections to any errors we find after publication)

Frequently Asked Questions

Click Support on the Linksys home page, and then click the icon for FAQs to see a list of informational documents that cover the questions and topics

C

most frequently asked by users. Just click a listing to read the fact-filled document.

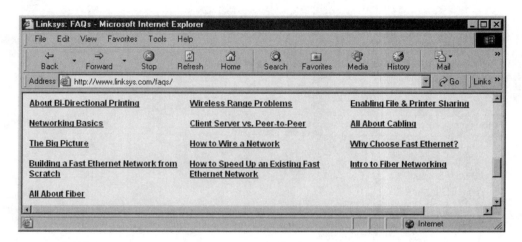

Product Registration

Click Support on the Linksys home page, and then click the icon for Registration to register your Linksys products. Just fill out the form to receive all the benefits of registration.

Warranty and Returns

Click Support on the Linksys home page, and then click the icon for Warranty Info to see a list of articles that explain your warranty and the return policy for your Linksys products (see Figure C-3).

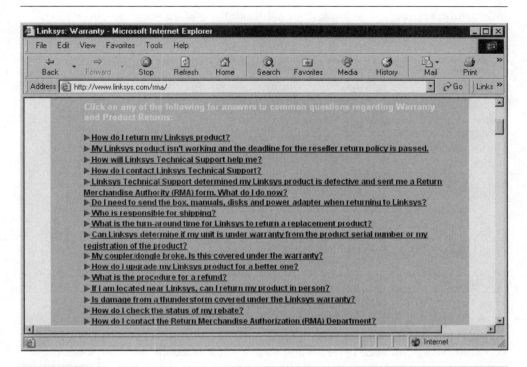

FIGURE C-3   Everything you need to know about Linksys warranties and return
              policies is available online

Network Configuration Assistance

Click Support on the Linksys home page, and then click the icon for Configurator
to learn about your networking options. These pages are terrifically helpful for
planning your network. Choose Small Business or Home to focus your quest for

C

information appropriately. Walk through the configuration windows and supply the requested information.

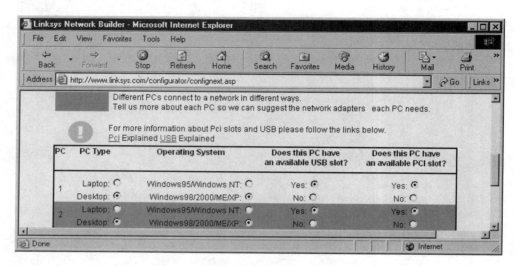

As you step through the pages, you'll find plenty of links that define terms and supply other additional information that you'll find useful. When you're finished, you know what you need to buy. Then you can download the documentation, read instructions, and collect other informative data before you actually put your network together.

Online Product Pages

For a quick overview of all the Linksys products, click the Products icon on the Linksys home page. The Products window displays all the product categories (see Figure C-4)—just click the appropriate link to learn more!

Each category page presents listings by subcategory and by product (see Figure C-5), so it's easy to drill down to exactly the product information you need.

When you select a product, the page you see offers an explanation of the product's use and also provides links to its documentation and support pages.

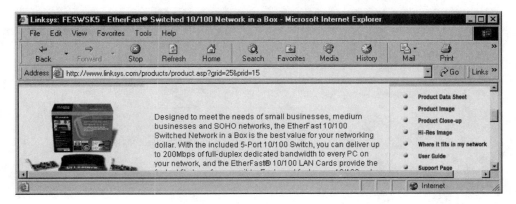

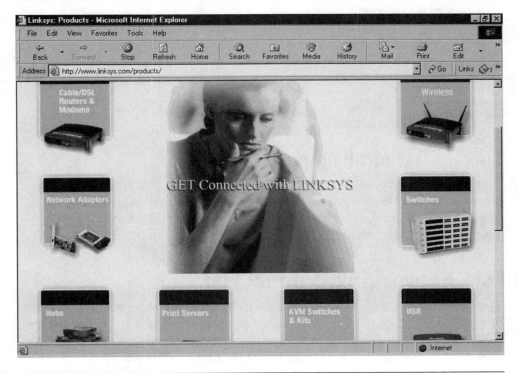

FIGURE C-4   Start your research by choosing a category

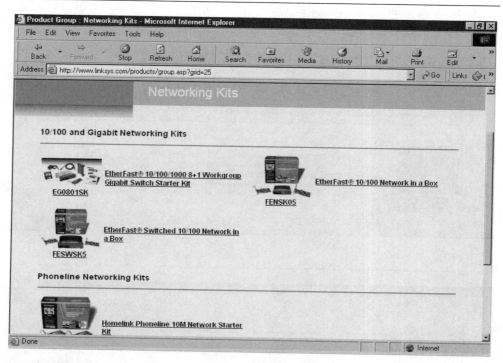

FIGURE C-5   I'm looking for kits, which contain everything I need for a small network in one product box

Linksys Technical Support

Linksys has technical experts ready to help you if you run into a problem. Each product category has its own specialists, who are knowledgeable and helpful. You can contact the right technical expert via a toll-free telephone number, which is found in the documentation included with your Linksys product.

Linksys Networking Product List

This section presents a list of Linksys networking products, along with explanations of each product's use in your home or business network. This list is presented by model number, so you can select the appropriate product code when you want to obtain more information about a product on the Linksys Web site.

BEFSR41

The Linksys EtherFast Cable/DSL Router with a 4-Port Switch is the perfect option to connect multiple PCs to a high-speed Broadband Internet connection or to an Ethernet hub/switch. Configurable as a DHCP server for your existing network, the EtherFast Cable/DSL Router with 4-Port Switch acts as the only externally recognized Internet device on your local area network.

BEFSR11

With its 10/100 Ethernet port, the Linksys EtherFast Cable/DSL Router is the perfect option to connect multiple PCs to a high-speed Broadband Internet connection or to an Ethernet hub/switch.

BEFSR81

This Linksys EtherFast Cable/DSL Router with 8-Port Switch is the perfect solution for connecting PCs to a high-speed Broadband Internet connection. Configurable as a DHCP server or a network node.

BEFSRU31

Connect computers to the EtherFast Cable/DSL with USB and 3-Port Switch Router through its new Plug-and-Play USB port. Then, enjoy a secure, high-speed Cable/DSL Internet connection. It's that easy, without even installing a network card!

BEFVP41

The Instant Broadband EtherFast Cable/DSL VPN Router from Linksys is the ideal solution for remotely accessing a network securely over the Internet using cutting-edge encryption and authentication methods.

Built from the popular standard Linksys 4-Port Router Model BEFSR41, the VPN Router expands its functionality and security features by utilizing 56-bit DES and 168-bit 3DES encryption, and Internet Key Exchange (IKE). A built-in IPSec coprocessor from Hifn allows for complete data privacy for the access and exchange of your most sensitive data from your home to your corporate network or between remote branch offices, without the additional cost of IPSec VPN client software for each computer. Mobile workers can also connect to a corporate network

C

using an IPSec-based VPN client software solution. The EtherFast Cable/DSL VPN Router is capable of conducting up to 70 simultaneous IPSec VPN tunnels.

BEFSX41

The Linksys Instant Broadband EtherFast Cable/DSL Firewall Router with 4-Port Switch/VPN Endpoint is the perfect solution for connecting a small group of PCs to a high-speed broadband Internet connection or a 10/100 Ethernet backbone. For enhanced protection against intruders from the Internet, the Router features an advanced Stateful Packet Inspection firewall.

BEFW11S4

The EtherFast Wireless AP + Cable/DSL Router provides the ideal solution for connecting your wireless network to a high-speed broadband Internet connection and a 10/100 Fast Ethernet backbone. Configurable as a DHCP server for your existing network, the EtherFast Wireless AP + Cable/DSL Router acts as the only externally recognized Internet gateway on your local area network.

WAP11

The Wireless Access Point from Linksys delivers the freedom to configure your network your way. Utilization of state-of-the-art wireless technology gives you the ability to set up workstations in ways you never thought possible; no cables to install means less expense and less hassle.

The Wireless Access Point's high-powered antennas offer a range of operation of up to 300 feet indoors that provide seamless roaming throughout your wireless LAN infrastructure. An advanced user authentication feature ensures a high level of network security. The Wireless Access Point is easy to install (just plug it in and you're ready to go!) and easy to use—Windows-based diagnostics and statistic tools ensure that you'll always be in control.

WPC11

Put the "mobile" back into mobile computing! Whether you're at your desk or in the boardroom, the Linksys Instant Wireless Network PC Card allows you to share printers, files, and other resources anywhere within your LAN infrastructure, increasing your productivity and keeping you "in touch."

The Instant Wireless Network PC Card now has a new higher-powered antenna that provides greater ranges than ever. The increased sensitivity helps filter out interference and "noise" to keep your signal clear. Improved error correction in the chipset keeps you operating at higher transmission rates for longer distances.

WUSB11

The Plug-and-Play Wireless USB Network Adapter connects directly to any USB-ready PC—just plug it in and you're ready to share data, printers, or high-speed Internet access over your existing wireless network. For desktop installation, you don't even have to open your PC's case. And user-friendly software makes it simple to set up.

Not only is the Instant Wireless USB Network Adapter easy to install and use, it's also powerful. You can send and receive data at speeds up to 11 Mbps, and a new higher-powered antenna provides greater ranges than ever. The increased sensitivity helps filter out interference and "noise" to keep your signal clear. Improved error correction keeps you operating at higher transmission rates over longer distances.

WMP11

Put your desktop computer wherever you wish. The Linksys Instant Wireless PCI Card allows you to share printers, files, and more within your wireless LAN infrastructure, increasing your productivity and keeping you on the network.

The Instant Wireless PCI Card gives you the freedom to work your way, from wherever you want. A high-powered built-in Diversity antenna means that you're covered at distances of up to 457 meters (1500 feet). Ready to run in any PCI-equipped desktop PC.

WPS11

Hook up a printer to the Wireless PrintServer from anywhere in your workplace and control print jobs with its remote management utility. A 256KB memory buffer handles your graphics jobs effortlessly, while an easy installation gets you printing in just minutes.

WCF11

Experience the same speed and ease of wireless networking with your CompactFlash Type II ready personal digital assistant as you do with your laptop or desktop computer with the Instant Wireless Wireless Network CF Card. This Type II CompactFlash card connects directly to your PDA—just plug it in and you're

C

ready to share data, printers, or high-speed Internet access over your existing wireless network. User-friendly software makes it simple to set up.

WCF12

The Wireless CompactFlash Card is not only easy to install and use, but also powerful. Your PDA can send and receive data at speeds up to 11 Mbps. A high-powered, built-in antenna keeps you connected at distances of up to 984 feet. The Wireless CompactFlash Card is also versatile and easily configurable through your PDA.

WET11

Tailor-made for the home or small office network, the Instant Wireless Wireless Ethernet Bridge extends wireless connectivity to any Ethernet-ready network device, such as a printer, scanner, or desktop or notebook PC. The Wireless Ethernet Workgroup Bridge simply and efficiently transmits data between the wired and wireless segments of your LAN.

The Wireless Ethernet Bridge gives you the freedom to place any standard network resource virtually anywhere in your office. A high-powered, built-in antenna means that you're covered at distances of up to 300 meters or more.

WAP51AB

The Instant Wireless Dual-Band Wireless Access Point works simultaneously with both 802.11a and 802.11b wireless standards to bring you the ultimate in wireless freedom. This means you can enjoy the broadest spectrum of wireless networking now without the worry of a costly upgrade later.

The Dual-Band Wireless Access Point's high-powered antennas enhance reception and provide seamless roaming through your wireless network. An advanced user authentication feature and security encryption of up to 152 bits give you the highest level of network security. It's easy to install (just plug it in and you're ready to go!) and easy to use.

WAP54A

The Instant Wireless Wireless Access Point from Linksys delivers the freedom to configure your network your way. Utilization of "state-of-the-art" wireless technology gives you the ability to set up workstations in ways you never thought possible; no cables to install means less expense and less hassle.

The Instant Wireless Wireless Access Point's high-powered antenna offers a range of operation of up to 328 feet indoors, providing seamless roaming throughout your wireless LAN infrastructure; an advanced user authentication feature ensures a high level of network security. The Instant Wireless Wireless Access Point is easy to install (just plug it in and you're ready to go!) and easy to use.

WPC54A

This wireless PC Card has a new higher-powered antenna that provides greater ranges than ever. The increased sensitivity helps filter out interference and "noise" to keep your signal clear. Improved error correction in the chipset keeps you operating at higher transmission rates for longer distances. Ready to run in Type II or III PCMCIA CardBus-equipped notebook PCs running Windows 98, Millennium, 2000, and XP.

EFG80

Insert 80 gigabytes of storage space into your network with the EtherFast© Instant GigaDrive. Compact and powerful, this Network-Attached Storage (NAS) device adds gigabytes of storage to your network without adding the cost, space, and maintenance hassles of a typical file server.

The Instant GigaDrive provides solid data transfer for multiple client connections. It is also equipped with a built-in Print Server for the quick and inexpensive addition of a network printer and an extra drive bay so you can add an additional drive as your network needs demand.

EFSP42

The Linksys EtherFast 10/100 2-Port Switched PrintServer—the first PrintServer to offer integrated 10/100 switch ports—is the easiest way to both expand and simplify your departmental, small office, or home office network. The EtherFast 10/100 2-Port Switched PrintServer houses two high-speed printer ports and four standard 10/100 switch ports, allowing you to connect up to two printers and four PCs (or a hub/switch) to your network.

PPSX1

The Linksys EtherFast 10/100 PrintServer is the easiest way to add one printer to your 10BaseT or 100BaseTX network. This PrintServer adjusts itself to either 10 Mbps or 100 Mbps speeds automatically. It's a stand-alone unit, so it doesn't

C

require a dedicated print server PC. Equipped with Direct Memory Access (DMA) technology, a 128KB buffer, and automatic collision control, it can handle even the most complicated print jobs up to 50% faster than regular print servers! Fully compatible with regular laser, bubble jet, ink jet, and dot matrix printers, the PrintServer also supports bidirectional printers that let you keep track of a print job's status from anywhere on the network.

EPSX3

The Linksys EtherFast 10/100 3-Port PrintServer is the easiest way to add up to three printers to your 10BaseT or Fast Ethernet network. This PrintServer adjusts itself to either 10 Mbps or 100 Mbps speeds automatically. A stand-alone solution that doesn't require a dedicated print server PC, the PrintServer houses three high-speed parallel ports that can handle incoming print jobs concurrently.

PCM100

Connect your notebook computer to a 10BaseT or 100BaseTX network in just minutes. The EtherFast 10/100 PC Card automatically adjusts its speed and duplex to match any 10BaseT or 100BaseTX network. The card also features low voltage operation, a 32KB file buffer hot swap capability, and unmatched compatibility with brand-name laptop PCs.

PCMLM56

Blazing 10/100 networking performance and the power of a 56K faxmodem in one integrated card! The EtherFast 10/100 + 56K Modem PC Card is the answer to your most demanding networking and telecommunications needs. A single integrated card that requires only one PCMCIA slot.

PCM200

If you have a high-performance 32-bit CardBus slot, the EtherFast 10/100 PCM200 Card will allow you to share files, printers, Internet connections, and more. The EtherFast 10/100 PCM200 Cards automatically adjust their speed and duplex to any 10BaseT or 100BaseTX network. The PCM200 also features low voltage operation, a 32KB file buffer hot swap capability, and unmatched compatibility with brand-name laptop PCs.

LNE100TX

Built to run with the fastest network applications, the EtherFast 10/100 LAN Card is a high performance network adapter for desktop computers with 32-bit PCI expansion slots. The EtherFast 10/100 LAN Card is ready to run with both 10BaseT and 100BaseTX networks right out of the box—the card's 10/100 combo RJ-45 port automatically detects your network's maximum speed and adjusts itself accordingly. This card also features Wake-On-LAN (WOL) event management.

EZXS55W

Surge your network with surefire data transfers in full duplex mode with the EtherFast 10/100 Autosensing Switches. Each of its independently switched 10/100 ports yield up to a remarkable 200 Mbps bandwidth in full duplex mode, and protect your PCs from downed network segments through auto-partitioning.

EZXS88W

The EtherFast 8-Port 10/100 Workgroup Switch is a quick and easy way to run your network at 10 Mbps, 20 Mbps, 100 Mbps, and an incredible 200 Mbps!

EZXS16W

This 16-port switch features a complete suite of advanced data error detection and correction features for surefire communication every time. Auto partitioning, data-collision control, signal regeneration, and incoming frame retiming ensure that not a single bit of data is lost, even during heavy network traffic.

BEFCMU10

This EtherFast Cable Modem with USB and Ethernet Connection provides you with the perfect solution for a fast and easy Internet connection.

PLUSB10

Network your PCs with Linksys PowerLine Networking, which allows you to turn the powerlines in your home or office into your network cable. The easiest way to integrate any PC or laptop into such a powerline network is with the Instant PowerLine USB Adapter. The Plug-and-Play USB Adapter connects directly to

C

any USB-ready PC—just plug it in and you're ready to share data, printers, or high-speed Internet access over your existing powerlines.

PLEBR10

The Linksys Instant PowerLine EtherFast 10/100 Bridge offers a complete Internet connection solution for your home powerline network. The PowerLine Bridge makes sharing your broadband access easier than ever.

EG1032

Unprecedented speed is now available over your existing network cabling! Built to run the fastest video, publishing, and database network applications, the Instant Gigabit Network Adapter is a high-performance network adapter for PCI local bus computers. Boasting an incredible maximum data throughput of 2000 megabits-per-second in full duplex mode, it includes a 10BaseT/100BaseTX/1000BaseTX port, which means that you can begin using Gigabit now!

EG1064

Built for desktop PCs equipped with 64-bit PCI slots, this card reaches speeds of 1 Gbps, up to ten times faster than regular 100 Mbps Fast Ethernet. Standard copper CAT5 Ethernet cabling can be used with the EG1064, instead of costly fiber-optic cabling and fiber-optic modules.

EG0801W

This new compact 10/100 Switch from Linksys provides blazing transfer speeds for your network applications with integrated Gigabit connectivity. Apply this switching power to your current Ethernet network, and your data traffic efficiency will improve several times over. Connect your workstations to the Switch's 10/100 ports, and speed up access time for all your users in just one move. Connect to your server through the single Gigabit port for full-duplex, dedicated bandwidth of up to 2000 Mbps.

EG0801SK

With the EtherFast 10/100/1000 8+1 Workgroup Gigabit Switch Starter Kit from Linksys, you can now move up to the new standard for network speed—1000 Mbps! The Kit comes with all you need to upgrade your network in minutes—one

Instant Gigabit Network Adapter, an EtherFast 10/100/1000 8+1 Workgroup Gigabit Switch, and one Category 5E network cable. Plug in the card, install the software driver, connect to the switch, and go!

FESWSK5

The EtherFast 10/100 Switched Network in a Box is the best value for your networking dollar. With the included 5-Port 10/100 Switch, you can deliver up to 200 Mbps of full-duplex dedicated bandwidth to every PC on your network, and the EtherFast 10/100 LAN Cards provide the fastest file transfers possible. Each card features a 10/100 auto-sensing twisted pair port, support for Wake-On-LAN management, and full duplex capability.

C

Index

425

INTERNATIONAL CONTACT INFORMATION

AUSTRALIA
McGraw-Hill Book Company Australia Pty. Ltd.
TEL +61-2-9415-9899
FAX +61-2-9415-5687
http://www.mcgraw-hill.com.au
books-it_sydney@mcgraw-hill.com

CANADA
McGraw-Hill Ryerson Ltd.
TEL +905-430-5000
FAX +905-430-5020
http://www.mcgrawhill.ca

**GREECE, MIDDLE EAST,
NORTHERN AFRICA**
McGraw-Hill Hellas
TEL +30-1-656-0990-3-4
FAX +30-1-654-5525

MEXICO (Also serving Latin America)
McGraw-Hill Interamericana Editores S.A. de C.V.
TEL +525-117-1583
FAX +525-117-1589
http://www.mcgraw-hill.com.mx
fernando_castellanos@mcgraw-hill.com

SINGAPORE (Serving Asia)
McGraw-Hill Book Company
TEL +65-863-1580
FAX +65-862-3354
http://www.mcgraw-hill.com.sg
mghasia@mcgraw-hill.com

SOUTH AFRICA
McGraw-Hill South Africa
TEL +27-11-622-7512
FAX +27-11-622-9045
robyn_swanepoel@mcgraw-hill.com

**UNITED KINGDOM & EUROPE
(Excluding Southern Europe)**
McGraw-Hill Education Europe
TEL +44-1-628-502500
FAX +44-1-628-770224
http://www.mcgraw-hill.co.uk
computing_neurope@mcgraw-hill.com

ALL OTHER INQUIRIES Contact:
Osborne/McGraw-Hill
TEL +1-510-549-6600
FAX +1-510-883-7600
http://www.osborne.com
omg_international@mcgraw-hill.com

Linksys.com

Your link to all of the latest information about Linksys and your products!

Promotion	**Now Shipping**	**Coming Soon**

See special values available for a limited time only.	Keep up-to-date on the latest wireless and networking products.	Be the first to buy new products as soon as they're available.

Products

Detailed information about all Linksys Products including pictures, data sheets, and much more.

Where to Buy

An up-to date list of Retailers, E-Commerce, Business Solutions, and Distribution partners selling Linksys products.

Support

Keep informed of new drivers and firmware updates, search our Knowledge Base for answers to your questions, register your product on-line, and more.

 LINKSYS®